LEGEND TRIPPING

The Ultimate Adventure

Robert C. Robinson

Other books of Interest

Yetis, Sasquatch & Hairy Giants
The Mystery of the Olmecs
Abominable Snowmen
Things and More Things
More Far-Out Adventures
Technology of the Gods
Pirates & the Lost Templar Fleet
Lost Continents & the Hollow Earth
Lost Cities & Ancient Mysteries of the Southwest
Lost Cities of China, Central Asia & India
Lost Ciies & Ancient Mysteries of Africa & Arablia
Lost Ciies & Ancient Mysteries of South America
Lost Ciies of Ancient Lemuria & the Pacific
Lost Ciies of North and Central America
Lost Cities of Atlantis, Ancient Europe & the Mediterranean
Atlantis & the Power System of the Gods
The Enigma of Cranial Deformation
The Crystal Skulls
Ark of God

LEGEND TRIPPING

The Ultimate Adventure

By Robert C. Robinson
Foreword by Loren Coleman

Legend Tripping: The Ultimate Adventure

ISBN 978-1-939149-64-0

Published by Adventures Unlimited Press
One Adventure Place
Kempton, Illinois 60946 USA

Thanks to Alex Harris for the illustrations

www.adventuresunlimitedpress.com
www.legendtrippersofamerica.blogspot.com/
www.wexclub.com

TABLE OF CONTENTS

Message from David Lynn Goleman
Foreword by Loren Coleman
Introduction: Something IS out There!

Chapter 1: Legend Tripping 1
Chapter 2: Bigfoot 13
Chapter 3: Other Cryptids 35
Chapter 4: Bigfoot Legend Trip 55
Chapter 5: Aquatic Cryptids 95
Chapter 6: Aquatic Cryptid Legend Trip 107
Chapter 7: Haunted Sites and the Paranormal 123
Chapter 8: Paranormal Legend Trip 141
Chapter 9: UFO Sites and Ghost Lights 157
Chapter 10: Extraterrestrial Legend Trip 171
Chapter 11: Treasure Legends 183
Chapter 12: Treasure Legend Trip 191

Chapter 13: Mysterious Places 203
Chapter 14: Day Legend Trips 213
Chapter 15: Critical Thinking 231
Chapter 16: Outdoor Survival 241
Chapter 17: Equipment and Tools 259
Chapter 18: Your Legend Trip Begins Now! 287
Chapter 19: Who's Who in Legend Tripping 291
Chapter 20: Legend Tripping in Popular Fiction 303

Author's Bio

ACKNOWLEDGMENTS

This book wouldn't have happened if it wasn't for the assistance of the following people. I can't thank them enough for the help they gave me.

Loren Coleman, David Hatcher Childress, Kent Holloway, Lyle Blackburn, David Lynn Goleman, Stacy Brown, David Lauer, Josh Watson, Emmette Kessler of SasquatchHunters.com, Charlie Carlson, Craig Woolheater, Jeff Belanger, Nick Redfern, Ken Gerhard, Glen Shelt, Nick Tudor, Marc DeWerth, David Bakara, Gary Fisher, Dana Holyfield, Scott Mardis, Chris Simoes, Josh Gates, Dr. Jeff Meldrum, Kevin Jackson, Matt Moneymaker, Cliff Barakman, James Fay, Ranae Holland, Edward Meyer and the entire Ripley's Inc. staff, Catherine McDonald, Dialne McCall, and my entire family and my wife Tracy.

LEGEND TRIPPING

The Ultimate Adventure

Foreword
By
Loren Coleman

Take a Legend Trip Today

I first became aware of Rob and Tracy Robinson in 2010, as they were preparing for their reality television appearance as the so-called "Bigfoot Family" on ABC-TV's Wife Swap series. For 23 semesters, I taught an undergraduate course in documentary film at the University of Southern Maine, and discussed the importance of such series in our cultural framework. I also would weave cryptozoology on television into my course. The Robinsons' firsthand experiences were important to me, as this merging of television and cryptozoology was significant. It was unfortunate, of course, that the network made the Robinsons sound like they actually were Sasquatch.

The Robinsons were being promoted as a "Bigfoot family," but, technically, they are not members of the unclassified primate species called Bigfoot. The Robinsons, who live in Florida, are nice folks who happened to be "Swamp Ape Seekers" or "Skunk Ape Hunters."

Rob Robinson said to me before the program aired, "I believe I gave monster hunting a good representation on the show."

They did.

The production company, needless to say, gave an overblown view of the life of people involved in searching for Skunk Apes. I said soon after the episode broadcast that the show was "a rather good accounting of cryptozoology and correctly reinforced the interest in that topic as a gateway for the family's children being involved in nature studies."

Since then, I have grown to know Rob and his family, learned of his inspiration from my 1983 book, *Mysterious America*, and worked with him around various events in Saint Augustine, Florida.

Rob Robinson now has delivered a good book for others interested and involved in what he calls "legend tripping."

Robinson is a member of the new generation of monster hunters, cryptozoologists, Bigfooters, and Skunk Ape seekers who come to the field with an open mind. You will want to use this as a handbook to assist you.

Famed British Columbia Sasquatch chronicler John Green once wrote, "Let's get this business about belief straight. The believers aren't the scientists, they're the ones who are clinging to a belief. The people who think that there are Sasquatch, are the ones who are investigating – the ones who have become convinced on evidence. The scientists are the ones going on pure faith and don't actually know much about it and make darn sure they don't know anything about it."

As many in the media have quoted me, I have shared, "Belief is the providence of religion, and believing has more to do with faith than science. I accept or deny the evidence, the patterns of reports, the eyewitness testimony, and those investigations inform me as to whether or not I feel this is an event, a hidden animal, and/or a cryptid of interest to cryptozoology."

In *Mysterious America*, I stressed, "Pursuers of the

unknown, Forteans all, believe in non-belief."

An "open-minded attitude to the many unexplained situations," I feel, is "the stock and trade of the Fortean."

Robinson, myself and our peers can, as I wrote in *Mysterious America*, "accept concrete answers, actual flesh and blood critters as the foundation to monster accounts."

However, I must observe that "a psychological answer may be at work with some of these accounts, and the rational conventional undiscovered animal answer may not be viable for all reports." I see there is "room enough to consider many possibilities."

But again, I must emphasize that as a cryptozoologist I do not "believe" in monsters. Cryptozoology, I reiterate, is "not about 'belief.'"

You will find Rob Robinson explores in this book the hard and fast facts about collecting the evidence pointing to the finding and reality of new species, new animals of interest to cryptozoology, and other explorations of the unknown. "Believing" is "the realm of religion," but "cryptozoology, like all sciences," is "about gathering the data and evidence to develop trends, patterns, and evidence which lead to hard facts and discoveries" (from *Mysterious America*).

In *Mysterious America* and other books of mine, I suggest, for example, on the one hand that quite probably "some monsters in America are chimpanzee-like dryopithecines," "some cats and maned lions are relict populations" of Panthera atrox, and "some lake monsters are unknown long-necked seals."

However, I also know that investigation shows search beyond their own bias, and feel there is also "room" in my "cosmic joke box" for "teleporting alligators, Dover Demons," and "phantom clowns that imitate UFO's in all aspects but flight," as I noted in *Mysterious America* which inspired Rob Robinson.

Last but not least, Robinson and others are wise to not be unafraid to say "I don't know."

Enjoy your journeys "legend tripping" with Robert Robinson, wherever your treks take you.

Loren Coleman
Director, International Cryptozoology Museum
Portland, Maine
March 14, 2016

INTRODUCTION
Something IS Out There!

A chill shot down my spine as I looked through the night vision goggles toward the swamp and saw two large glowing eyes. The eyes appeared between two cypress trees. I blinked a couple of times to make sure my eyes weren't playing tricks on me. I looked again and the glowing eyes were still glaring. My goggles only had a range of fifty feet, so whatever this animal was, it was just out of range. All I could see was the two large glowing orbs surrounded by blackness. "What could it be?" I wondered. The trees had no extending branches, so that ruled out a raccoon or an owl. Using my height as a reference, I judged that the animal glaring at me was at least eight feet tall; too big to be a bear or panther. Searching my memory, I ran out of animals that I hoped it could be. Had I really found the legend I was looking for?

Huge cypress trees filtered out most of the moonlight and cast the Florida swamps into almost complete darkness with dancing shadows. The pungent smell of the decomposing swamp floor filled my nostrils. The whole scene could have been in a horror movie as a glowing mist crawled its way through the palmettos and dead trees, like a ghostly entity weaving through the foliage. I felt helpless and hypnotized by the sight of these strange luminous eyes. I felt something bad would happen if I looked away. It reminded me of a stare down contest, only I didn't know who my opponent was.

The hair stood up on the back of my neck as I saw whatever it was blink. It wasn't my mind playing tricks on me. It was a living animal, and I was in its swampy domain. Just a few moments earlier, my attention had been drawn to the location of the eyes by the sound of something large moving through the dank water, pushing its way through the thick swamp, knocking over small trees and bushes with little effort to get through thick vegetation. It didn't seem to care how much noise it made in contrast to the silent setting where not even a cricket was chirping, amplifying the sounds of the mysterious movement. Though I couldn't see anything but the eyes, I could now hear it. A heavy breathing of an animal filling huge lungs with each inhalation.

A sudden thought struck me, "Where is my son?" I furtively looked around. Did he get scared and run back to the vehicle? The thought lingered in my mind as I prepared to call out to him. A strange noise broke the silence. I strained to see my son's shape through the darkness. I then looked back, and the glowing eyes were still there, piercing through the darkness. I remember thinking, "It knows I'm here." I wondered if it could be the legendary being I came to look for. Had IT ventured to this part of the swamp? Is IT glaring at me right now, from the darkness?

This whole night's adventure started a couple days back, when a hunter contacted me and related that he had seen a strange creature from his hunting stand. In fact, the creature walked right by him, stopped, looked up at him, and then ran off on two legs. This mysterious animal, or being, has become a legend in these parts. It is supposed to have made its home in a deep area of the dark, sinister swamplands known as the Devil's Creek Swamp. A lonely part of the Green Swamp, it has taken on a legendary status from tales of its hauntings, missing persons, buried treasure, and strange lights. This particular legend is something so terrifying and monstrous that any mention of it is kept in whispers among the local townsfolk.

This legend is called the Swamp Ape. Eight feet tall and covered in dark, matted, hair, it is said to prowl the swamps of Florida. This southern cousin to Bigfoot is reported to give off a smell so toxic that it freezes hunting dogs in their tracks. Yet, scientists say an animal of this kind cannot possibly exist. The locals say differently. The hunter took me to the area of the sighting and showed me which direction the creature had taken when it ran off. I checked a map to see where the creature had gone. Based on that, I found an area where I believed the creature would be, or at least would be traveling through. I told my family of the sighting and of my plan to go out there that weekend. Not wanting to go alone, I asked them if they would accompany me to the area.

We arrived shortly before sunset. As I turned the vehicle off, I noticed how deathly quiet it was. Even though the sun was not completely down, it was almost totally dark out there. The only lights were the small red beams from the headlamps we wore. I felt a chill in the air; the autumn season was coming on, and the nights were cooling off. It was amazing how the darkness could make you feel so alone and vulnerable. Looking around this dense, isolated swamp, you could see how it got the name Devil's Creek Swamp. Every entity from my nightmares could have been out here.

The Green Swamp is part of the Southwest Florida Water Management area, and is just on the outer edge of civilization, forty-five minutes west of Orlando. It was hard to believe that nearby, people were enjoying the theme parks of Walt Disney World and Universal Studios.

Hundreds of stories come out of Devil's Creek Swamp about the Swamp Ape every year, and tonight we would add our adventure to them. I divided the family into two teams: my son, Josh, with me on one team, and my stepdaughter, Kera, with my wife, Tracy, on the other. We then bravely departed for our areas in the darkness of the swamp. Half an hour later, Josh and I were deep in the swamps where humans rarely roam. With us so isolated, so far from civilization, the only sounds that could be heard were the occasional croaking of frogs and gators. The humidity turned my sweat ice cold, and I shivered with each trickle down my back. While trying to present a confident in-charge front, I found myself nervously looking up at the dark cypress and palm trees and then back down at the eerie rolling mist covering the swamp floor. I had this feeling that someone or something was watching us. I kept straining my eyes to focus on anything visible. I wondered, "How could this area look so beautiful by day, but look so menacing at night?" I could see my breath turn to mist as I exhaled slowly into the night air.

As we ventured down a remote game trail, I suddenly stopped dead in my tracks. I could hear something large moving through the swampy water to the left, splashing as it moved. I stopped, and the splashing noise stopped. I looked around and noticed that my son was gone. As I looked for him, I had this overpowering feeling that something was watching me from the swamps. Then I realized that all animal noises had ceased leaving me feeling even more alone. I started moving down the trail again and, as before, the splashing started. I immediately stopped and listened. There was an uncomfortable silence all around me. I took out my nightvision goggles and looked in the direction of the splashing. Then I saw them: large glowing eyes staring right at me. I stood there, paralyzed.

Suddenly, a noise came from behind me! The hairs

on my neck went up as I felt something staring at me from behind. A thought shot through me: "Oh, crap, now there are two of these things!" Had one of them gotten my attention while the other snuck behind me? I slowly turned around. I don't know what I was prepared to see or do. If this situation went bad, which way was I going to retreat?

"Oh, thank God! It's my son," I thought with relief as I took a breath. Even in the darkness I could see by the look on his face that he had also heard the noise. (Later, I found out he had been there the whole time; he was next to a tree and I didn't see him.) I cautiously signaled to him and pointed to my ear and then to where the activity was coming from. We stared at each other and listened intently. A crashing sound rang through the swamp again, and my son's mouth fell open. Again I stopped breathing, and I didn't dare swallow. I could hear the thing moving again, but now it sounded like it was moving away from us. I cautiously looked back to where I had seen the glowing eyes. It's funny, but you only think about finding it; you never stop to think what you're going to do if you *actually* find the beast. I pulled my camera out of my pocket and turned it on. I prayed it wouldn't light up and give away my location. It seemed like minutes before I saw the small red light come on. I repositioned myself behind a large cypress tree to get in a safer position to see what was out there in the darkness. I brought the camera up to scan the area in front of me.

There was nothing there but the darkness. The glowing eyes were gone. Whatever it was, it was moving away from us. After a while, the sounds of the frogs and alligators returned. I slowly exhaled and looked over at my son. I had started to say something to him when an ear-piercing scream echoed through the night. It sent shivers up my body. I know every kind of animal in the swamps, and the sounds they make, but this scream wasn't any animal sound I had ever heard. That is the best way I can describe it. It wasn't a roar or a yell. It didn't sound like a cat or a bear; it sounded almost apelike.

I tried to calm down and come to my senses by telling myself, "This is why I am here tonight, and I may never get an opportunity like this again." I ordered myself to breathe and think. Using my camera, I scanned the area, but nothing showed up—just cypress trees and darkness. The noise pierced again through the swamps—this time, louder. Something was getting closer. My son slowly leaned over and whispered to me, "Maybe we need to leave and go back to base camp." I slowly nodded in agreement as I scanned the darkness for any sign of movement. We both slowly and cautiously walked out of the swamp, looking around. I was relieved when I could make out the dirt road in front of us. Neither of us said a word as we walked back to camp. I found myself continually looking over my shoulder, as I felt like we were being watched. I scanned the dark swamps, ready for something to jump out at us. But there wasn't any movement or any glowing eyes. I realized I still had my camera ready.

Suddenly, a third scream echoed through the night, and this time it sounded closer to us than before. Somehow, my legs did all the thinking, and my son and I found ourselves running down the dirt trail toward our base camp. I felt a little relief, as I could finally see the outline of the vehicle. I tried to slow down and start walking while I tried to catch my breath. I could hear my son doing the same. I could see dark silhouettes moving around the vehicle as we approached. "Thank God, its people! It's the rest of the family," I thought. The silhouettes stopped moving as we approached.

A voice that sounded like my wife's called out, "Who's that?" I quickly answered back with my name, between breaths, and my son did the same. The same voice asked, "Did you guys hear that scream?" With a smile, I replied, "We were right next to it." Then everybody started talking at once. A new voice asked the question, "Where were you?" I pointed down the dark road, knowing perfectly well nobody could see me.

My son and I related our little adventure, trying not to leave out anything. When I brought up the scream, everyone chimed in excitedly about it, each one with his or her own explanation.

Suddenly a fourth scream pierced the night. Everybody froze. After a couple of seconds, we looked around into the darkness of the swamp and then at each other. It didn't sound far away. I don't know who said it first, but it was suggested that we call it a night and leave. It didn't take long to get everyone in the vehicle.

Once we were out of the swamp, we started laughing at how we had acted, and what could have made that sound, and what it was that I saw with the glowing eyes. I can't honestly say I saw the Swamp Ape. But I racked my brain as to what it could have been if it wasn't the Swamp Ape. All I do know is that whatever it was sent chills up my spine that night and will remain lodged in my memory forever. My family and I all came to the same conclusion that night: "Something IS out there!"

Chapter 1
Legend Tripping: 101

I believe legends and myths are largely made of 'truth,' and indeed present aspects of it that can only be received in this mode; and long ago certain truths and modes of this kind were discovered and must always reappear.
— *J.R.R. Tolkien*

Bigfoot, flying saucers, haunted houses, ghost lights, and the Bermuda Triangle are legends which have survived the test of time. Some of these tales are just as popular now as when they first began. Our world is full of mysteries which not only mystify and scare us, but also create intrigue. Not everything on this planet is black and white. There is gray area of things which defy normal explanation. These enigmatic tales have been passed down for generations and have become legends. When I say legends, I'm not talking about if George Washington really cut down a cherry tree, or if Paul Revere really made his famous midnight ride. I'm talking about the legendary beings and objects still around today.

Did you know almost every state in the union has stories of large, hairy, bipedal creatures, roaming the forests and swamps just on the edge of civilization? Besides Bigfoot, stories around the campfire tell of strange creatures called MoMo, the Yeti, the Fouke Monster, and the Skunk Ape. There are large aquatic sea serpent-like creatures dwelling in lakes and rivers around the country. People report seeing Champ,

1

a large unknown aquatic creature lurking in the depths of Lake Champlain in New York and Vermont; Altamaha-ha, the sea serpent seen in the Altamaha River in Georgia; and OgooPogoo (also known as OgoPogo), seen in Lake Okanagan in Canada. On the Internet you can read tales of strange alien-like beings roaming around our very backwoods, such as the Mothman and the Dover Demon.

There are stories of ghosts and mysterious apparitions that haunt various locations all over our nation. Did you know almost every lighthouse in Florida is reported to be haunted? There is a paranormal investigation being conducted nearly every weekend somewhere in the United States.

To this day, people all over the world report seeing strange objects flying across the sky. Some have seen these objects land and the evidence is still there to see. There are tales of alien-like beings seen wandering around backyards and forests. Some of these beings have been seen actually floating.

Did you know there are lost treasures from pirates and the American Civil War, worth millions, still waiting to be found? Stories have been passed down from generation to generation of buried treasure still out there undiscovered, possibly in our backyards. There are places here in the United States where mysterious events happen to this day which defy explanation. There are places in the US where gravity is in turmoil and strange lights haunt mountain tops.

As you can see, these legends are as exciting as they are mysterious. Today these legends are gaining popularity as people discover the thrill of going out and looking for them. The best part is, it is not difficult to do, and you can enjoy it with your entire family. Monster and ghost hunting groups are popping up everywhere on the Internet as people search for the truth behind these legends. Every day you hear how people have seen things they can't explain and now they are feeling the adventurous spirit to investigate them.

Have you ever looked into the darkness of the woods and asked yourself, "Is something mysterious out there?" and have you ever thought about what you would do if you saw something that was unexplainable? If you have an adventurous spirit, then legend tripping is for you.

Wikipedia defines legend tripping this way: "Legend tripping, also known as ostension, is a name recently bestowed by folklorists and anthropologists on an adolescent practice (containing elements of a rite of passage) in which a usually furtive nocturnal pilgrimage is made to a site which is alleged to have been the scene of some tragic, horrific, and possibly supernatural event or haunting. The practice has been documented most thoroughly to date in the United States." It looks to me whoever wrote this was trying to use as many big words as he or she could to confuse everybody.

The best way to define it is to break it down. The definition of legend is "non historical or unverifiable story handed down by tradition from earlier times and popularly accepted as historical" (thefreedictionary. com). Tripping is simply an extension of the word "trip," meaning a physical journey to another place.

My definition is simple:

Legend tripping is to go on, or participate in, a quest or adventure for something that is defined as a mystery or legend and is not verified or explained by science.

Legend tripping was given a bad name when kids were going into abandoned buildings and underground

3

facilities and were calling themselves legend trippers. Some of the kids got hurt. In July 2012, teenagers snuck into the old, abandoned Ravenswood Hospital (in Chicago, Illinois), and one teenager died when he fell from the second story onto a concrete floor. That was not legend tripping; that was trespassing. When paranormal investigators go into abandoned buildings, they first get permission. There are many abandoned buildings I would love to go into, but I don't because I know it can be dangerous; usually, it's illegal. I'm not going to teach my kids how to break the law. Legend tripping is looking for and experiencing a legend and doing it the right way.

Do you want to be a legend tripper? Then ask yourself this: Are you one of those unique people who brave the woods at night to search for the large enigmatic creature known as Bigfoot or other cryptid creatures? Do you like to explore old run-down haunted places or graveyards, and conduct a ghost hunt? Do you investigate areas where sightings of strange unknown flying aircraft and landing sites have been reported? Are you one of those people who search for legendary lost treasure left behind by pirates or soldiers? If you do any of that, then you are a legend tripper.

You've heard the saying 'Think outside the box.' With legend tripping, you 'look outside the box.' You go out and search for things out of the norm. Let's be real, Bigfoot and ghosts are not what we call normal. In fact, it is why they are called paranormal. If you look up and see strange lights moving in an irregular pattern, and say 'It's probably a plane,' then you are not looking outside the box. If you say, 'it might be a UFO,' then you are. Legend trippers aren't discouraged by what scientists have to say. They know everything isn't always explainable. There are still things out there we don't know. A legend tripper braves the night to find the truth behind these legends.

Now, a person who looks for just cryptids is a cryptozoologist, and a person who looks for ghosts is a paranormal investigator. A legend tripper does not go by these labels. They eat, drink and live legends and spend every available minute researching and exploring the stories behind the legends. My passion lies in the thrill of the search for the unknown, the unexplained, the mysterious, and the weird. To a legend tripper, it is not a job but a passion. It would be nice to have a job looking for legends and mysteries. Legend tripping is a chance to get out and away from the everyday routine of life, and experience something above the norm.

On a side note, if you are one of those people who are looking to get famous, then legend tripping is probably not for you. Today, there are too many people to count out there looking for Bigfoot and/or ghosts, just to get what is referred to as the "money shot" (one photograph nobody, including scientists, can dispute), and to gain a large amount of money for being the person who took it.

The truth of the matter is there is no money shot. Today, with the many hoax videos on the Internet, people want proof they can actually see and touch. So, unless somebody brings in a live or dead specimen, then the photo or video is going to be ridiculed and branded a fake. The famous Bigfoot film is the 1967 Patterson-Gimlin film of a supposed female Bigfoot, and it is to this day, still considered by scientists to be a fake. No matter how many legend trippers say it's real, scientists say it is a person in a specially built gorilla suit. With the paranormal and extraterrestrials, unless you can get the ghost or UFO to show up at the same spot for scientists, your photo is going to be called a fake. But

5

a legend tripper doesn't care. It is not about making money and fame; it is about experiencing something nobody else gets to experience. It is the opportunity to look for something unique. It's a chance to step out of the normal day-to-day routine of everyday life and look for something that might help us reexamine how we look at certain scientific theories. Legend trippers are not out to prove science wrong, but that some of these legends have fact behind them.

Where do legend trippers go to explore legends? The quick answer is everywhere. There are legends in every one of the fifty states in the US. Every state has legendary haunted places. Washington Irving's famous short story "The Legend of Sleepy Hollow" is based on a real legend of a headless specter who is doomed to search for his head forever. The cave with the bottomless pit and hidden treasure in Mark Twain's book *Tom Sawyer* is based on a real legend. Unidentified flying objects are seen almost daily in every part of the world. Look on MUFON's website to see the daily UFO sightings. Cryptids are seen daily in various parts of the country and include Bigfoot, the Mothman, werewolves, and lake/river serpents. Native Americans have stories of these strange creatures going back centuries, and they are still reportedly seen today. A legend tripper knows where to look.

A legend tripper is not one of those people who are content to just lie on the couch watching television every weekend. They don't spend all their money at theme parks for excitement. A legend tripper lives to find weird places and explore them. Legends are all around us, you just need to research and find one close by and go on a legend trip.

Is everything on this planet explainable? Scientists will say, "Yes." Well, what I say to that is: have them explain why the rocks sound like bells when you

6

hit them at Ringing Rocks Park in Pennsylvania. Ask them what causes the ghost lights in the Blue Ridge Mountains of North Carolina. Not everything is explainable!

Have we documented every known animal on this planet? The answer is "No." Every year, scientists discover new kinds of animals, new plants, even new planets. The world around us is still full of mystery. We still don't know what is at the bottom of the oceans. We don't really know how the pyramids were built. Who made the large drawings on the Nazca Plains, out in the desert in Peru? Not every report of a UFO has properly been explained. Are we the only intelligent species on this planet, or in the universe? Are experienced hunters mistakenly seeing a bear instead of a large bipedal humanoid creature walking around our forests and swamps? Are there large aquatic creatures lurking at the bottom of some of the deepest lakes in the world? If not, what are people seeing? What happened to all those aircraft and ships which disappeared off the coast of Florida, in the area known as the Bermuda Triangle?

Every day, people are seeing animals they cannot identify or have never seen before. Hunters are seeing a large hairy bipedal animal that walks like a human. A scientist's quick response is they are seeing bears walking on their hind legs. I don't know any hunter who does not know the difference between a bear and a Bigfoot. People are seeing something they cannot identify.

When it comes to UFOs and extraterrestrials, I like Ivan T. Sanderson's acronym UAO instead of UFO. UAO stands for Unidentified Aerial Object. It makes sense because these strange object are not flying with the use of wings or rotors like birds, helicopters and planes. They are not displacing air but are instead moving through an unknown form of propulsion. For practical purposes I will still use the acronym "UFO" in this book.

As a kid I loved the movie *Close Encounters of the Third Kind* and read a lot of books on the subject like Ivan T. Sanderson's *Uninvited Visitors* and *Invisible Residents*. For the record, I do believe we are being visited by beings not from this planet. For my own adventures, I try to find out where the last UFO sighting took place see if it shows up again. Sometimes they do and sometimes not. But when it comes to extraterrestrials, what excites me the most is to visit and explore supposed UFO landings and crash sites, and locations where there have been sightings of alien-like creatures.

Today, there are numerous groups who go out and look for monsters, conduct paranormal investigations, and look for UFOs. In fact, there are so many I can't begin to count them. If you want to join one of these legend tripping groups, make sure it is one you want to belong to and the beliefs are the same as yours. The great thing is, most of these groups will allow you to come on an investigation and see what they are about. They are excited about having new people along to share in their investigation. On the flip side, there are some groups who keep everything internal. What I mean by is, if you find anything, you can only share it with them, and the group will announce the finding to the community.

The great thing about legend tripping is there are all kinds of legends to go look for, and each one is just as exciting to look for as the other. In this book, I will break the legends down into four categories:

Cryptids
- Bigfoot

- Lake monsters
- Large birds and flying humanoids
- Alien animals
- Misplaced animals

Paranormal
- Haunted places
- Ghosts

UFOs and Extraterrestrial Encounters
- Sightings
- Landing sites

Hidden or Lost Treasures
- Treasures are located in the US and Canada

Mysterious Places
- Ghost lights
- Gravity hills
- Other mysterious places

I will be more in-depth about these legends in the following chapters and describe how to conduct a legend trip to look for them. Unfortunately, I can't go over every legend out there, because it would take up volumes. I will however go over some popular legends as well as some little-known. There are plenty of books and websites on legends and myths making the research of legends easier. There is a complete list at the end of this book.

I've designed this as a guidebook on how to actually conduct and go on a legend trip. I organized this book by first going over the legend and then explaining how to look for it. Each legend trip works the same in the East or the West of the United States. The only thing different is the location. Some of these trips can be just a day trip, like looking for ghost lights. Ghost hunts are generally an overnight trip. Some, like Bigfoot hunting, can take longer. I will go over what I have found is good to take with you on the trip and things to be aware of when planning a legend trip.

One last thing before I share my excitement with you. Being retired military, I tend to use a lot of military terms. I do this out of habit and to shorten sentences. A few examples would be the word "rucking," which is nothing more than hiking with a backpack on. A "ruck" is a backpack and "snivel gear" is what the military calls rain gear like a poncho. "Static posts" or "observation points" are where you set up in the area of investigation and just wait, watch, and listen. ASAP is short for "as soon as possible."

Here is a quick list of dos and don'ts I want to stress before we go over legend trips. It's important safety be your major concern when you are out there in the woods.

Legend Tripping Dos and Don'ts

Do make a complete plan for the legend trip and have a Plan A and a Plan B.

Do make a supplies/equipment list and make sure you get everything on it.

Do brief the plan with the team and make sure everybody understands it.

Do plan for the worst.

Do bring wet-weather gear.

Do let other family members know where you are going and when you expect to return.

Do have everybody wear a safety necklace at night.

Do bring cell phone chargers for the vehicle and a solar powered charger for hiking.

10

Do carry water and purification tablets.

Do have proper fishing licenses.

Do stay put and do not move, if you get lost, and contact base camp.

Do bring extra batteries.

Don't treat the legend trip as if it were a walk in the park.

Don't assume there are stores in the area to buy supplies.

Don't be in a rush to leave—otherwise you will forget something important.

Don't trespass on private property; it's against the law!

Don't wear new boots for hiking trips; you need to break them in before hiking.

Don't always believe the weather reports.

Don't try out all new equipment before you go.

Don't drink untreated water.

Don't bring and drink alcohol on expedition.

Don't not go near wild animals.

Don't Leave trash behind.

Chapter 2
Bigfoot

There is a famous story about Alexander the Great. After conquering a region in India, Alexander had ten philosophers, or wise men, in his custody. These philosophers were believed to have caused some unrest in the Indian nation. Alexander stated if they were indeed wise men, they would be able to answer his questions and avoid execution.

He asked one of the wise men, "What animal is the most cunning animal in the world?"

The wise man answered, "The one that avoids man." This wise philosopher lived.

The word "cryptozoology" is defined as "the search for and study of animals whose existence or survival is disputed or unsubstantiated." There is some controversy on who actually coined the term. Bernard Heuvelmans is credited with it in his book *On the Track of Unknown Animals*, but he actually states Ivan T. Sanderson was the first to coin the term "cryptozoology".

"Cryptid" is a term derived from cryptozoology for an animal whose existence has not been verified by science. Some animals are no longer considered cryptids, such as the giant squid, which Japanese researchers confirmed through deep sea video in 2012. It's funny, but when they are still a legend they belong to cryptozoology, and when they are proven to exist, they then belong to zoology and biology.

Some books categorize cryptids differently. I

want to keep it as simple as I can for those who are new to cryptozoology. I have arranged them with the popular monsters first.

The best-known type of cryptid is the large hairy humanoid. The most famous of these are known as Bigfoot. I decided to dedicate this whole chapter to the cryptid giant. First, because it is the only cryptid that is in almost every state in America and second, I love to plan my legend trips looking for this elusive creature.

Bigfoot.

For those who don't know anything about this cryptid, this is a short, down and dirty summary of it and other cryptids. I could fill a whole book on the subject of this beast, but I didn't want to deprive you of reading some awesome books on the subject (which I will name at the end of each cryptid summary).

Bigfoot are described as large (between six and ten feet tall), bipedal, humanlike creatures covered in reddish-brown hair. They look like hairy Neanderthal men and sightings of them are reported in almost every part of the world. Even Europe has reports of large hairy animals roaming the forests. They are located in nearly every state in the Union except Hawaii. These animals tend to avoid human contact so sightings are rare. Because these animals live in the woods, their senses are heightened, especially their sense of smell. They usually leave when they smell humans.

Stories and legends about these animals go back

for centuries. During the 19th and early 20th centuries, newspapers in small towns around the United States and Canada occasionally featured accounts of hairy wild men seen by locals, sometimes giving warnings. They are said to mostly nocturnal (active at night), which a lot of cryptids seem to be. In contrast, most apes, like chimpanzees and gorillas, are by nature diurnal (active during daytime). Bigfoots' size is often associated with their location. On the west coast through to the northern east coast, they are said to be about ten feet tall, while those on the southern east side of Florida are about six or eight feet fall. There has been some controversy about whether these animals are violent or not. The ones located in Texas, Ohio, and Arkansas are known to have a mean streak and have grabbed at humans or thrown rocks at them. Hunters and ranchers are less squeamish and tend to shoot at the animals there, which may explain the aggression. If somebody was shooting at me, I'd get mean as well. Out of all the cryptids, these have gained the most popularity, due partly to books and publications but mostly to television shows and commercials.

Bigfoot has become the poster boy for cryptozoology.

Bigfoot has also gone by different names here in North America. The Native Americans have a long history of Bigfoot and each tribe has their own name for it, the popular one being Sasquatch. In this

15

Legend Tripping

An early photo of Bigfoot taken by Zack Hamilton in 1965.

16

chapter I'm going to go over some of the different Bigfoot which are said to inhabit the United States; some of the names you might recognize.

The first one I want to talk about is the classic Bigfoot which makes its home in the forests, mainly in the Pacific Northwest. This one is usually referred to as Sasquatch. There have been stories of wild

San Francisco Chronicle
THE VOICE OF THE WEST

FINAL HOME EDITION ★   MONDAY, DECEMBER 6, 1965   10 C

The Mountain Giants

A comparison of a man and the "man-animal," compiled from reports based on the numerous eyewitness sightings of the strange mountain creatures.

Hamilton's photo appeared in this Dec. 4, 1965 article in the *San Francisco Chronicle*.

17

men among the natives of the Pacific Northwest coast for hundreds of years. Native American tribes had their own name for the creature featured in the local version of such legends. Many names meant something along the lines of "wild man" or "hairy man." About one-third of Bigfoot sightings are located in the Pacific Northwest, Washington state having the most sightings, with California second for the region. The state of Oregon is actually fourth for Bigfoot sightings.

Some Bigfoot proponents like anthropologist Grover Krantz and primatologist Geoffrey H. Bourne believed Bigfoot could be a relict population of Gigantopithecus. This is an extinct genus of giant ape that existed from perhaps nine million years to as recently as one hundred thousand years ago, in what is now China, India, and Vietnam.

A major event happened in October 1967. Roger Patterson and Bob Gimlin were in the Six River National Forest filming a Bigfoot documentary. On the morning of the 20th, the two were riding on horseback came to an area known as Bluff Creek. All of a sudden a large hairy creature stood up from the creek and looked directly at them, spooking their horses. Patterson was thrown from his horse but quickly recovered and grabbed his camera and started filming as the creature retreated from the area, back into the woods. The fifty-three second film made Bigfoot history. You can clearly see a large hairy figure that appears to be a female due to the prominent breasts, walking away and glancing back at them as it leaves. This film has been ridiculed by scientists, who claim it is nothing more than a man in a suit. But oddly enough, nobody to date, can successfully recreate it. The film is easy to find on the Internet and is probably the most compelling evidence the animal does exist.

18

Today with popular television shows and commercials, Bigfoot has become an icon. More and more people are out looking for this elusive beast. Bigfoot hunting groups are in almost every state except Hawaii and Rhode Island, the most popular of these groups being the Bigfoot Field Research Organization (BFRO) run by Matt Moneymaker. BFRO has one of the most comprehensive and up-to-date website detailing all the latest Bigfoot sightings as well as historical accounts. BFRO also has Bigfoot hunts you can participate in for a fee. You can go on their website to find where the next Bigfoot expedition is going to be. If you have a sighting and make a report the BFRO, a contact is usually sent to record your account of the sighting and look for additional evidence.

The second cryptid I want to talk about is the Florida Skunk Ape. Believe it or not Florida is the second highest state for overall Bigfoot sightings. The Skunk Ape has been reported in virtually every part of Florida except the Keys. It is reported to look a lot like its western cousin, all covered with dark brown hair, extremely muscular and a cross between an ape and a human. The only real difference is the Skunk Ape in Florida is reportedly not as tall as Bigfoot observed in California and Oregon.

The term "Skunk Ape" actually originated in Arkansas in the late 1800s, but when the early settlers came to Florida and reported a strange primate-like creature prowling the forests and swamps and its nauseous smell, it too was called the Skunk Ape. Some cryptozoologists refer to it as the Swamp Ape, the Seminoles refer to it as Esti Capcaki (Cannibal Giant) and one town in Florida calls it the Bardin Booger. The Skunk Ape is pretty widely known here in Florida, and is probably the state's most famous

19

legend. Sightings of these elusive beasts range in the thousands. Unfortunately, most of these sightings go undocumented by hunters and hikers, who do not wish to be ridiculed.

Although Bigfoot is traditionally associated with the Pacific Northwest, most people do not realize it was actually well known in the South decades before its first documented appearances in Washington and Oregon. During the 19th century, sightings of large hairy creatures were often reported as the frontiers of the United States rapidly spread out from the Atlantic seaboard. People of that day and age, however, called it the "Wild Man."

The first recorded sighting of an unknown primate in Florida was in 1818. The sighting occurred at Apalachicola of a five-foot baboon-like figure. While some experts dismissed this as fiction, it should be noted the first zoo and circus in Florida opened in 1927. The second recorded sighting occurred in the winter of 1883-1884, which was originally reported as a wild man who had appeared at Ocheesee Pond, a large wetland covering nearly nine square miles in southeastern Jackson County. Located below Grand Ridge and Sneads in the southeast corner of Jackson County, Ocheesee Pond was a focal point for early settlers. Most of the pond is covered by a vast cypress swamp, although there are some stretches of open water—most notably its southern arm. The strange humanlike creature was often spotted roaming the swamps or swimming from place to place.

As more sightings occurred in the remote area, the local residents, many of them former Confederate soldiers, decided to launch an expedition to capture this Wild Man. In August of 1884, they succeeded! Newspapers at the time, were silent on the eventual fate of the Ocheesee Pond Wild Man. It was reported his body was covered in thick hair, but the captors believed he was a human who had probably escaped from an asylum. No asylum reported such an odd escapee, however, and his captors became even more baffled by the Wild Man. The last account has the strange beast being sent to Tallahassee and then back to Chattahoochee after scientists could not identify it and, unfortunately, so ends the report.

The next reported Swamp Ape sightings happened in 1942 where a large apelike figure jumped in front of a vehicle in the town of Branford. It was then supposed to have jumped on the running board of the moving vehicle and clung on for at least half a mile. It looked into the vehicle and then dropped off and ran into the nearby woods.

In 1947, in Lakeland, a large hairy bipedal creature was seen by a four-year old little boy, who stated he saw the strange creature standing behind an orange tree, watching him. He quickly went back into his home and related what he saw to his mother. While you may think the boy was seeing things, misidentifying a bear, or just flat out making it up, remember the first story I related happened at the Green Swamp which is just north of Lakeland.

In August 2004 schoolteacher Jennifer Ward was driving on a rural road in Southern Florida, two weeks after Hurricane Charlie had hit central Florida. She had just been visiting a friend; the sun was setting and she was now on her way home with her two daughters asleep in the back seat.

Something on the side of the road caught her attention. She first thought it was an animal of some kind, but could not tell what. It appeared to be crouched in a ditch on the roadside. It was something large. She slowed the car to get a better look. As she neared it, the creature noticed her and stood to its full

21

height on two legs. Something she had never seen before. "When it saw me, the animal looked just as surprised as I was," she later told the news press. "I didn't stop because I was scared. It was almost dark, but I could see it and I did get a good look at it."

What Jennifer described was a mysterious creature that has been seen in virtually every state of the Union, but has never been scientifically classified. It stood six to eight feet tall, she reported, and was covered in dark hair about two inches long. The area around its eyes was whitish and its full lips had the color and texture of the pad on a dog's paw.

The Bigfoot Field Research Organization has more than two hundred and eighty sightings recorded on their website in Florida alone. The creature is seen in all parts of Florida from up in the panhandle, to the central area not far from Orlando, down in the Everglades, and even in an area close to Cape Canaveral and the Kennedy Space Center.

While I don't have the room to go over every sighting (there have been over 600 in Florida alone) I do however want to go over some photos taken of the large cryptid. One of the most talked about picture is the Myakka Skunk Ape photo. In 2000, two photographs and a letter were sent by an anonymous woman to the Sarasota County, Florida, Sheriff's Department. The photographs showed a large hairy bipedal creature standing next to a large palmetto plant. In the letter, the woman claims to have photographed an ape in her backyard.

The woman wrote on three different nights an ape had entered her backyard to take apples left on her back porch. She was convinced the ape was an escaped orangutan. It should be noted the witness in question at no time called the creature a Skunk Ape but simply refers to it as ape, which she believed

22

to have escaped. Escaped exotic animals are not uncommon here in Florida. During Hurricane Andrew in 1992, animals from the Miami zoo got loose and some were never recovered.

As far as the pictures go, the jury is still out on this one. Believed to be a real animal, cryptozoologists can't decide if it is, in fact, an orangutan, or an unknown primate. Without the witness coming forward and showing exactly where the sightings took place, the photos will continue to stay unsolved.

On May 8, 2012 Bigfoot hunter Stacy Brown Jr. of Sasquatchhunters.com was out Bigfoot hunting with his dad in Northern Florida, when something exciting happened. They went out equipped with night vision and a FLIR thermal scope. At about midnight, after hearing some knocking, Stacy's dad spotted something large on the FLIR scope. A large bipedal

One of three Skunk Ape photos taken in 2000 in Myakka, FL.

23

creature was standing behind a tree and appeared to be watching them. Then all of a sudden, the animal moved from behind the tree to another tree. The FLIR picked up the total thermal outline of the creature as it moved.

A Swamp Ape.

The video is available to watch online and you can see the perfect outline of the creature as it moves. Stacy took me out to the sighting location. My wife filmed me at the same location doing the same movement and you can see whatever it was, was a lot larger than me. In fact, it is estimated the creature is about eight feet tall. Next to the famous 1967 Patterson-Gimlin film of Bigfoot, this is the best evidence to date of the unknown cryptid. The video can be viewed at SasquatchHunters.com

In March 2013, Mike Falconer and his son were visiting Myakka River State Park in Sarasota County, when he saw a large hairy bipedal creature roaming around a large field next to a lake. He immediately pulled his truck over and he and his son took off running after the creature. Falconer had his cellphone video going the entire time. He did capture a large figure on his cellphone camera in the field. It is hard to see what is really out there. I viewed Mr. Falconer's video and found the same problem as with other video. Cellphones do not offer the best quality for filming and objects appear further out than they really are. I believe Mr. Falconer did see a large bipedal animal and he did attempt to film it. The area of Myakka has a long history of Skunk Ape sightings.

As you can see, Florida has no shortage of Skunk Ape encounters. Who knows, there might be more footage of this rare creature will surface right after I finish this book. This animal which defies science continues to make its presence known in the Sunshine State. Its legend goes

The author with a Swamp Ape statue.

back before the settlers came to Florida, when Native Americans occupied the land. Today there are still vast swaths of forests and swamps offering refuge for this cryptid. Today science is continually discovering new species of animals. As man encroaches more into the last of Florida's forests and swamps, the day will come when the world will see these fantastic creatures do exist along with other cryptids.

Along the Tamiami Trail, in the southwest corner of Big Cypress National Preserve, is the bump in the road known as Ochopee, consisting of one hole-in-the-wall restaurant, a miniscule post office and the world's only Skunk Ape Research Headquarters owned and operated by one Dave Shealey. Dave is Florida's self-appointed Skunk Ape expert. Slim, in his mid-forties, he wears dark, wraparound sunglasses, a hat with a band of alligator teeth, and no shoes. "There's never been a documented case of anyone ever being physically attacked by a Skunk Ape," he says, reassuringly. "But also, there's a lot of people

25

that go into the Everglades and never come out."

Dave has been studying the Skunk Ape "pretty much all my life" and describes it as six to seven feet tall and 350 to 450 pounds. He guesses there are between seven and nine of the creatures around here, in a waterlogged and bug infested wetland of buzzards and alligators.

As I describe more fully in the Introduction to this book, after a witness related the sighting he had in central Florida, he took me to the area of the sighting, and I looked at the direction the creature was going. Later the same night, I took my family out there. With the help of my son's night vision goggles, my son and I encountered something large moving through the swamp. It seemed to keep up with us while we walked a fire break trail. When we stopped, it stopped. I looked through the night vision goggles and saw two glowing eyes. The creature then let out a scream I can only describe as sounding like a gorilla. My son and I decided to head back to our vehicle. I know what a bear, panther and hog (known animals in the area) sound like and whatever it was, was moving through the swampy area. The goggles only have a range of fifty feet so we did not get a positive look at what it actually was.

Recently a new photo and video of the legendary beast surfaced on the news and the Internet. The

The 2015 Tampa, FL, Swamp Ape photo.

26

photo was taken by a fisherman near Tampa in 2015. The beast even has a white streak going through the top of its hair. There was also a video that supposedly showed the animal wading through the swamps of Lettuce Lake. The photo and film proved to be a hoax.

If you ever find yourself in the early evening, venturing into the swamps of Florida, don't be surprised to see a large hairy creature prowling through the swamps. You just saw the Florida Skunk Ape.

Probably one of the most famous of Bigfoot-like creatures is the Fouke Monster. This cryptid is often referred to as the Boggy Creek Monster or the Southern Sasquatch. The creature has the same description as a classic Bigfoot with the exception it is reported to have three toes. Sightings of this cryptid actually originated in the 1940s when it was first referred to as the Jonesville Monster. Apparently the creature made its presence known by breaking into chicken coops and stealing pigs from farms. The creature made headlines in the summer of 1971, when it terrorized the home of Bobby and Elizabeth Ford late on the night of May 1. The Fords reported they fired several shots at the creature and believed they had hit it. Later, no traces of blood were found, but strange three-

The Fouke Monster.

toed footprints were located near the house. It attacked Bobby Ford later that night.

Since then, there have been numerous sightings of this cryptid. It is mostly seen crossing Highway 71 and around the

Three-toed print.

Sulfur River bottoms. A radio station KAAY posted a $1,000 bounty on the creature, which nobody collected. Attempts were made to track the creature with dogs, but canines refused to track it after getting its scent. When Charles B. Peirce's now classic movie *The Legend of Boggy Creek* was released in 1972, a renewed interest in the creature began.

If I were to pick a particular moment when I got bitten by the legend tripping bug, it would probably be when I first saw *The Legend of Boggy Creek*. This movie really changed where I focused my interests, and changed my life. I can remember the first time I saw the movie. Yes, I've watched it more than once. In fact, to date, I think I've watched it more than one hundred times. The first time was in 1974 at a local drive-in theater in Hattiesburg, Mississippi when I was twelve years old. I remember escorting my little brother to the restroom before the movies started. As we passed the concession stand, I looked up and saw a movie poster of the large hairy monster walking in the creek, as if toward you. I thought to myself, "What the heck is walking through the water in the woods?" Actually, it is a pretty awesome poster. The artist who painted it is known for his art for the *Star Wars* movies today. I own an original copy of the movie poster proudly hanging in my office.

After the previews were shown, the movie started, and what was the first thing came on the screen? "This is a true story." I remembered the movie poster

28

and thought, "Holy cow, there is a real hairy monster walking around out there!" Then the terrifying scream rang through the drive-in. I stared wide-eyed at the movie screen, at the image of a young boy running through a huge field, and thought, "Oh my god, this thing eats little boys!" I won't ruin the rest of the movie for those who have never seen it, but long story short, the movie was terrifying, but exciting to me. After it was over, I thought about the Fouke Monster the whole car ride home. It is actually a simple documentary movie, no elaborate special effects or expensive monster suit. Mr. Pierce did what nobody else has done; he made a simple documentary-style movie which made you feel like you were right there next to those people being terrorized by an unknown creature.

Later, I found out I wasn't the only one who got his wits scared out of him. It did however, get me reading books about Bigfoot, the Fouke Monster, and the Yeti. Lucky enough, in my school library there were a lot of books on the subject of the unexplained. I think I ended up doing all my book reports on the unexplained and I found I was becoming a young expert on the subject. My dad would often bring me into an adult conversation if it pertained to the subject of Bigfoot or any other cryptids.

In 2015, I had the privilege of speaking at the third annual Boggy Creek Festival in Fouke. It was an honor to be there and meet people like Loren Coleman and Lyle Blackburn who are quite prominent in the cryptozoology world.

Lyle Blackburn wrote what is

probably the best researched book on the Fouke Monster phenomenon called *The Beast of Boggy Creek: The True Story of the Fouke Monster*. It is one of my favorite books. Lyle took me around Fouke and down around Boggy Creek. I know this is going to sound cheesy, but I consider Boggy Creek my Graceland. The whole reason I got into legend tripping was because of the movie. For me to go walking around the creek looking at the wood line was exciting, and I had a great time and made a point of grabbing a rock out of Boggy Creek. Lyle also took me to all the areas where sightings happened

The author in Fouke, AR.

in the movie. Unfortunately, some of the homes have been torn down. Later I went down around the Sulfur River bottoms and walked around there. The Fouke Monster has been seen in that area as well.

The residents of Fouke are extremely nice and they are pretty much OK with you asking about the monster. I found a lot of them do not believe in the legend, but they won't tease you about it. The focal point of Fouke is the Monster Mart, which is also a museum on the local legend and is easy to find. There is a large bust of the creature gracing the front entrance of the store/museum.

Another Bigfoot-like creature which recently gained popularity is the Ohio Grassman. For almost

150 years Ohio residents have reported sightings of these creatures lurking about rural farms and fields. This large hairy monster is said to inhabit Ohio and Western Pennsylvania. It allegedly eats wheat and other tall grasses, hence the name. As far as appearance goes, the Grassman looks pretty much like the classic Bigfoot, but is also said to be aggressive. There is one report where five of these animals were seen at one time.

During the 70s, if you were lucky enough to be growing up along the upper east coast of the United States, chances are you saw an incredible and popular roadside attraction making the rounds at carnivals and shopping malls. It was kept in a trailer; you walked into one end, looked at the attraction and then exited the other. This attraction featured a large rectangular glass container in a trailer. In this container was the body of a large hairy bipedal creature frozen in ice. The animal appeared to have died of still visible gunshot wounds. This animal fit the exact description of what witnesses reported Bigfoot looks like.

Frank Hanson, the owner, claimed it was real and he had purchased it after it was found floating in the South China Sea. He later made claims he had in fact shot the animal on a hunting trip in Minnesota. It was investigated by Ivan T. Sanderson and Bernard Heuvelmans. They declared the animal was authentic. This side show oddity was known as the Minnesota Iceman.

After the FBI got involved, over the display of a real cadaver, the attraction was revealed to be a fake. Mr. Hanson later stated he substituted the real one for a fake one he had constructed in Hollywood to avoid problems with the authorities. There has always been speculation about whether the creature was real or a hoax. It was thought to have been lost, but was then discovered in a closed down carnival. You can see this rare oddity of the cryptozoology world at its permanent home at the Museum of the Weird which I mention in Chapter 15: Day Legend Trips.

The first Bigfoot sighting I investigated was the Missouri Bigfoot, MoMo. The name MoMo is short for 'Missouri Monster.' Unlike the classic Bigfoot appearance this cryptid is reported to have a large, round-shaped head, with a furry body, and hair covering the eyes. MoMo has been spotted up and down the Mississippi River. While reports of this creature started in the early seventies, the Native Americans have legends of this beast that go back hundreds of years. The first modern report was July 1971, in Louisiana, Missouri when Joan Mills and Mary Ryan were picnicking down by the river, and saw this strange animal. The story goes, the beast came walking up on them and the two ladies quickly fled to their car. They both forgot the car keys and watched the beast eat their food. They had to wait for the animal to leave before retrieving the keys. There are still reports of these cryptids roaming around the area.

I decided to put swamp monsters in the same category as Bigfoot, instead of aquatic cryptids, due to their similarity. These creatures are Bigfoot-type creatures with the exception they are three-toed. These large, hairy animals are seen mostly in the southern states and seem to prefer the security of the swamplands. The most famous of them is the Honey Island Swamp Monster. This creature was first seen in 1963 by Harlan Ford, a retired air traffic controller who was out hunting. Native Americans call this creature Letiche and have legends of these swamp creature going back to the time when they first came to the area. In 1974, the monster gained national fame after appearing on an episode of the popular television show *In Search Of.* In the episode Ford and his friend Billy Mills claimed to have found unusual footprints in the area, as well as the body of a wild boar whose throat had been gashed. Ford continued to hunt for the creature for the next six years. After his death in 1980, his granddaughter Dana Holyfield found a reel of Super 8 film showing the creature. On a side note there is a bizarre legend of a train wreck in the area. A travelling circus was on the train, and from it a group of chimpanzees escaped and interbred with the local alligator population. Dana wrote an excellent book appropriately called *The Honey Island Swamp Monster* which is the most comprehensive investigation and study done on this cryptid.

It just seems odd every animal that is bipedal has five toes, yet these bipedal animals only have three. I realize some birds are bipedal and have three toes like the penguin. It might be possible they are not anthropoid in nature and might be something else. Unfortunately, we're not going to know until we find one of these animals and examine it.

As you can see there seems to be a small population of hairy giants inhabiting our woodlands and swamps around Northern America. Scientists still insist all these witnesses are seeing bears. But Bigfoot is not the only mysterious creature roaming around the United States. Next up, more cryptids.

The author with his specially-equiped Legend Tripper vehicle.

Chapter 3
More Cryptids

The second most popular category of cryptid is giant birds and flying humanoids.

The Jersey Devil

Probably the most famous of these is the Jersey Devil (or Leeds Devil), which has been seen for more than two hundred years in the Pine Barrens of New Jersey. This unique cryptid is often described as a kangaroo-like creature with the head of a goat or horse, leathery bat-like wings, horns, small arms with clawed hands, cloven hooves and a forked tail, but there are as many variations in descriptions as there have been reported encounters. One thing over 2,000 witnesses have agreed on is the Jersey Devil emits a "bloodcurdling scream." Each region of New Jersey has its own version of the origin of this cryptid, but the most popular legend dates back to 1735 when a witch named Mrs. Shroud lived in Leeds, New Jersey with twelve children. On a stormy night Mrs. Shroud gave birth to her 13th child. She was said to have been so angry about having another child she wanted it to be a devil. When the baby

The Jersey Devil.

The Jersey Devil.

was born, it was said to be misshapen and deformed. Mrs. Shroud looked down at the terrifying creature she gave birth to and screamed. The creature then flapped its wings and escaped out the chimney and was never seen by the family again. One version says the Devil killed Mrs. Shroud and the midwife, before flying away.

There were then varied reports coming in of witnesses seeing this strange winged creature flying around the Pine Barrens. One famous witness was Joseph Bonaparte, elder brother of Napoleon, who claimed to have witnessed the Jersey Devil while hunting on his Borden town estate around 1820. A famous Naval hero, Commodore Stephen Decatur, was said to have been testing cannon balls on the firing range when he saw a strange beast flying across the sky. It was also reported he fired and hit the creature but it kept right on flying. Hard core scientists believe the Devil is nothing more than misidentification, believing it is was either a large owl or crane. Sightings of the Devil are still being reported today. Most don't know this but the Pine Barrens encompassed over one million acres, so it is possible an unknown animal could make its home there. A paranormal television show on production in the Pine Barrens filmed, with a thermal imaging camera, a large bipedal winged animal. This cryptid is so popular New

36

Jersey named its hockey team after it. Mark Sceurman and Mark Moran, who created the best-selling book *Weird New Jersey*, included the most up-to-date sightings of the devil.

The Mothman of West Virginia

Another popular flying figure is the Mothman of Point Pleasant, West Virginia. Even though it was only seen for a short period of time, it gained a reputation for appearing before major disasters. According to legend and newspaper articles, the whole affair with the cryptid started on November 12, 1966, when five men who were digging a grave at a cemetery near Clendenin, WV, claimed to see a man-like figure fly low from the trees over their heads.

It made the headlines on November 15, 1966, when two young couples from Point Pleasant, Roger and Linda Scarberry, and Steve and Mary Mallette, saw a large white creature whose eyes "glowed red" when the car headlights picked it up. The animal was described as a "large flying man" with ten-foot wings following their car while they were out joyriding in an area outside of town known as 'the TNT area.' This was the site of a former World War II munitions plant. A terrifying en-

WANTED

REWARD OFFERED FOR THE CAPTURE, DEAD OR ALIVE, OF THE LEEDS MONSTER, ALSO KNOWN AS THE

JERSEY DEVIL

THE CREATURE IS OFTEN DESCRIBED AS A KANGAROO-LIKE PATCHWORK WITH THE FACE OF A HORSE, THE HEAD OF A DOG, LEATHERY BAT-LIKE WINGS, HORNS, SMALL ARMS WITH CLOVEN HOOVES AND A FORKED TAIL. IT HAS BEEN REPORTED TO MOVE QUICKLY AS TO AVOID HUMAN CONTACT, AND OFTEN IS DESCRIBED AS EMITTING A "BLOOD-CURDLING SCREAM."

APPROACH WITH EXTREME CAUTION

$250,000 REWARD!

counter occurred on November 16, 1966 when the Thomas family spotted a "funny red light" in the sky which moved and hovered above the TNT plant. A neighbor, Mrs. Bennett, drove to the Thomas house a few minutes later and

Mothman.

got out of the car with her baby. Suddenly, the cryptid stirred near the automobile. Mrs. Bennett went on to say it rose up slowly from the ground. She stated is was a big gray thing with terrible glowing eyes. The animal horrified Mrs. Bennett and she dropped her little girl, but quickly recovered, picked up her child and ran to the house. The Thomas family locked everyone inside but hysteria gripped them as the creature shuffled onto the porch and peered into the windows. The police were summoned, but the cryptid had vanished by time authorities arrived. Mrs. Bennett never psychologically recovered from the incident.

On December 15, 1967, tragedy occurred when the Silver Bridge connecting Point Pleasant, WV to Kanauga, OH collapsed resulting in the death of 46 people. This famous tragedy gave rise to the legend that the Mothman is seen right before a disaster, forever connecting the sightings and the bridge collapse. This cryptid has also been associated with the paranormal and a possible extraterrestrial origin. There have also been strange UFO sightings and reports of "Men in Black" intimidating witnesses. There has been no evidence such as tracks or clear photographs of this cryptid. Yet, witnesses swear the animal exists. There is an annual Mothman festival in Point Pleasant to celebrate their local cryptid.

Loren Coleman wrote a very detailed book on the Mothman phenomena called *Mothman and other Curious Encounters*. The most famous book was John A. Keel's 1975 *The Mothman Prophecies* which was later made into a movie. Several paranormal television shows have visited Point Pleasant interviewing old and new witnesses, visiting the old TNT munitions site and even employing a psychic to address every aspect of this legend.

Thunderbirds and Other Giant Avians

For centuries there have been legends of birds so gargantuan they were reported to have tried to carry off small children. In the cryptozoology field, these large birds are referred to as Thunderbirds. According to Native American legend, the Thunderbird was capable of creating storms and thunder while it flew above. Clouds were pulled together by its beating wings, creating thunderous reverberations while sheet lightning flashed from its eyes with each blink, and individual lightning bolts shot from glowing snakes carried in its talons.

Modern descriptions have the giant birds with wingspans of up to 20 feet wide, hooked talons and razor-like beaks. With recent sightings of this airborne cryptid, there has been a renewed interest in folklore and documentation. A fantastic story associated with the Thunderbird occurred in 1977 in the town of Lawndale, Illinois. On July 25th, two giant birds were observed by witnesses above the town. The birds were observed circling and swooping in the area. Then without warning the birds attacked three boys who were playing in the backyard of Ruth and Jake Lowe. One of the Thunderbirds grasped the shirt of ten-year-old Marlon Lowe with its talons and attempted to fly off

One of the fake "Dead Thunderbird" photos.

with the small boy. Marlon's cries brought his mother running outside. She stated what when she came outside, she saw the bird actually lift the boy from the ground and into the air. Apparently her screams and the boy attempting to fight his way loose caused the bird to finally release Marlon. It had carried him, at a height of about three feet, for a distance of about forty feet. She was sure if she had not come outside, the bird would have been capable of carrying the boy away. Luckily, Marlon was not seriously injured although he sustained numerous scratches and was horribly frightened.

Today there are numerous sightings reported on the Internet of avian behemoths all over the United

States. Various sightings of large birds made the headlines in Texas during the 1970s. It all started when two police patrolman from Harlingen reported a giant bird with a 10-foot wingspan gliding over their patrol car.

The Dover Demon.

On January 7, 1976, a terrifying incident occurred near Brownsville, Texas. Raymondville resident Armando Grimaldo was sitting outside smoking a cigarette one evening. Suddenly, he heard the sound of great, flapping wings and was attacked from above by a beast which scratched at him, ripping his clothes. Grimaldo was transported to the Willacy County Hospital and was treated for shock.

One sighting made headlines in Texas when two civilian workers from San Antonio's Kelly Air Force Base spotted a 5-foot-tall winged creature sitting on a stock tank on a 400-acre ranch north of Poteet.

These flying creatures have been described as looking like a large condor and other times like a prehistoric flying dinosaur, or pterosaur.

As recently as 2002 reports from *Anchorage Daily News*, also picked up by the wire services, have reported "a giant winged creature like something out of Jurassic Park" sighted several times in southwest Alaska. Ken Gerhard wrote an excellent book on the subject called *Big Bird: Modern Sightings of Flying Monsters* published in 2007.

Alien Animals: The Dover Demon and More

Another type of cryptid is the alien animal. These animals appear to have come out of nowhere and might in fact be extraterrestrial in nature. The first one that

41

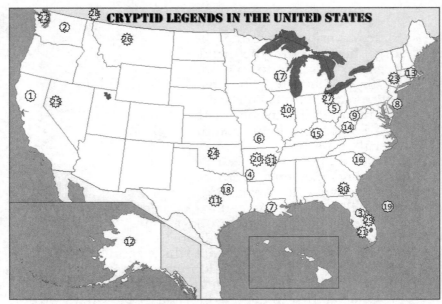

CRYPTID LEGENDS IN THE UNITED STATES

comes to mind is the Dover Demon. It was first reported on April 21, 1977 by seventeen-year-old William Bartlett. He claimed to have seen the strange large-eyed creature on top of a broken stone wall, while driving on Farm Street outside of Dover, Massachusetts. He described the creature as four feet tall, white in color with large glowing eyes and tendril-like fingers. Two fifteen-year-olds, John Baxter and Abby Brabham, also reported seeing the same creature, the same night, but at different locations from the original sighting. I remember when the sightings made all the newspapers. There has been an additional sightings of this strange cryptid but witnesses have been reluctant to come forward.

This incident was investigated by noted cryptozoologist Loren Coleman who traveled to Dover to investigate. He christened the creature the Dover Demon. He concluded "we have a credible case, over 25

42

1. Bigfoot, CA
2. Sasquatch, WA
3. Skunk Ape, FL
4. Fouke Monster, AR
5. Grassman, OH
6. MoMo, MI
7. Honey Island Swamp Monster, LA
8. Jersey Devil, NJ
9. Mothman, WV
10. Thunderbird, IL
11. Giant Bird, TX
12. Pterosaurs, AK
13. Dover Demon, MA
14. Flatwoods Monster, WV
15. Hopkinsville Goblins , KY
16. Lizard man, SC
17. Werewolf, WI
18. Lake Worth monster, TX
19. Chupacabras, PR
20. Gowrow, AR
21. Sanibel Island monster, FL
22. Cadboro Bay sea serpent, BC
23. Champ, NY
24. Oklahoma Octopus, OK
25. Tahoe Tessie , NV
26. Flathead Lake monster, MT
27. South Bay Bessie , OH
28. OgoPogo, CAN
29. Astor Monster, FL
30. Altie , GA
31. White River Monster, AR

hours, by individuals who saw something." Loren interviewed all three teens within a week of the reported sightings and said he was convinced they had not concocted a hoax. It should also be noted Farm Street has a history of unusual activity. There is a legend of a buried treasure nearby, and was supposed to be guarded by a supernatural entity, like a ghost or demonic animal.

In 2011 a picture surfaced on the Internet of what was supposedly the Dover Demon. It was reportedly taken with a game camera. Later it was revealed to be a viral marketing stunt for the upcoming PlayStation 3 exclusive *Resistance 3* game. I can't confirm it, but a few gaming websites have said it was, and it does look like the zombies in the game, but it also oddly follows the exact description of the Dover Demon.

Another alien animal is the Flatwoods Monster seen in 1952 in Braxton County, West Virginia. This strange being was seen by six children after they observed a strange light descend into the nearby forest. On September 12, 1952 the kids got together and decided to go up into the hills and see what had landed. When they got there they saw this strange hovering figure. It was at least seven feet (2.1 m) tall, with a black body and a dark, greenish glowing face. Witnesses described the creature's head as being elongated and shaped like a sideways diamond. It was said to have nonhuman eyes with a large, circular cowl appeared behind the head. The creature's body was inhumanly-shaped and clad in a dark pleated exoskeleton, later described as a shadow. They also reported a pungent mist which made their eyes and noses burn. When the being began making a hissing noise and started coming toward the children, they immediately fled the area and told their parents of the sighting. The local sheriff with his deputies, after taking a statement from the oldest boy, went up into the hill to investigate. They did not find anything, except the lingering odor and two marks on the ground. The children later reported being sick for about a week after the sighting. Also, it was reported more people came forward and related they too had seen the strange floating being.

The US Air Force, upon investigating the incident, stated it was probably a meteorite and the being was actually a large owl. Ivan T. Sanderson investigated the incident but because of lack of evidence was unable to conclude what the children had seen. There have been no more sightings of this type of being. To celebrate this strange event, Flatwoods had a three-day festival to celebrate the "Green Monster."

There is the famous and terrifying story involving alien-like beings called the Hopkinsville Goblins Case. I remember first reading about the incident in Loren Coleman's book *Mysterious America*. It has been featured on nearly every television show and movie about UFOs and extraterrestrial beings. The 1978 television show *Project UFO* did an excellent recreation of the incident.

According to reports the event started in the summer of 1955 in the small town of Hopkinsville, Kentucky, when the Sutton family and their guests claimed, after observing strange lights in the sky, their farmhouse was terrorized by an unknown number of creatures similar to gremlins, which have since often been referred to as the "Hopkinsville Goblins." The small alien-like cryptids were described as being three feet tall, silvery metallic in color, with upright pointed ears, small thin legs, long arms and clawlike hands. Their movements

44

at times seemed to defy gravity with the creatures floating above the ground and appearing in high places, and they "walked" with a swaying motion as though wading through water. Although the creatures never entered the house, they were seen looking into the windows and appeared at the front doorway. One of the cryptids was reported to have been hiding on the roof and grabbed the men's hair when they walked outside. This ordeal woke up all the children in the

The South Carolina Lizard Man.

house causing a hysterical frenzy. The men stated they fired their guns at the entities to no avail. The families fled the farmhouse in the middle of the night. Noted cryptozoologist Ivan T. Sanderson investigated the incident and while finding no physical evidence, did find the witnesses credible in their ordeal. One ridiculous theory put foward to explain the incident involved a group of monkeys painted silver. On a side note, Steven Spielberg planned to make a movie about the incident, but it then was rewritten into the popular *ET* movie.

Like the Dover Demon and the Flatwoods Monster, these strange little creatures were only sighted once. Research shows this is a common occurrence with alien-type animals.

45

The Lizard Man of South Carolina

The South Carolina Lizard Man is another possible alien animal. Also referred to as the Lizard Man of Scape Ore Swamp, it is a large reptilian humanoid cryptid with red glowing eyes and clawed hands. It is said to inhabit areas of swampland in and around Lee County, South Carolina and the sewers in towns near the swamp. The creature has an incredible degree of strength, more than capable of ripping into a car.

This strange creature was first reported by 17-year-old Christopher Davis on a lonely country road on the

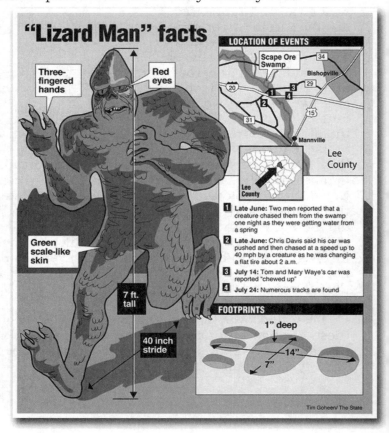

"Lizard Man" facts

Three-fingered hands

Red eyes

Green scale-like skin

7 ft. tall

40 inch stride

LOCATION OF EVENTS

Scape Ore Swamp

Bishopville

Mannville

Lee County

Lee County

1 **Late June:** Two men reported that a creature chased them from the swamp one night as they were getting water from a spring

2 **Late June:** Chris Davis said his car was pushed and then chased at a speed up to 40 mph by a creature as he was changing a flat tire about 2 a.m.

3 **July 14:** Tom and Mary Waye's car was reported "chewed up"

4 **July 24:** Numerous tracks are found

FOOTPRINTS

1" deep

14"

7"

Tim Goheen/ The State

evening of June 28, 1988. The story goes Chris had stopped to fix a flat tire. Upon finishing, he heard a strange noise and saw this peculiar animal standing bipedal in a nearby field. The creature then started running towards Chris, who quickly got back into his car. As Chris raced off, the creature was said to have jumped on top of the car and started clawing at the roof, in attempt to get at him. Chris attempted to swerve the car and the creature either fell or jumped off and ran back into the swamps. Chris got home and told his parents about the incident. The car's side view mirror was found to be badly damaged, and scratch marks were found on the car's roof, though there was no other physical evidence of the incident. Deputies found three-toed footprints in the area. Some tracks later turned out to be fakes. Lyle Blackburn trekked down to the town of Bishopville and did an investigation into the Lizard Man which is detailed in his best-selling book *The Lizard Man: The True Story of the Bishopville Monster*, a book I highly recommend.

According to legend, a race of extraterrestrial lizard people called the Reptilians, or the Anunnaki, live in an underground base in Mount Shasta, California, and kidnap humans and eat them. Some have theorized all the people who have gone missing in national forests are victims of the Reptilians.

Another category of cryptids is misplaced animals. These animals appear in areas where they shouldn't be, as in the famous "alligator in the sewers" stories. Though often thought to be urban legend, there are documented stories of alligators being found alive in sewers in northern states such as New York and Chicago. These stories have appeared in newspapers with accompanying pictures of the dead alligator. Nile monitor lizards have been seen in Cape Coral. Kangaroos and even mongooses have been seen

47

wandering around the continental United States. There are mongooses in Hawaii, but they were imported in the nineteenth century to combat the snake problem. Florida has reported a problem with Burmese pythons in the Everglades. But a lot of Florida's misplaced animal problems are a result of pet owners letting the animals loose in the wild.

Miscellaneous Cryptids

My final category is Miscellaneous Cryptids. These are unknown animals which do not fit in the other categories. The first one I want to go over is werewolves. Believe it or not, there have been reports of large bipedal wolflike animals seen in various parts of the United States. Author Linda S. Godfrey has written extensively on the subject, including one such man-beast seen in Wisconsin. Her bestselling book *The Beast of Bray Road* is the most complete investigation ever done on this cryptid.

According to Linda's book, the first sighting to make the headlines occurred in 1936 when Mark Schackelman noticed someone digging in a field off the side of the road while he was driving along Highway 18 just outside of Jefferson, Wisconsin. As Schackelman slowed down to get a better look, the "man" turned around and faced him. It turns out it was a hairy creature which stood up on two legs. He described the creature as looking like a mix between an ape and a dog. The creature had the general shape of a large man, long ears standing up with a snout and large canine teeth. As you might guess Mr. Schackelman quickly departed the area. In 1964 Dennis Fewless saw the same creature run in front of him on Highway 89. In 1972 a woman in Jefferson County called 911 and stated a large hairy canine creature standing on two legs was trying to break into her home. Investigation revealed large unknown footprints outside the house. Also in 1972 police in Defiance, Ohio were told to be on the lookout for a werewolf-like creature. In 1989 the town of Elkhorn, Wisconsin reported numerous sightings of the creature. Linda went on to state she didn't believe it was a person who had changed (shapeshifting) into a wolflike creature. She believes it was a type of canine that was

American Werewolf.

able to walk/run upright on its hind legs. Maybe there is something to these werewolf legends. The popular television show *Mountain Monsters* did an episode on the beast. Dr. Colm Kelleher and George Knapp wrote in their 2005 best-selling book *Hunt for the Skinwalker* about their scientific investigation of a northeastern Utah ranch where reports of a strange "misshapen" wolflike creature would attack humans or mutilate livestock. When shot at, the creature was reported not to respond to bullets.

Werewolves have also been seen in West Virginia. Some cryptozoologists have theorized maybe the witnesses are actually seeing a Bigfoot-type creature with an attitude. Linda Godfrey did a follow up book *Real Wolfmen: True Encounters in Modern America* which covers werewolf sightings in other states.

Along the lines of half-human half-animal comes another miscellaneous cryptid called the Lake Worth Monster. This cryptid is described as being half man and half goat which is why it is sometimes called the Goatman. The story goes in July of 1969 a young couple sighted this strange creature by Lake Worth, just

49

outside Fort Worth, Texas. The creature immediately made the headlines.

Then on July 12, 1969, Tommy Burson not only saw the strange creature, but he went on to say it landed on his car after jumping out of a tree. The police found an 18-inch gouge on the side of his car, when Burson reported it to them. Then in October a report came in of the creature hurling a tire at some bystanders. A photograph (and perhaps the only one) of the creature

The Lake Worth Monster photo.

was taken by Allen Plaster in October 1969 near Lake Worth during the tire throwing incident. Sallie Ann Clarke wrote a book about the unknown cryptid called *The Lake Worth Monster*.

The next miscellaneous and famous cryptid in this category is the Chupacabras. This legendary cryptid is said to inhabit various parts of the Americas but was first reported in Puerto Rico. Chupacabras translated from Spanish is "Goat Sucker," and the creature is so named due to its habit of attacking and drinking the blood of livestock, especially goats. The description of the creature has gone through some drastic changes since its original sighting. The original description reports the creature to be lizard-like, about the size of a small bear, with a row of spines reaching from the neck to the base of the tail. It is reported to have sharp claws, long fangs, and large glowing eyes. The sightings in Puerto Rico started in March 1955 when some farmers reported their livestock killed with the blood drained from

50

the animals. Later witnesses reported seeing the creature in the Puerto Rican town of Canóvanas. 150 farm animals and pets were reportedly killed in town during this time period. There were also animals killed in the same manner reported in the Dominican Republic, Argentina, Bolivia, Chile, Colombia, Honduras, El Salvador, Nicaragua, Panama, Peru, Brazil, and Mexico.

Then in July 2004, a rancher near San Antonio, Texas killed a hairless dog-like creature which was attacking his livestock. The animal

A Winged Chupacabras.

was then called a Chupacabras, for reasons unknown. Now every feral, wild canine is referred to by this name.

In 2006 the Chupacabras was seen in Russia. Reports beginning in March 2005 tell of a beast which kills animals and sucks out their blood. Neighboring villages reported 30 sheep were killed and had their blood drained.

In 2007, a series of reports from Colombia claimed more than 300 dead sheep in the region of Boyaca. Then reports started flooding in from other countries

51

of animals found dead with their blood drained. The Chupacabras was blamed for all these incidents.

Whatever the creature is there are still reports of reptilian-like creatures attacking livestock and drinking the blood. There are also numerous reports of unidentified feral dogs also killing livestock. On a side note: a friend of mine who grew up in Puerto Rico related to me that growing up he was told the Chupacabras was sort of boogeyman creature and was used to keep children from venturing deep into the jungle. Either way the legend of the Chupacabras is still out there.

The last miscellaneous cryptid is the Gowrow. I left this one for last because it is also one of my favorite legends. There is a cave, right outside the small town of Self, Arkansas called the Devil's Hole. Self is located about 20 miles (32 kilometers) southwest of Yellville, near the Arkansas and Missouri border.

According to legend in the early 1900s the owner of the land where the cave is located decided to check out the place, after hearing weird stories about the cave. Upon entering the cave, it immediately bottomed out to an unknown depth. He climbed down a rope about 200 feet to a ledge where the shaft narrowed to a point that could only be crawled through. He suddenly heard a vicious hissing from the darkness, perhaps like a large lizard would do, and he made a hasty retreat. The story was recreated in the 1975 movie *Encounters with the Unknown*. This low budget movie, narrated by Rod Serling, features three different stories about the supernatural. The cave was changed to a sinkhole in the movie, and at the end of the tale the landowner emerges from the hole, stark raving mad at what he saw. The movie goes on to say all the stories are based on real events.

I remember being a young twelve-year-old, glued to the screen waiting to see what was in the sinkhole.

52

I always wondered how true this story was. I thought to myself, "Is there really a sinkhole with something in it that makes people go mad when they see it?" One day I saw an article about bottomless caves and I remembered the movie and the sinkhole story. I started researching the story and I found the source of the tale and the legend of the Gowrow.

The Gowrow is one of several unknown creatures reported in Arkansas popular lore.

The Gowrow.

Not only does the Fouke Monster prowl in this state but now I find another legend lurks there. I found the Gowrow is a creature twenty feet in length with two tusks, large webbed feet ending in claws, a row of short horns along its back, and a long thin tail with a blade on the end. It makes its home in the Devil's Hole. Supposedly Native Americans in the area know about the large lizard and stay away from the cave. They relate the lizard is a maneater.

Later, I located a book (*From Flying Toads to Snakes with Wings*) by Dr. Karl P.N. Shuker, who wrote about the Gowrow. In it he states the areas near the Mystic Cave system are littered with limestone caves and are possibly linked to the cave system. He goes on to relate an incident, sounding very familiar, that took place during the early 1900s at Devil's Hole Cave. A landowner by the name of E.J. Rhodes wanted to find

53

out what was causing all the commotion down in the cave on his property, so he descends by rope to a ledge 200 feet below ground. He finds a shaft going deeper but it is too tight to penetrate farther. So with the help of some men, he probes the rest of cave with a long rope. They secured a flatiron to the rope and let it down into the hole. A vicious hissing rose out of the hole, as if from some large, angry animal. The men pulled up the rope and found the handle of the iron had been bent, and was even thought by some to show teeth marks. A large stone was then lowered with the rope. When the rope was drawn up, the stone was gone, and the rope was neatly bitten off.

The Gowrow lizard beast has never been photographed and no physical evidence has ever been taken. I did find the cave but there are no pictures of the cave entrance, even though it is supposed to be popular with spelunking clubs. But I could not find much information on the beast. Whatever the case, it is a neat legend that never seems to go away. There is also a cave called the Devil's Den located at Devil's Den State Park, near Fayetteville, Arkansas.

These are not the only cryptids out there. I just wanted to go over the popular ones and I only touched on some of the numerous sightings to give you a better idea what these creatures are. You can research and find the ones in your area.

Chapter 4
Bigfoot Legend Trip

One of most exciting legend trips you can go on is a Bigfoot/Cryptid legend hunt. It is like a roller coaster, some of it is scary and some of it will give you an adrenaline rush. It is also one of the easiest and most popular legend trips to do.

My first Bigfoot legend trip was during my senior year of high school. After reading *Creatures of the Outer Edge* by Loren Coleman and Jerome Clarke, I got excited and wanted to go check out some of the legends near me. I talked two friends, Rob and Phil, into going with me on a road trip to check out the legend in Louisiana, Missouri. I had read about some sightings of a Bigfoot-like creature called Momo prowling along the banks of the Mississippi river. Oddly enough the town of Louisiana is about twenty-five miles from Hannibal, the birth place of Mark Twain.

It turned into an overnight trip and because we didn't properly prepare ourselves for our excursion, we ended up sleeping in the car. Long story short, the townsfolk were not too cooperative. In fact, most of the residents didn't really believe in Bigfoot. We talked to some local teenagers and they were nice enough to show us where the sighting occurred. We walked around the riverbanks that night hoping to see it. Unfortunately we didn't see Momo or anything weird or strange. We did have a good time and enjoyed the freedom of going out on our own and going on a real adventure.

This adventure did make me realize investigating

cryptid sightings was not going to be easy, and a lot of people did not believe in Bigfoot or other cryptids. I also realized I needed to plan out my legend trips. We were not prepared to spend the night and it ended up costing more money than we anticipated. As the expression goes, "Lesson learned!"

Today, one of my favorite legend trips is to search for the Skunk Ape in Florida. While I do not consider myself an expert on the cryptid, I do read everything I can find on the subject. Every day I check the BFRO (Bigfoot Field Research Organization) website scouring reports to find out where the animals have been seen and what they have been observed doing. I also check out other websites for the most recent Bigfoot sightings.

In this chapter I will go over how to conduct a Bigfoot legend trip and share some things I have learned. This kind of legend trip can also be applied when you are out looking for other land based cryptids like the Jersey Devil or the South Carolina Lizard Man, so I will call these trips "monster hunts." I will go over aquatic cryptid (lake/river monster) legend trips in Chapter 6.

Monster hunting is not something you should do on a whim. You have to do some research and preparation as there is nothing worse than going on a trip without proper planning. You get there in the woods and end up forgetting something, like a camera. You'll find as you go out on any kind of trip, be it of the camping or legend variety, when you forget something, your adventure comes to an abrupt halt.

For planning purposes, I'm going to use a Bigfoot hunt as an example, because most of my legend trips are monster hunts and it is what I like to do. Being a military retiree, I learned to have everything planned out before going out on a legend trip. Before leaving, I lay out all the equipment and check and make sure all my electronic devices work. I usually keep most of my gear in a footlocker so I have everything needed kept centrally located so I don't have to run around looking for everything. I've compiled a quick list of equipment you'll need at the end of this chapter and a more detailed list of equipment in Chapter 17.

When it comes to research, you'll need to decide where you are going to look for this cryptid. You can't just jump in your car and drive to the first wooded area and hope there is a Bigfoot or the Lizard Man hiding nearby. You're probably asking, "Where can I find the research data for a legend trip?" The answer is, "It's everywhere on the Internet." There are hundreds of sites and thousands (yes, thousands) of books on the subject. The most up-to-date information on cryptids and paranormal is definitely on the Internet. If you are new to legend tripping, search the Internet for recordings of alleged Bigfoot calls and download them if you can. If you know what they sound like, you will know them when you hear them.

When I learn of a sighting, the first thing I do is check the map and look for the nearest water source (i.e., river, stream, or creek). Again, research has shown these animals like to travel along the waterways. For example, the Fouke Monster stays close to Boggy Creek. My theory is some Skunk Apes travel north in the summer and south in winter using favored water landmarks to guide migration. The animal is reported to primarily travel at night, being the best time to avoid human contact, a common pattern of most Bigfoot-type creatures. I also look to see how far it is from a town or campgrounds. I look at the details of the sighting to see which direction the animal moved. I consider the time of the year and try to make an educated guess on where the animal is or where it is traveling to. If you research past sightings in the area, you might be able to pinpoint where it will be seen next.

Legend Tripping

Every animal on Earth has a behavior pattern. Humans all the way down to insects have some kind of pattern to the way they live day to day. When you read about past sightings, you can see a general pattern these animals seem to be displaying. They are usually seen at a certain time of the year and at certain places. Researching Bigfoot, I have found the animal is nocturnal and mostly nomadic. In other words, it mostly moves around at night and does not stay in one place but moves from one location to another, generally following a water source, such as a river. There are some beliefs these animals do stay in one area where they will probably encounter low human contact.

When it comes to other cryptids like the Jersey Devil, werewolves, or the South Carolina Lizard Man, their behavior is still being studied and hypothesized by cryptozoologists. The only thing they have determined is, like Bigfoot, these creatures seem to be nocturnal. With that in mind, use the same process to look for these cryptids as you would looking for Bigfoot.

The best time of the year to do a Bigfoot legend trip is spring or fall. I highly recommend you do not do it in the winter. While in the military, I attended cold weather training in Italy, and it was not a pleasant experience. I have now developed a hatred toward the cold and will not go camping in extreme cold or snow. There is nothing more agonizing then being cold and wet the entire time you're out there. Your legend trip companions are not going to have a good time if they are cold. In fact, it's darn near impossible to get them away from the campfire.

Dangerous situations can arise more quickly when camping in the winter, hypothermia being the worst of the threats. When that happens, the legend trip comes to a halt and you need to seek medical attention. This happens more to people who have never been camping during the winter months. It is OK to do a Bigfoot hunt in the daytime, but I would not advise camping overnight in the snow.

If you go in the summer, you run into the heat, and you will have to deal with the mosquitoes and other irritating insects. If you do decide to go on a Bigfoot hunt in the summer, you may end up staying at lodgings, where you will pay more in the summer. Also, if it is really hot and if you don't have a pool nearby, your team may become miserable and will lose interest in the legend trip quickly.

Bigfoot hunters primarily do their monster hunts at night, when animals are more active. Most sightings have taken place in the evening. These large hairy cryptids have been seen many times at night, crossing a road or highway. You can look during the day if you are just looking for evidence such as footprints and broken branches, but these are smart animals and they continually stay alert to avoid humans. When these animals come into contact with humans, they immediately leave and never return. You might get a whiff of their lingering odor. I used to wonder how these animals can smell us when they stink so badly. The smell is quite overpowering. But I've learned these animals have heightened senses. In other words, they hear, smell and see better than humans.

When monster hunting, one thing to consider is if there is a water source nearby. By "water source," I mean a flowing body of water, such as a river or creek. These animals usually stay close to rivers and creeks. This is not so much a source of drinking water as a route for them to travel and not be seen.

When trying to predict where it might be seen again, consider the nearest water source. My theory is Bigfoot and other bipedal animals hang around lakes at night, but do not stay long. Rivers and creeks seem to be their comfort zones. Also, there are fewer mosquitos around flowing water than stagnant water. Roger Patterson filmed his now-famous Bigfoot footage at Bluff Creek.

The next thing you need to consider when determining a good expedition location is whether it is away from the general population. Like I said earlier, Bigfoot seems to avoid human contact as much as possible, so look for a wooded area away from towns and cities. There are many national forests in the US, and the great thing is most of them have had Bigfoot sightings. Yosemite National Park has had some Bigfoot sightings. It's good to go to an area that is nice to look at even if you don't see Bigfoot or anything. I also want to say, never—and I mean never—go rucking or hiking by yourself. A lot of bad things can happen when you are by yourself. You always hear stories about people who do and are never seen again. If you can't find anybody to go with you, then wait till you do. I cannot stress this point enough. Never go into the woods by yourself. Also, check there are no designated hunting areas in the location. If there are, then make sure everybody is wearing orange. Usually, if hunters are present then Bigfoot won't be. Remember, it usually stays away from humans.

For Scout Masters and Venturing Crew guides, most Boy Scout camps have stories of Bigfoot sightings and haunted areas. You should look into this when you are planning your weekend outing and make it part of the experience.

Conducting a Witness Interview

If you do come in contact with a witness, there are things you need to know whenever you conduct an interview about a sighting. As a military policeman, I learned some great interviewing techniques I now use them with legend tripping. I know legend tripping is supposed to be fun, and it can be, but when it comes to probing deep into a legend, you need to take it seriously.

It has been my experience when a person really sees Bigfoot or a ghost, it is a lifechanging event for them. They become really emotional after the sighting and sometimes when they are recounting it to you. They are very sure about what they saw and don't add to it. In other words, if I ask the witness if they saw what the animal's eyes looked like, they either did or they didn't. They don't say, "I think they were brown in color." They will say either, "I didn't get close enough to see them," or "They were really dark." They know what they saw and there is no doubt. Now some will say, "I can't believe I really saw it."

With that being said, you need to also remember even good people lie; sometimes they do it to try to make sense of what they saw. In other words, they will add things so they don't look stupid about what they saw. Some people like the attention, and some like to make legend trippers look foolish, as if they will believe anything. Whatever the outcome with the witness, do not become aggressive if you feel the witness is lying. Let the person tell the story and then thank him or her. After the witness leaves, go over the story with your team or family and explain your conclusions about the interview.

I often refer to my military police experience and describe how I conducted my interviews. The first thing I would do when I arrived at a scene was to gather up the witnesses. I would separate them and interview each one in a location where they could not be overheard by the other witnesses. I would make sure they were comfortable (either standing or sitting) and let them tell their stories without interrupting them. If I had questions, I would write them down and wait for the witness to finish. If I suspected a witness

61

was lying, I would have him or her tell me the story again. I would then ask my questions, and then ask him to tell his story again. A liar cannot retell a story without changing it. The only exception to this is when the event took place more than a week earlier. Then, witnesses have had time to get their stories straight.

It's the same with monster or ghost hunting. If you have more than one person who saw something, try to separate them and talk to them individually. It is a great idea to make a list of questions prior to the interview. If they can't describe what they saw, do not help them. In other words, don't put words in their mouths. If they really saw something, they will be able to tell you what they saw. Always look at them with your full attention. Occasionally nod in acknowledgement and encouragement. Try not to show any emotion except attentiveness. If you show signs of disbelief, like rolling your eyes or shaking your head, they are liable to stop their story, and could end the investigation.

Don't go into an interview thinking you've got a hoaxer. Let the person tell his or her story. Body language can show you if a person is lying. Most people look up when answering questions. Those who I believe they have had a real sighting will look you in the eye when they tell you their story. Have a map available so they can show you exactly where the sighting occurred. Have them use a marker so you can get an idea of the size of what they saw. You can do this for both a monster and ghost investigation. If people see something strange, they will be able to describe it to a T. If they aren't sure, because it was moving behind some vegetation, then they should at least be able to show you where they saw it and describe exactly what they saw.

When it comes to questioning a witness, there are different styles of questions. These are as follows:

- Open-Ended Questions: questions do not limit or direct the answer. An example would be, "Tell me what happened to you," or "Tell me everything that happened that night."
- Closed-Ended Questions: questions require a brief answer or a yes or no answer. An example would be, "What time was it when you saw it?" or "Were you alone during this time?"
- Follow-Up Questions: questions probe deeper into the event, after the witness tells his or her story. An example would be, "Where exactly did you see this thing?"
- Direct Questions: questions are reserved for a witness who might be lying. An example would be, "After you saw it, what exactly did you do?"
- Control Questions: questions bring you back in control of the questioning. An example would be, "We're almost finished, but I have a few more questions I'm not clear on."
- Leading Questions: questions used to guide the witness through the interview. I frown on this type of question. A witness might not be able to positively identify the thing, but through leading questions, you can have the witness believing he or she actually did see something. This type of question is useful in law enforcement but not when it comes to legend tripping. I've seen this technique used a lot by monster hunters.
- Confrontational Questions: questions are accusatory, typically being confrontational in nature, when you believe the witness is lying. Since legend tripping should be fun and exciting, I highly discourage this type of questioning. It would be best not to challenge the statement. Just because you think the witness is lying doesn't make it so.

63

When you resort to this type of questioning, there is no going back to being friendly.

The first time you interview a witness, it will be best to use what is called the oblique approach. This method is suited for an interview in which the witness tells the story without prompting. Let him or her tell the story while you're silent but attentive. When witnesses are telling me about their sightings, I like to nod, maybe smile, and I will say things such as, "OK" or "I'm listening." Try to keep eye contact.

If I write down the story, I like to go over it with the witness and make sure I heard it right which works as another method to detect if the witness lying. If you are interviewing a child, always have the parent present. It will make everybody more comfortable during the interview. The only drawback is sometimes the parent will interrupt the child. If this happens, be patient and keep your attention on what the child is saying. If a witness becomes emotional, be patient and wait for him to compose himself. I like to say, "I believe you saw something." It will help the witness compose himself more quickly and continue with the story.

Another thing I have observed is the witness will change or embellish their sighting if they are being filmed, with the possibility of being on television. Sometimes it's not their fault. The television interviewer will try to get them to say certain things to make the sighting more exciting.

Don't get discouraged if you interview a witness who is obviously lying about a sighting. It happens. It actually is good training. It shows you what to look for.

Physical Evidence

On a legend trip, one of the goals, and admittedly one of the exciting parts, is finding tangible evidence. What

64

can be more exciting than looking on your camera and seeing a strange apparition gliding along a dark room, or looking on your game camera and seeing a large hairy animal walking past? You go out into the woods and, lo and behold, you find some large footprints are not a bear, a deer, or a panther. You just might have found some prints made by a Bigfoot! You might find some strange hairs on a fence where somebody saw the creature go over it.

There are two kinds of proof you want when you go legend tripping: video proof and physical proof. With both monster and ghost hunting, you want to get video proof. With monster hunting you also want physical proof or evidence of the animal's presence.

Base Camp

When you arrive at the area where you are going to conduct your research and investigation, you are going to set up your base camp. I'm going to show you how I set up my base camp. I have a checklist to make sure I set up everything we need. Again, you can do it the way you want, because everybody is different. This checklist has worked for me, and I've been doing this for years. Most of the time, I like to go out Bigfoot hunting, so this checklist is used for a Bigfoot legend trip.

I like to pick an area for my base camp with numerous areas to see, not just one. I have gone to areas full of hunters, so you need not just one area but many, just in case one of them has human activity. Check to make sure it is not private property. Try to find posted campsites. They often have bathrooms and trash bins. If the area is full of campers, it might be a good idea not to tell everybody you are Bigfoot hunting.

When you arrive at your actual campsite, the first thing to do is unload your camping gear and get your home base (camp) set up. I like to first put up a tarp,

Stacy Brown making a casting of a suspected Bigfoot track.

just in case it rains when we are unloading our gear, and it makes a good shade area when there aren't any others.

If you are the team leader, then you need to make sure everybody gets the camp set up before it gets dark. Do not go wandering around yet, wait until later. It is important to get all your gear set up, especially the tents. Do not set up near a lake, because the mosquitoes or other insects will drive you crazy. Rivers are different, because the fish eat the mosquitoes. Otherwise, make sure you have the mosquito candles ready. When the sun goes down, they come out to play. You need to have the bug spray ready.

The first thing to set up is the tents. Find a good spot and put them up. After you've got them up, put down some ant repellent around each tent. Fire ants love tents. If you brought cots, then get them up and assembled. The next thing is to inflate your air mattresses if you brought them. When you put your sleeping bags out, don't unroll them. They attract bugs

66

and snakes. Get your light source, i.e., lanterns, ready in each tent. Then get your eating area set up. I always keep the food locked up in the back of the car. I keep the cooler there as well. It keeps bears and raccoons and other pesky animals away from the food.

I also get a garbage bag set up away from the tents. When you go out at night, make one stop a trash point so you won't have garbage around the area at night. Raccoons can destroy a camp, so make sure you get rid of the trash or secure it in a vehicle for the night.

Get your folding chairs set up. I usually put them near the campfire. You don't want to sit on the ground. If the campgrounds have a trash drop-off point and bathrooms, then go find out where they are. If I bring my family, my kids always find the bathrooms the second we get to the campgrounds. I guess is a standard family ritual, after a long trip.

Start gathering up wood for a fire, if you are permitted. Make sure you can have a fire. In some parts of the country, during the dry part of the year, and in other places where it is really dry, campfires are prohibited, so make sure you have your lanterns ready. Also, do not chop down trees; it might be against the law and you can be fined. Search for dead wood and make sure you get plenty of it. Wood burns fast and it can be a problem when you run out in the middle of the night. Make sure you collect a good supply. I have always found when you think you have enough firewood, you don't. Go get some more. You will require three times as much as you think you need. If the wood is really dry, it will burn quickly. You can never have too much wood, and if you leave it in a nice pile, somebody else can use it. Also, watch out for snakes when you are gathering up wood. They like to hide in deadfall.

Lay of the Land

Now you've got your base camp set up, it is time to scout around the area and see what's out there. Get your map out and, with your team, plot where you want to look. Also, you might want to check and see where the nearest hospital is, just in case. If you have a GPS—and most cell phones have one on them—then find out where the nearest emergency personnel are located such as the Ranger Station. This is also the time to see what else the area has to offer, in terms of things to see and do. As I said, most monster hunts are done at dawn or dusk, so you have a whole day to fill. Your legend hunting team will appreciate having something to do. Swimming, hiking and canoeing are great family friendly activities to do during your down time.

Go and scout the area. In the military this is called a reconnaissance or "recon" for short. You should take the team with you when you go over the area you intend to search. It's easier than going back and explaining it on a map. Something can get lost in the translation or a member of the team could be directionally challenged. Make sure everybody knows what they should look for, such as tracks in the dirt, broken branches or weird branch configurations.

There are things you need to be on the lookout for to let you know one of these cryptid animals is in the area. First and foremost, look for tracks. Look for loose soil or muddy areas where tracks are easy to see. Looking near rivers or streams is a good idea. You also need to look to see if there are any torn-down branches. The theory is Bigfoot tears down branches to either mark its trail or warn others of human activity. People have found what they claim to be Bigfoot nests which might be something to look for as well. Be aware of strange configurations of branches. These are broken tree

68

branches arranged in a pattern, usually interwoven with each other off the ground, referred to as stick structures. I observed one of these configurations while on a Bigfoot expedition. Recently on a trip near the Georgia/Florida border, we found a stick structure miles from any human habitat or roads.

Another thing to be conscious of is smell. These animals during certain parts of the year give off a pungent smell which most of the time will catch you off guard. You'll be walking through the woods when the smell will hit you like a tidal wave and you'll stop dead in your tracks. The smell is bad. It reminds me of dead wet dog.

You need to realize the area in the woods or forest where you are conducting your legend trip is this animal's home, and it knows the woods better than you do. Its senses are a lot more acute than a human's. In other words, it can hear and smell you when you enter the woods. Do not have any misconceptions that these animals just sit around and wait to be seen. They actually are very intelligent and need to be treated that way. If they were stupid, we would see them a lot more.

As I said before, there is a ninety-five percent chance you are not going to actually see Bigfoot or the monster you are looking for. Now you are asking, "Why go look for them then?" My answer to that, and what I tell everybody is, "The five percent." If you don't look, you're never going to see them. Only patience and determination pay off in this field. As of this writing, I have witnessed glowing eyes and a large shape in a thermal. I have seen physical evidence, such as large tracks and strange stick structures. Something is out there. I realize there is only a slight chance I will get a good look at it, but I believe if I continue to look, my efforts will eventually pay off. Plus, I enjoy the thrill of the hunt.

Safety Considerations

When you are in the woods be careful of what is around you. In the eastern part of the country, which is very hilly, there are a lot of cliffs, which are difficult to see if you're going lights out during a hunt. There have been numerous accidents with hikers. I recently read a story where some hikers found an injured person who fell from a cliff next to a waterfall. Because it was night, he didn't see the end of the ledge and fell and broke both his legs. Luckily the hikers came by the next morning and found him. He had to be airlifted by helicopter.

If you're conducting your legend trip in the swamplands, you need to be exceptionally vigilant. For example, in the swamps there are cypress trees and their roots do not grow straight down but rather to the side and up. This happens because most of the time the swamp is flooded and the roots grow up above the water line. These roots are called knees. They look like stalagmites and can be sharp. These are especially dangerous at night which is why my team and I stay on the dirt roads once darkness falls. I have heard many stories of hunters falling and becoming impaled on them. Also, there are sinkholes which you can't see, and you can't tell how deep they are, which presents a dangerous situation. Make sure you go over all of this with your team before you enter the area.

Also, during this time frame you need to choose a rally point—a designated area for everyone to meet back up again after the hunt. You need to decide where to set up observation points (OPs) and where to place your trail cameras. Daytime is the best time to find an OP. Use trail markers or orange 550 cord to mark your OP (trail markers work best because you can see them at night).

This is also a good time to see if you can find footprints

and stick structures. If you do find prints of known animals, such as deer or raccoon, show them to team members who are new to the woods so they can learn something about the animals in the area. As I stated earlier, loose soil or muddy areas are where you're going to finds tracks, especially near rivers or streams. Stick structures are usually easy to see. They stand out pretty well in the forest. Take plenty of pictures of them and mark on the map or GPS where you find them.

A Bigfoot casting.

Making Castings of Footprints

One of the most popular things to look for during a Bigfoot legend trip is footprints made by the cryptid creature. Recently I attended a cryptozoology conference and talked with Cliff Barackman. Cliff is one of the hosts of the popular television show *Finding Bigfoot* on the Animal Planet channel. He made a comment that really made sense. He stated, "The footprint is not the shape of the foot. It's the shape of the damage done to the ground by the foot." That is why all Bigfoot prints look different. There are different kinds of terrain that affect a print and how long the print has been there.

If you or somebody on your team finds a footprint you cannot identify, then you need to make a plaster cast of it. Here are the steps you need to do to make a successful casting. The items you will need are listed in Chapter 17. You need to keep all the cast-making items in one location. I keep all the casting material in plastic storage tubs. You can also use these tubs to store the finished castings.

If this is the first time you have ever done any casting, then I recommend you start off using plaster casting powder. It is inexpensive and you can find it at any home improvement or hobby store. There are other casting powders, but some dry really fast. You can also use foam, but you'll need to put something on top of it. I have experimented with other materials and I come back to plaster. You will likewise need a pail or a large, strong, and sturdy plastic bag. And you will need plenty of water to mix into the casting powder. To make a barrier around the print, you will need a large plastic or bendable copper strip about two inches by twenty-four inches or two pieces of two-inch by thirteen-inch. You will also need some hairspray.

First you need to take a picture of the print. In fact, take a bunch of pictures. Make sure you have something in the picture to compare the size, such as a ruler or even a dollar bill. It helps to give an idea of the size of the print. Then scout around and see if you can find more prints. You need to find all the footprints you can. Unless this creature is one-legged, there should be more than one print. If it has a right foot, it obviously has a left foot. It is better to get both left and right footprints. When a person finds only one print, it automatically seems suspicious. If you brought out plenty of casting powder, you need to cast as many of the prints as you can. Use small sticks with orange tape to mark the prints; this way everybody in the party will know where the prints are and won't accidently step on them.

You then need to move some of the large items like branches away from the print. Leave the tiny twigs or leaves, because they might have hair on them for

Glan Shelt with casting of track found in Florida.

73

Picture 1 | Picture 2 | Picture 3 | Picture 4 | Picture 5

Picture 7 | Picture 8 | Picture 9 | Picture 10 | Picture 11

Picture 13 | Picture 14 | Picture 15 | Picture 16 | Picture 17

Picture 18 | Picture 19 | Picture 20 | Picture 21 | Picture 22

analysis. Set up the barrier around the print. Make it at least one inch from all the borders of the print. If the print is near water and is flooded with water, try to channel the water away from the print and also use an oven baster, which looks like a large eye dropper, to carefully drain the water out of the print. Do not be in a rush when you do this.

Once you have the print ready, make sure the barrier is set up and is not going to move. I put small sticks on the outside of the barrier to keep it in place. I like to use the sticks with the orange tape on them, so they have a dual use. Next, take the hairspray and spray the print and around the print. Use a generous amount and let it dry. The hairspray acts as a kind of glue and will keep the print intact, especially if it is in sand.

You then need to get the casting powder ready. First, put your rubber gloves on, and then put the

74

powder in the pail or plastic bag. Remember, you are casting a larger than normal human-style footprint, so you will use a lot of the powder. I recommend four cups of powder and three cups of water. Then, wearing rubber gloves, use your hand to mix it up. Make sure you mix it well and get rid of all the clumps. It should have a soup-like consistency. Now carefully and slowly pour the mixture into the print. I recommend starting at the heel and working your way up to the toes. Some people like to add branches to the back of the print to add strength. I have never done that, and all my prints came out strong and solid. Do not try to push some of the mixture around with your hands; it will damage the print. Let it dry and start on the next print.

It will probably take about an hour to dry. Do not mess with it during the drying period. After the hour is up, first check the top of the casting to see if it is all the way dry which you will recognize when the casting is hard as a rock. Rainy or damp weather can affect the time it takes for the plaster to set. If you are in the swamps, it will take longer to dry because of the moisture in the air.

When you are satisfied the casting is dry, carefully pick it up. It will be covered in dirt or sand. Take a soft brush and carefully clean the loose sand or dirt off the print. I always take a picture of it after I do this. Then wrap the print with bubble wrap and secure it in a container where you know it will not get broken. As I stated, I always bring large plastic tub containers to put the prints in. If you get more than one print, make sure you use plenty of bubble wrap to protect them.

In order to be able to do this process correctly and effectively, you need to practice. If you do it for the first time when you find a print, you are going to ruin the print. Sometimes I will do a casting of a known animal just to keep in practice. Have your family do it as well.

It's actually kind of fun to do. Messy, but fun. My kids love doing castings of prints. They feel like CSI agents solving a crime. A word of caution: the plaster casting mixture can ruin your clothes if you get it on them, so be careful. It is a pain getting it out of your hair. My stepdaughter found out the hard way.

Setting Up Trail/Game Cameras

Trail (game) cameras should be set during the day. You really need to think about where to set up these cameras. You've got to remember you are not trying to photograph deer or wild pigs. You are dealing with an extremely smart animal that shies away from human contact. You are going to have to put the camera deep in the woods away from roads. You will not have good results if you put it in an area that has a lot of human traffic.

Be careful: I have found game cameras out in the boonies that were left out there by owners who forgot where they placed them. Make sure you put a lock on it. Some people think because they put the camera up deep in the woods, nobody will see it or take it. I am here to tell you from experience you may think you have the perfect hiding place, but some hunter or kid riding his ATV will see it and take it. When I set up cameras, I always secure them with a lock, and I mark where I put them with my GPS so it is easier to recover them. They cost a lot, and you don't want to lose them out there.

The best place to set them up is on game trails. These are paths animals have cut through the grass and continue to use. They are not hard to see during the day. I put camouflage netting around the camera to help hide it. I spray anti-scent on it to mask my human odor. Even with anti-scent, it will take at least two weeks for the human scent to go away completely, so be prepared to leave your camera out for a while unless you are just doing a weekend legend trip. Set up some kind of trail marker close by so you can find them to later retrieve.

Do not put the trail marker right next to the camera, otherwise your camera will be gone. I also put a camera in an area where I want the animal to go or I think it will go. In other words, I will place the camera in the area I want to walk around in the evening. I know if this animal is around it will leave when it knows we are there. Looking at a map of

Setting up a trail camera.

the area, I try to guess which direction this animal will go and I put my camera there so when it vacates the area it will go by my camera, trip the beam, and get its picture taken.

Make sure you know how to use your trail camera before you set it up outside. You will not want to set up your camera in night vision mode. If the flash on the camera goes off, every animal in the area will see it and stay away. Some cameras have timers; if yours does, make sure you don't have it set, otherwise the batteries

77

will run down faster.

If you are going to look in multiple areas, then make sure you have at least two people on each team, including an adult. The teams need to know their prescribed distance (five-hundred feet is usually the best distance) before coming back to the rally point. Each team will have a working radio with fresh or extra batteries or cellphone. I've gone over with the teams to always return to the rally point when they can't get reception on the radios. In other words, if they can't pick up anybody on the radio then turn around and come back. If they see panther or bear tracks, then they are to radio it in and return to the rally point. I go over all of this with everybody, before each team moves out to their assigned area or path.

Dangerous Animals

I want to bring up the subject of dangerous animals. They are very real and should be considered when venturing into the woods. This part is for anyone who has never been in the woods. I am not an expert on animals, but I do know there are dangerous animals out there. You probably have heard stories about attacks on humans by animals. There is some truth to those stories. It is imperative to understand this land is the

animals' home, and they will protect it. Do not underestimate any kind of wildlife, even small foxes and armadillos.

While out in the woodlands of the United States there are dangerous animals you need to be aware of. The most dangerous animals are bears, large wild cats, wild pigs, alligators, snakes, and certain insects. They are extremely unsafe and should be avoided at all costs. I will go into detail on each animal. It is important all team members know what animals they can run into.

Bears are located in nearly every region of the United States. Reports of bear attacks have been on the rise as urban sprawl continues to soak up habitat. If you go to a place where there are reports of roaming bears, I recommend you go look somewhere else. Bears can be particularly mean, especially in the fall before hibernation as well as in the spring when waking up hungry from a long winter's nap. Bears are typically solitary animals. There are two species in the lower United States, the black bear and the brown bear (grizzly). They can be active during the day (diurnal), but are very active during the night (nocturnal) or twilight (crepuscular), particularly around humans. They have been known to come into camps when they smell food. Bears are aided by an excellent sense of smell. Bears may at times look slow-moving because of their heavy build and awkward gait, but they can run quickly and are adept climbers and swimmers. Bears use caves and burrows as their dens. During the winter some bears sleep for a long period (up to a hundred days) in a state similar to hibernation. Bears should be considered dangerous and not messed with. I always make sure I have my bear mace when I go into woods or swamps. This highly-concentrated pepper spray is also good on large cats, wild boar, and even snakes. I go more into bear mace in my equipment chapter.

Panther/Mountain Lion

Black

Bear Tracks

Grizzly

Wolf tracks

Wild Pig

Gator tracks

Another extremely dangerous group of animals and one you don't hear a lot about are the large cats of United States. Mountain lions, pumas, and panthers are found in many habitats, from Florida swamps all the way up to the Canadian forests. Believe it or not, these large cats are all the same animal, and can be extremely dangerous. Because they are rarely seen most people do not take the proper precautions when they are out in the woods. I am here to tell you they are out there. I was lucky enough to see one in the

80

wild, from the safety of my car, and it was a beautiful animal. Panthers are on the endangered species list. While these cats do shy away from humans, they have been known to stalk hikers which is why travel in pairs or groups when out in the woods is always a dependable safety strategy. If you are told of a panther sighting in your expedition area, relocate immediately. Their tracks are easy to distinguish from other animals with a distinctive "M" shaped pad and three lobes on the rear of the heel (dogs only have two lobes). Their claw marks do not show in the track.

The Montana Fish, Wildlife and Parks Department came up with some great tips on what to do if you ever encounter a large cat such as a mountain lion or panther. They are as follows:

- Avoid the animal if at all possible; in other words, do not approach it
- Do not run or turn your back. Make eye contact, and if you have children, pick them up while maintaining eye contact with the animal. If you have sunglasses on, take them off.
- Try to appear larger than you are by opening your jacket and by raising and waving your arms
- Speak firmly and try not to sound afraid (I know this is easier said than done)

Bottom line: if you see these animals, leave the area and do your legend trip somewhere else. Remember, personal safety is a priority.

There have been reports from time to time of black panthers roaming around the Florida swamps, but Florida Fish and Wildlife will tell you they are false. Most people who say they have seen them are in fact seeing the black bobcat. It is possible there are black panthers.

81

Legend Tripping

Following hurricanes, zoos and rescue centers have reported losing animals, including black panthers. Though these animals shy away from humans, they can be dangerous when encountered.

Wild pigs (also known as wild hogs, wild boar, or feral swine) are not native to the Americas. The first wild pigs in the United States originated from domestic stock brought to North America by early European explorers and settlers. Many years later, Eurasian wild boar were introduced into parts of the USA for hunting purposes. In areas where domestic pigs and Eurasian wild boar were found together in the wild, interbreeding occurred. Today, hybrid populations exist throughout the wild pig's range. Wild pigs have been reported in at least forty-five states. They will eat almost anything and are extremely dangerous. A mother pig will aggressively protect her young, and all wild pigs will defend themselves when they feel they are cornered or injured. They have rock hard snouts, which they use to burrow in the ground for insects. Wild pigs usually come out at dawn and leave when humans show up. They are extremely fast-moving animals. If you hear them out there, I recommend you leave and have the bear mace ready. Wild pigs cannot climb trees, so if you come into contact with an aggressive pig, immediately seek shelter in a nearby tree.

Alligators are located in the southeastern part of the United States (i.e., Florida, Georgia, Alabama, Mississippi, Louisiana and Texas. These reptiles are extremely dangerous and should be avoided at all times. When they attack humans, they get hold of a limb and drag them into the water. They will then do a death roll, which twists the limb off and drowns the victim. They are especially aggressive during the mating season with is April through May. I recommend you do not plan any of your legend trips where these animals are. If you find yourself lost and there is a shallow body of water you must cross, then you must do the following. When you start walking through the water, you need to drag your feet along the bottom. This will kick up the mud and silt which will camouflage you, and if you do kick an alligator, because they can't see you, they will think it is another alligator and move. This does not work during mating season. They will attack anything that touches them. Again this extremely dangerous and should be done as a last resort.

When it comes to snakes, there are four dangerous species in the United States: rattlesnake, copperhead, coral snake, and water moccasin (cottonmouth). I cannot stress enough: snakes should be left alone if you come into contact with them, even the nonvenomous ones. If a team member gets bitten by a venomous snake, your legend trip is over.

The most common venomous snake is the rattlesnake, which is the largest of the venomous snakes in the United States. They can accurately strike at up to one third their body length. Their venom is neurotoxic (it affects the nervous system), leading to everything from seizures to death. Neurotoxic bites are the deadliest. Rattlesnakes use their rattles or tails as a warning when they feel threatened. They sun themselves near logs, boulders, or in open areas. Their habitats include mountains, prairies, deserts, and beaches. Florida has pygmy rattlesnakes, and they are just as venomous as the big ones.

The next venomous snake is the copperhead and these are recognized by their reddish or tan color with hourglass-shaped colored bands. Their venom causes hemorrhaging in their prey, mostly small mammals. Adults are usually eighteen to thirty-six inches long. They are not normally aggressive, but will bite if someone steps on or near them. Copperheads live in forests, rocky areas, swamps, and near water.

Coral snakes are probably the most underrated and the most poisonous snake in the United States. They are scarce; I have never seen one in the wild. Oddly enough, they do not have a camouflage pattern. They are red, yellow, and black in color. There is a rhyming verse which helps people know the difference between the coral snake and the nonvenomous king snake: "Red on yellow kills a fellow. Red on black is friend to Jack."

Coral snakes are primarily located in Arizona, Texas, and Florida. They reside in the wooded, sandy, and marshy areas, and spend most of their lives burrowed underground or in leaf piles. In the southern part of the United States, they are known to live in old tree trunks. They are not aggressive, and they tend to shy away from humans. When a person is bitten, which is rare, it's because the person sat down next to one or stepped on one. Coral snakes have small mouths so their bite seems like a nibble. Unfortunately, they are more poisonous than both the rattlesnake and the water moccasin. Believe it or not, coral snakes are related to the cobra and sea snakes. There is little or no pain or swelling at the site of the bite, and nothing will happen for up to twelve hours. The venom is a neurotoxin, which messes with the nervous system and can lead to muscular paralysis and respiratory or cardiac failure. In other words, it can make your heart stop beating.

If you find one of these snakes, you need to stay away from it. It was recently reported the supply of antivenin for coral snakes is dwindling. Recently a man in Miami was bitten and had to be airlifted to Tampa because the Miami hospital was out of antivenin. Of course, the best rule of thumb for any snake is to just stay away from it. Like my dad used to say, "It's not messing with you, so don't mess with it."

Water moccasins are probably the most aggressive

of the venomous snakes in the United States. These snakes are pit vipers in the same family as copperheads and rattlesnakes. Their venom is hemotoxic, which means the venom affects the blood and organs, causing a breakdown or inflammation in the body. Hemotoxic bites are the most painful kind. These snakes average fifty to fifty-five inches long as adults and are dark tan, brown, or nearly black, with vague black or dark brown cross bands. Juveniles have brown or orange cross bands and a yellow tail. Cottonmouths are frequently found in or around water. They are not easily scared, and they will defend themselves if they feel threatened. They are the only snakes known to chase people and climb on boats.

There are also dangerous arachnids you need to know about. The first one is the scorpion. The Arizona bark scorpion is the only species in the United States potentially dangerous to humans, and thankfully they're only native to the Sonoran Desert, which is located in parts of Arizona, New Mexico and California. They like to hide under rocks, in wood piles, or under tree bark (hence their name) during the day, while at night they come out to actively hunt for prey. These scorpions actually prefer to be upside down, so this means many stings are from someone reaching under an object with their hand. Even though the annual number of stings is estimated to be in the thousands, only two fatalities have been recorded in Arizona since 1968. A sting from an Arizona bark scorpion should not be taken lightly, though, especially with children or the elderly, and medical attention should be sought immediately.

The next is the black widow spider. These are one of the most recognizable, and most feared spiders and inhabit the entire United States. The females usually measure between ½ to 1-½ inches in length, are a glossy black color, with the signature red hourglass marking on either the top or the bottom of the abdomen or none at all. Their venom is strong enough to drop a cow. Although human deaths are fairly rare, a Colorado resident died after being bitten 19 times on the foot in 2011. The good thing is these spiders are not aggressive, so in others words, if you leave them alone, they'll leave you alone. Most bites are caused by accidental encounters in places like wood piles, trash dumps, sheds, gardens, and under rocks, or if they get trapped in a sock or shoe. If someone gets bitten, it can take over 30 minutes for symptoms to take effect. Watch for redness and swelling, an overall "achy" feeling, weakness, vomiting, headache, and nausea. Always seek medical attention as soon as possible.

The next dangerous arachnid is the brown recluse spider. This spider is difficult to identify since it has no discernable markings on the body, although they sometimes have a violin pattern, which cellar spiders and pirate spiders can also have. The best way is by their eyes, if you can get close enough to see them; these spiders have six eyes instead of eight. Their range is from Texas to western Georgia and from Louisiana to southern Iowa. These spiders are not aggressive as their name suggests and tend to only bite if trapped in clothing, gloves, or bedding. If someone does get bit, it usually isn't even felt initially. Pain and itching can follow within 2 to 8 hours; pain worsens over the next 36 hours, and a visible wound will develop within a few days. Immediate treatment is to place an ice pack on the bite area and seek medical attention. Do not cut open the wound and squeeze the pus out, as this will only make the bite area worse. If left untreated, the tissue around the bite becomes infected and rots. I myself have been bitten by one of these and it took weeks for the bite to heal up. I didn't even know I had been bitten until I went to the hospital for a large swollen bump on my leg. I now have a permanent scar from this encounter.

A dangerous insect is the bee and I really want to address the African honey bees, also called killer bees. They were accidentally released by a Brazilian beekeeper in 1957 and these deadly bees spread through most of South America, Central America, and up into Mexico. They have now been located in Texas, Georgia, Arizona, Nevada, New Mexico, Florida, Arkansas, Louisiana, Utah, and California. These honey bees are much more aggressive than the European honey bee in the United States. Killer bees, as a swarm, will chase a victim over a mile and attack within a quarter mile of their hive (which can be underground). Their sting actually has the same potency as a European honey bee's, but since they attack in such larger numbers, this makes them much more dangerous. One to two deaths per year are usually credited to killer bees.

In 2012, an Arizona resident was killed by a swarm in a Tucson city park; it is important to note the victim was allergic to bees. Of course, to someone who is allergic to the sting, any bee can be deadly. When I was down in Panama, my group had a run in with these insects. We ran a couple of miles before the bees stopped attacking. Luckily nobody in my team was seriously stung and better yet no one was allergic. If you happen to run into a nest of Africanized bees, don't make any sudden movements, keep animals away, and avoid waving around jewelry or other flashy objects. On the other hand, if the bees begin to attack, run! And don't stop running until you're sure they are not swarming after you. Try to protect your face from being stung, run into the wind, and head towards the nearest shelter such as a house or tent—don't jump in water, since the bees will wait for you to resurface. It is a good

87

idea to know if any members of your legend tripping group are allergic to bees or any other stinging insects.

The next dangerous insect and one everyone has had some kind of encounter with is the wasp. There are over 100,000 species of wasps but the two most common are the yellow jacket and the hornet. The hornet is larger than the yellow jacket, but the most common difference is their color. Hornets make their nests in trees where yellow jacket make theirs in the ground, which accounts for most yellow jacket stings on the bottom of exposed feet. Hornet stings are usually more painful than yellow jacket stings. Again like bees, multiple stings can cause shock and sometimes death. If you see them, leave them alone.

The Hunt

After you finish the recon, head back to camp and get ready. There you will eat dinner and wait for the early evening. Make sure everybody helps with the camp chores and cleans up. When it is time to move out, then get the teams ready, load up the vehicle(s), and drive to the research location. Before you head out, always double check the radios, flashlights/head lights, and survival necklaces. Once you get to the rally point, park your vehicles so it is easy to get out. This can be a challenge at nighttime.

Instruct all teams to keep their video cameras on and recording, and then send them to their area. You never know when something will happen, and when it does, it happens quickly. By the time your camera is up and running, what you want to film is gone or the noise has stopped. If this happens and you don't get anything, erase the recording. Each team should stay on their paths or dirt roads. I know the woods look pretty inviting during the day, but once the sun goes down, everything looks different. It is better to stay on dirt paths and roads that are easy to see at night, so it will be easy to backtrack to the rally point. Each team will move to their OP (observation point) and wait and listen.

Have some of the teams do wood knocks or call blasting. There is a theory that Bigfoot will alert other Bigfoots that humans are in the area by knocking on wood. I have heard these knocks. You can never be one hundred percent sure it is Bigfoot making these knocks. I know some people will take a baseball bat to do the wood knocks. If you do the wood knocks, make sure every team knows it is happening, otherwise one team will do the wood knock and the other team will hear it thinking it's a Bigfoot and do a wood knock back. Then you'll have two teams thinking they've got a Bigfoot in the area.

"Call blasting" is where you take a recording of a supposed Bigfoot scream or howl and play it on a loudspeaker and see if you get any response. I have tried this technique. I don't set up an elaborate sound system to do the call blasting. I simply put the recording in my vehicle sound system or outdoor speaker, turn up the volume, and wait. Sound travels farther at night, so as long as everybody is silent, the call blast will go out. If you do get a call back, first of all, you won't know one hundred percent it is a Bigfoot making the call, and second, what if the Bigfoot is calling to tell the other Bigfoots to stay away from the area?

When I first started writing this book, I was not a big fan of humans attempting to make Bigfoot yells or screams. I thought for some time it was a waste of time when people tried to imitate a Bigfoot yell. It reminded me of a person meowing to a cat. The cat looks up at the human and doesn't even twitch an ear at the sound. The cat is thinking, "Why is this human trying to sound like us?" With Bigfoot, I thought the effect was the same.

89

Legend Tripping

These animals are smart and I'm pretty sure they can tell the difference between a human and one of their own. But on one of our late-night outings, we had a young female investigator, April, do some screams and oddly enough we heard something call back. I think you can get more positive results if female members do the scream. I think the big guy has a thing for the ladies. There are investigators who swear these screams provide positive results. Many Bigfoot investigators with whom I've been on expeditions like to do the yells when we're out in the woods. Again I'm going off of my own experiences when I go out monster hunting.

You can now buy game calls that will broadcast animal yells. You can record Bigfoot yells and broadcast them with the game caller. It will save you from losing your voice.

If you can afford it, a thermal imager is a great tool to use when looking for Bigfoot. These expensive devices will scan an area and pick up heat signatures. In other words, if there is something alive and giving off heat, this device will pick it up. It works great at night when you can't see your hand in front of your face. Thermal imagers come in a variety of designs, but they are all expensive. All the thermal imagers you see on these monster hunting and paranormal shows are rented. As I said, they are great for monster hunting, but they are expensive and fragile.

When I was in the military, a huge one was used to scan the outside of the base to make sure nobody was trying to infiltrate us. I keep looking on the online auction sites for one at a decent price. No luck so far, but I'll keep looking.

After the teams have walked around for a couple of hours, I usually call them in when the sun goes down and it gets dark. An exception to the rule is when a team starts to see or hear things. If you or one of your teams hears something, then have everybody stop what they're doing and listen. Remember, always keep the video camera in record mode. You can talk and explain where you are and what time it is. There is a theory Bigfoot is attracted to a child's voice. So have your children act like they are taping a television show and you never know, you might hear something. Again, it makes the kids feel like they are part of the investigation.

When you get all the teams back, inventory all the gear. If your team is late getting back, as a safety measure, call on the radio and let the base know you have stopped and are listening for something. Give them your location as well. It only takes a couple of seconds to do this. If a team does not show up at the prescribed time, don't panic. First, call them on the radio and see where they are. On the way back, a team will hear something and stop to listen. If they don't answer (radio/cellphone) and it has been a while, then send only one team with a member who knows the area.

When you are out in the woods and your team radio stops working, then you need to immediately come back to base or the rally point. You can't depend on your cellphones. Sometimes they lose their signal deep in the woods. This is something all of your teams need to know: if your team gets lost, first stop and then contact the base and tell them the situation. If at night, have every team member turn on their light, which is located on the safety necklace, and form a circle pattern, facing out and flashing away from the center. That way when the search party comes looking for the team, they can be easily seen. You probably are thinking this will blow the whole legend trip and scare the Bigfoot away, with all the lights flashing everywhere. Oh well, never jeopardize safety for the experience.

If you have night vision goggles, turn them on. They magnify any kind of light source and you can see from quite a distance away. It will make it easier to find the lost team. If you have done your briefing right and every team went and stayed in their assigned zone or road, then you will pretty much know the area in which they are located. Also, call out to them and see if the lost team can hear you. Sound travels better at night. Make sure only one team is calling out to them. If all the teams do this, then you won't be able to hear the lost team when they reply.

If the worst happens and you can't find them, then call 911. Fish and Wildlife officers will come out, and they often have helicopters equipped with heat detecting devices and will be able to find the lost team. When they arrive, give them the location where the team is supposed to be, which will give them an area to start their search. In the whole time I have been legend tripping, I have not lost a team. I always ensure each team has an experienced person with them, stays on the road, and has a working radio.

When all the teams are back at the rally point, then you do a quick briefing to find out what all the teams saw or heard. Make sure they know where it was they heard the noise or saw the object. That way you can come back in the morning and do a search of the area in daylight. You might find some evidence, such as footprints. Do a sketch, because things look different in daylight and your team might not remember the exact spot in daylight.

Once you finish your briefing, have everybody load up the vehicles. Assign an order of march for each team. In other words, in the first vehicle have a team member who knows the area and then have everybody follow that person. I like to be in the last vehicle; that way, if any vehicle breaks down or something goes wrong, I am there to fix it. If a vehicle breaks down, you may have to tow it with your vehicle. This is another reason

I own a Jeep; Jeeps are good for that.

Now when you get back to base camp, you get everyone together and go over the night's events. Talk about what you saw and heard. Go over all the pictures and recordings. If you or any of your team found footprints review the sections where I go over how to not only conduct interviews but also make castings of suspected footprints.

Last but not least here is a quick packing list for your legend trip. A more detailed list is in Chapter 17 Equipment and Tools.

Bigfoot Legend Trip Packing List:
- Camping gear, including tent(s), sleeping bag(s), lanterns, and cooking stove
- Fuel for cooking stove
- Water and items to clean water
- Food
- Trash bags
- Canteens
- Knife/machete/shovel
- Camera—one that has IR capabilities
- Flashlights/head lights/light sticks
- Batteries for all equipment devices
- Game camera—it is better to have more than one so you can put them in multiple places
- Outdoor clothing, including snake boots
- Sunglasses
- Rain gear—Gore-Tex is great because it also keeps you warm
- Bug spray/sunblock—bring a lot of it; you'll need it
- Anti-scent spray—start spraying this on your equipment before you leave on the legend trip
- GPS—this is good to use when you set up your game cameras; you can mark where you put them with the GPS

Legend Tripping

- Bionic ear device
- Evidence kit including footprint casting material
- Fishing gear
- Binoculars

Here is what I carry in the backpack I use for day trips. I carry this with me all the time in the back of my vehicle:

- Survival kit
- First aid kit—include poison ivy cream, moleskin for blisters
- Foot powder (cold weather)
- Petroleum jelly (hot weather and swamps)
- Extra socks
- Canteen with cup
- Flashlight (two)—always carry a headlamp and an extra flashlight
- GPS (with extra batteries)
- Compass—in case the GPS stops working
- Poncho (for use as a poncho or shelter)
- Rain gear
- Back-up knife
- Water purifier pump
- Plaster casting kit
- Pheromone chips (keep in sealed durable container)
- Binoculars
- Trail camera
- 550 parachute cord
- Marking kit
- Bear mace
- Machete
- Food (beef jerky, trail mix, peanut butter crackers, and an MRE)
- Solar wrap used to recharge a cell phone or GPS
- Toilet paper/baby wipes (you will need them)
- Sunscreen/bug spray
- Map of area
- Camera with night vision

94

Chapter 5
Aquatic Cryptids

Aquatic cryptids are in a category all to themselves, which is why I wanted to dedicate an entire chapter to the subject. Like Bigfoot, there are well documented lake monster sightings here in the United States with each of these water creatures having its own unique name.

One of the first and most popular books is Bernard Heuvelmans' 1968 *In the Wake of the Sea-Serpents.* Heuvelmans concluded there were unknown animals still in the oceans and seas and tentatively identified nine possible genera or species into which those that were sufficiently described might be classified. He also stated 600 claimed sightings were of unknown animals and about 10% were hoaxes.

In this chapter I will do a brief overview of aquatic cryptids in the United States and Canada. If I miss one you know of, I do apologize but my intent is to introduce to new legend trippers these aquatic cryptids. Some I will only briefly mention because there isn't a lot of data on them or sightings. Others, like most giant sea serpents, have only been seen once, so documentation and evidence is rather thin.

I used Loren Coleman and Patrick Huyghe's 2003 book *The Field Guide to Lake Monsters, Sea Serpents, and Other Mystery Denizens of the Deep* as a guide for this chapter.

The most famous of aquatic cryptid in the world is the Loch Ness Monster, which is located in northern

Scotland. In fact, next to Bigfoot, Nessie is one of the most popularized cryptids out there. This creature has been seen for centuries and still nobody has gotten a good picture of it. The famous "Surgeon's Photograph" was later reported to be a fake, though now there is some debate on it. Yet legend inspires imagination and fictional movies, such as *Water Horse*, tell creative and beautiful stories about the possible origins of this famed creature.

There are actually three kinds of aquatic cryptids. They are the sea serpent, the lake monster, and the river monster. Since bipedal swamp cryptids seem to have more in common with other bipedal cryptids, I covered them in my chapter on Bigfoot.

Sea Serpents

For centuries man has been reporting strange creatures in our ocean depths. There are legends of large aquatic reptile beasts attacking and sinking ships. When man first journeyed across the waves, any missing ship was blamed on sea serpents.

Today with 71 percent of the earth covered in water, there are aquatic creatures still unknown. When it comes to sea serpents, unfortunately, these aquatic beasts are most of the time seen once and never again. Today there are still reports and videos of large unidentified creatures in our oceans and seas witnessed by dependable observers.

On October 6, 2013, a couple vacationing on Florida's Sanibel Island, filmed a "monster" near the shore. They managed to capture some rather exciting footage of a large aquatic creature. It should be noted the creature moves too fast to be a manatee, and alligators are freshwater creatures, not to mention whatever it is, is too big to be either one. Unfortunately there have been no more sightings of this aquatic creature off Sanibel

An old print of a sea serpent from a Swedish manuscript.

Island.

Not all sea serpents make a solo appearance then disappear. In British Columbia there is a sea serpent seen frequently. It is believed to be a Cadborosaurus, named after Cadboro Bay where most of the sightings have occurred. Sightings of this sea serpent report the creature to be up to 30 feet long and sometimes showing front and rear flippers. The descriptions given by witnesses are consistent and have been reported for ages.

In 2009 a video of this sea serpent surfacing in the water was taken by an Alaskan fisherman in Cadboro Bay. In the film you can see a large object moving through the water.

Another type of aquatic cryptid creature that resides in the ocean and seems to be making more appearances is the giant squid. Though technically not a sea serpent, this large creature was first thought to be an old sailor's legend called the Kraken. Now it is science fact that large squid and possibly octopus

97

An old print of a sea serpent seen from the HMS Daedalus, 1848.

are living in the deepest part of our oceans. With the changing water temperatures in the oceans, these creatures are being seen more and more. In October 2013 a giant squid was found washed ashore on La Arena Beach in Spain and in May 2015, another one was found on a beach on New Zealand's South Island.

Sometimes reported sightings of aquatic creatures are vastly misconstrued creating excitement only to end with a "logical" explanation. For example, in 1937, a body of an unknown animal was found in the stomach of a whale captured by the Naden Harbor whaling station in the Queen Charlotte Islands, a British Columbia archipelago. Samples of the animal were brought to the Provincial Museum in Victoria. It was later identified as a fetal baleen whale.

Lake Monsters

The next kind of aquatic cryptids is lake monsters. They are located all over North America and descriptions of these creatures vary from lake to lake. Descriptions have ranged from a large snake, to a giant octopus, to a prehistoric serpent from the Jurassic period.

Probably the most famous of lake monsters in the United States is Champ. This large beast is said to reside in the depths of Lake Champlain in Essex and Clinton County in New York. Champ is often referred to as America's Loch Ness Monster. Lake Champlain is 125 miles long and though averaging a depth of only 64 feet, it is 400 feet deep at its deepest point. It is situated between New York and Vermont, with six miles extending into Québec. The Abenaki and the Iroquois tribes have legends dating back hundreds of years about this large aquatic creature. The Abenaki have stories of their horses being mysteriously pulled under by the creature they call Tatoskok.

On July 24, 1819 a boat captain reported he saw a creature black in color, about 187 feet long with a head resembling a seahorse. The witness's story relates the monster reared more than 15 feet out of the water on Bulwagga Bay. He went on to say the monster had three teeth, a white star on its forehead and a red belt around the neck. He related all this detail yet he was two hundred feet from the creature.

In 1873 a *New York Times* story reported a railroad crew had seen the head of an enormous serpent in Lake Champlain. At the time, Clinton County's sheriff, Nathan H. Mooney, reported an enormous snake or water serpent, 25 to 35 feet long. Later in August, the steamship *W.B. Eddy* ran into Champ and nearly capsized, according to the tourists on board.

Showman P. T. Barnum, upon hearing the reports, offered $50,000 for the monster—dead or alive. As

99

Legend Tripping

anyone can guess, nobody collected the reward.

In 1981, Sandra Mansi presented a photograph of Champ, she took while on vacation with her family on July 5, 1977. The photo does show what appears to be a large Plesiosaur-type animal in Lake Champlain.

Sandra Mansi's photo of Champ.

There had been over 180 sightings of the creature by over 600 witnesses. There are still sightings of this aquatic cryptid occurring today. Apart from Bigfoot, Champ is considered one the most popular cryptids in the United States.

There is a large freshwater octopus-like creature supposedly lurking in Lake Thunderbird in Oklahoma. Marine biologists will tell you there are no known freshwater octopi. If you ask the residents living around Lake Thunderbird in Oklahoma, they will give you a different answer. They are convinced a giant octopus dwells in the lake and it has been blamed in the numerous mysterious drowning deaths. Oddly enough, the same cause for drownings has been cited in Lake Oologah and Lake Tenkiller in Oklahoma. The description of the octopus sounds like your standard saltwater octopus with its brown skin tinged with red and a sprawl of tentacles, although reportedly it as large as a horse. There has been no physical evidence or pictures to back up the claim of this giant octopus, other than eyewitnesses. But as I searched on the Internet I found there is a large number of unsolved drownings occurring at Lake Thunderbird, Lake

100

Oologah and Lake Tenkiller. As the saying goes, "The jury is still out" on this one.

A strange creature named Tessie or Tahoe Tessie has been seen in Lake Tahoe, Nevada. This aquatic cryptid, according to the Washoe and Paiute tribes, is said to live in an underwater tunnel beneath Cave Rock, and sightings have continued into the modern day. Lake Tahoe is the largest alpine lake in North America, with a maximum depth of 1,645 ft. (501 m); it is the second deepest in the United States after Crater Lake. It borders California and Nevada and is a popular summertime recreation area. Tales of a large creature dwelling in this lake go back as far as the 1950s when two policeman first reported seeing a large hump pursuing a speeding boat. There were a rash of sightings of the beast in 1980. The most credible account was when two divers found an underwater cave. Upon closer examination of it, a strange creature suddenly shot out of the cave into the lake. The divers did not get a good look at it because of all the silt the creature stirred up in its escape. Some witnesses describe the lake monster as looking like a plesiosaurus, while others say it is more snakelike. I found this to be most common witness description of lake monsters from other parts of the country.

There is a large creature that has been seen in Flathead Lake, Montana. This beautiful lake is located in northwest Montana and is the largest lake in the western United States. Flathead Lake is approximately 28 miles long and 16 miles wide, with a maximum depth of 370 feet. It is on the southern tip of the Rocky Mountain Trench and was formed more than 75 million years ago when the state of Montana was covered by a vast inland sea inhabited by various shark species and aquatic reptiles. Fossils of massive sea creatures have been excavated nearby.

This creature has been described as being large,

101

brownish to blue-black in color, eel-shaped, with grayish-black eyes. Its body is round with a wavy movement like a snake and spans from twenty to forty feet. It has a long history with the Native Americans. Unlike other lake monsters, this cryptid does not have a catchy nickname. It's simply called the Flathead Lake Monster.

The legend of this lake monster started in 1889, when the captain and passengers of the *U.S. Grant,* a lake steamboat making its rounds between lakeside towns, reported seeing what they thought was a large log heading toward the boat. Since this initial report, there have been numerous sightings of this serpent by credible eyewitnesses such as mothers, doctors, lawyers, biologists, engineers, anglers and policemen. All have reported being witness to unusual happenings in the lake usually occurring between April and September.

A creature called Bessie apparently lives in Lake Erie, Ohio. Nicknamed South Bay Bessie or just plain Bessie, it is described as gray, snakelike, and 30 to 40 feet long. It was first sighted north of Sandusky, Ohio in 1793.

Canada has a famous lake monster called OgooPogoo. This cryptid makes its home in Lake Okanagan. I was first introduced to this cryptid when it was featured on an episode of the popular television show *In Search Of.* Lake Okanagan is in British Columbia, located 250 miles east of Vancouver. It is 84 miles long

A Lake Monster.

and 3 miles wide, with an average depth of 249 feet. OgooPogoo is described as being one to two feet in diameter with a length of 15 to 20 feet with a horselike head. It is referred to as N'ha-a-tik meaning "snake in the lake" by the Indian tribes. They also believe small, barren Rattlesnake Island on Lake Okanagan is the home of this cryptid. The first recorded sighting was in 1926 when about thirty carloads of witnesses saw it at Okanagan Mission beach. On July 2, 1947, a number of boaters saw the monster simultaneously. In 1968 Arthur Folden shot film footage of a large object moving in the lake. It was studied by experts and found not to have been tampered with. To date, there are over 200 sightings by credible people including a priest, a sea captain, a doctor, and police officers. It should be noted Lake Okanagan and Loch Ness are both on the same latitude line. They are both large deep lakes.

River Monsters

When it comes to river monsters, there are some in the United States still witnessed to this day. The first one I want to talk about is the St. Johns River Monster, also known as the Lake Monroe Monster or the Astor Monster, as it was seen in various spots in these neighboring watery Florida locales. This is the only aquatic cryptid found in both a lake and river. Legends of the Astor Monster, also called "Pinky," have been around for hundreds of years. In 1774 William Bartram, a famous American naturalist, traveled through Astor.

Bartram wrote he saw a strange unknown beast in Lake George which the local Native Americans told him was "the beast of the deep." He saw it around Volusia Bar where a lighthouse was built in 1886.

Over a hundred years after Bartram's experience, on August 24, 1896, the local press reported "something

103

dangerously large" overturned a fishing boat in Lake Monroe and a week later, the steamer *Osceola* was struck by something large near the same location.

In 1956, strange footprints were found in the mud along the river's edge. They were described as being about 10 inches long and reptilian in style, with three toes pointed to the front and two to the rear. Descriptions of the creature varied greatly, with some claiming it looked like a dinosaur with a horn in the center of the head. The police dismissed the reports saying it was probably a manatee or alligator.

During the 60s and 70s, the Astor Monster was seen repeatedly in the river and Lake Monroe. Some individuals claimed to have shot at it but missed. The last reported sighting of the monster was in August of 1987. Two men were fishing on St. Johns River when something about 35 feet long, greenish-gray with spikes on its back, struck their boat and then submerged into the river depths. Cryptozoologist Loren Coleman mounted a 2008 expedition, but was unsuccessful in learning more about the creature.

Georgia has a river monster named Altie that has been witnessed in the famous Altamaha River, one of the largest rivers in the state. According to Tama Indian legend there is a huge water serpent lurking in the rivers and tributaries. Sightings by the Tama date back before whites settled the area.

In the 1920s, timbermen reported sightings of the creature in the river. It was seen by a Boy Scout troop in the 1940s and two officials from the Reidsville State Prison the 1950s. The most recent report was in 2002 when a man pulling a boat up the river, near Brunswick reported seeing something strange in the river, over twenty feet in length and six feet wide, break the water. The animal seemed to emerge from the water to get air and then submerge again beneath the depths.

104

The sightings have all taken place near the town of Darien. Cryptozoologist Lyle Blackburn investigated the legend in 2012.

A large snakelike beast has been reported numerous times and even photographed at the White River in Arkansas. Sightings of the monster began in 1915, though legend has it that the creature is responsible for the overturning of a boat during the Civil War. The first sighting to make a newspaper headline was when a plantation owner saw a large, gray-skinned creature "as wide as a car and three cars long."

The author with a statue of Altie.

In 1937 a plantation owner, Bramlett Bateman, observed a strange creature rolling on the surface of the water in the river and described it as having the skin of an elephant, four or five feet wide by twelve feet long, with the face of a catfish.

During the summer of 1971 the creature was seen by numerous eyewitnesses who described it as "the size of a boxcar" with a bone protruding from its forehead. One eyewitness stated that it looked like the creature was peeling all over, but it was a smooth type of skin or flesh. The creature is reported to make strange noises sounding like a combination of a "cow's moo and a

105

horse's neigh."

In 1973, the White River Monster Refuge was created. The Arkansas State Legislature signed into law a bill by state Senator Robert Harvey designating the area located between the southern point on the White River known as Old Grand Glaize and a northern point known as Rosie. It is illegal to harm the monster inside the refuge.

Cryptozoologist and biologist Roy P. Mackal investigated the sightings and has suggested the creature is in fact a large male elephant seal that wandered mistakenly up the Mississippi River into White River. Most scientists believe the sightings are nothing more than mistaken identity, like a floating log.

As you can see, there is no shortage of aquatic cryptids to go searching for on a legend trip. The great thing is there are still sightings of these creatures as I write this.

Chapter 6
Aquatic Cryptid
Legend Trip

I went on my first aquatic cryptid legend trip back in 1975. My interest in these waterway creatures started at an early age with my mother, who was born and raised in Scotland. While I was growing up, she would tell me stories about the Loch Ness monster. When we finally visited Loch Ness in 1975, I walked the shores for hours looking for the famous lake beast. Unfortunately the weather turned bad and we had to leave. I remember that there weren't a lot of Nessie souvenirs to purchase back then and I remember seeing a team from *National Geographic* magazine out there looking for it. Still, it was an exciting trip and something I will always remember.

When I returned to the United States, I remember thinking that I wished there were lake monsters in North America. As luck would have it, I was watching the popular television show *In Search Of*, and the episode was about a lake monster in Canada called OgooPogoo. I went to the library and found some books on the unexplained and found that Lake Champlain in New York has a legendary lake monster called Champ. I continued my research and found that there were numerous other lake and river monsters in the continental United States. Legends of these aquatic cryptids date back to the time of the Native Americans, before the European settlers showed up.

Legend Tripping

In 1989, I went on my second aquatic cryptid legend trip. I was assigned to Fort Drum for Air Assault School. After finishing this training, I talked my travel partner into stopping by Lake Champlain on our way back to North Carolina and we drove around the lake. The lake also borders the state of Vermont where we found a monument to Champ. It wasn't very big and I almost didn't see it as it's a small granite block at the end of Perkins Pier. Like my trip to Loch Ness, I didn't get to stay long, but it was still exciting to visit. I entertained my friend, who had never heard of Champ, with stories about the legendary lake monster.

Conducting an aquatic cryptid legend trip has a similar preparation process, while also being very different from a Bigfoot legend trip. Both are equally exciting, but each offers its own challenges. In this chapter I will go over how to conduct a successful aquatic cryptid legend trip to be applied when you are out looking for either lake monsters or river monsters.

Like all legend trips, you need to know where you are going to look for this cryptid and pack the right equipment. As I said earlier, I like to have everything planned out before leaving on a legend trip. Being that this is an aquatic beast, my list of equipment is going to be different with items added like a canoe or boat. With a boat comes a lot of different things you need to plan for and have on your packing list. I've compiled a quick list of equipment you'll need at the end of this chapter and a more detailed list of equipment in Chapter 17.

There are differences to consider when looking for aquatic cryptids versus land-based cryptids. The big difference is the number of sightings between the two. When it comes to lake or river monsters, there are not a lot of sightings and some sightings are months apart, sometimes years apart. Most sightings are of strange humps moving up and down a river or in the middle of a

108

lake. Most witnesses don't get a really good look at what the creature is. Some sightings are misidentification of known animals (manatees and sturgeons) or rogue waves that look like humps. But some of these humps are too large to be from a known animal and can't be explained.

While land cryptids are primarily nocturnal, aquatic cryptids are seen both in the daytime and nighttime. Evidence suggests that lake/river cryptids are fish eaters and more active at night. Based on that assumption, you should try to look when the sun is coming up and going down because fish are very active and near the surface at these times. When the water surface is calm and the sun is out, there is less mixing of the waters from the different thermal layers and oxygen in the upper layers is greater, causing the fish to come closer to the surface to get their oxygen from the water near the surface (which is absorbing oxygen from the air). Presumably, these cryptids are following the fish into the upper layers of the water, which may explain why there are so many sightings in calm, sunny weather.

Sighting are primarily in the daytime, during the warmer parts of the year. This is primarily due to the fact that there are more people to make the sightings while enjoying recreational activities going on around the lakeside, i.e., canoeing, swimming, skiing and scuba diving. Like land-based cryptids, these animals seem to avoid human contact. In other words, when approached, these aquatic beasts submerge into the depths. However noise from boat engines seems to scare them. Which calls into question if these aquatic cryptids are reptiles or fish?

Where land-based cryptids have forests or swamps to hide, aquatic cryptids reside in deep lakes or rivers. Unlike land-based cryptids, these creatures are con-

109

The author on a nighttime aquatic hunt.

fined to the lake. But some of these lakes are miles long and very deep. River creatures are a different story. Rivers are miles long and these creatures are known for showing up at different locations, and sometimes they appear in the lake the river empties into.

Every animal on Earth has a behavior pattern. Reptiles all the way down to fish have some kind of pattern to the way they live day to day. When you read about past sightings, you can see a general pattern that these animals seem to be displaying. They are usually seen at a certain time of the year and at certain places. Some of these animals do stay at one area and that is due to low human contact.

When I hear or get wind of a sighting, like all cryptid sightings, I first check on the map where the sighting happened. If it's in a moving body of water like a river I look for where the river goes (i.e., lake or the ocean). I also check the feasibility of getting to the sighting location. Will I need a boat or can I walk along the banks to look for it? I look at the details of the sighting to see which direction the animal went. I consider the time of year and try to make an educated guess on where the animal is or where it might make another appearance. If you research past sightings in the area, you might be able to pinpoint where it will be seen next.

Crytpozoologists do their aquatic monster hunts during the day, primarily due to visibility of the creature (you can't see these animals at night), and safety reasons concerning being on a boat or watercraft. Anyway, that is when the animal seems to like to come to the surface and bathe in the sun.

With all legend trips you need to take into consideration the time of year you want to look for this creature. Summer is the ideal time for hunting as this is when most sightings occur. You can also plan other things around this legend trip, like water recreation fun, when you're not looking for the creature. If you are taking your family, I highly encourage you to do this. If you are scuba qualified, you might want to do some diving in the sighting location. If you do this, NEVER dive alone. Also if scuba diving in lakes, you will need the proper diving attire, i.e., dry suit as the water in the depths of some of these lakes can reach freezing levels. Make sure your air tanks are full prior to arriving. Some lakes do not have places to reload your air tanks. Also you will need the proper underwater casing for your cameras, and they are not cheap. Some of the casings will only allow you to go down to a certain depth so closely check your equipment parameters.

When you arrive at the lake or river, the first thing you need to do is decide where you are going to set up your base of operations. I like to find campgrounds that are close to the sighting area and with lake sightings, this is easy to do. Most lakes in the United States have campgrounds right next to them. Lake Champlain in New York not only has campgrounds on its shore but there is also a walking trail that goes around the entire lake. It's good to go to an area that is nice to look at even if you don't see the lake monster. Again I also want to say, never go rucking or hiking by yourself. If you can't find anybody to go with you, then wait until someone is available. I cannot stress this point enough, even if you are simply walking a trail around a lake. You won't have to worry about hunters as hunting is illegal near lakes or rivers on public land.

For Scout Masters and Venturing Crew guides, you need to see if there is a Boy Scout or Girl Scout camp near the lake and maybe incorporate a lake cryptid legend trip into your weekend outing. It adds to the excitement of the trip and gives you and your troop something to prepare and look for when they are hiking by the lake.

Setting up a base camp is pretty much the same as doing a Bigfoot legend trip. I always make a checklist to make sure I set up everything we need. Again, you can do it the way you want, because everybody is different. This checklist has worked for me, and I've been doing this for years.

I like to pick an area for my base camp that is close to the lake or river. I have gone to areas that turned out to be full of boats, so you need to plan for multiple locations in case this happens. As I stated earlier, motorboats scare these creatures away. Also if the area is full of campers, it might be a good idea not to tell everybody you are cryptid lake monster hunting. Additionally, you should locate the nearest hospital, just in case. It doesn't hurt to be proactive, especially with your family or young children.

When you arrive at your actual campsite, the first thing to do is unload your camping gear and get your base camp set up. Put your boat or canoe in a secure location with some way of securing it like a lock and chain to prevent theft. If your boat has an engine, cover

112

it with a tarp, just in case it rains when you are unloading your gear. Also be careful what tree you put your boat/canoe under. Some trees have branches that fall and can destroy whatever is underneath. Most campsites have secured areas to put your boat/canoe. Keep the life vests and oars in your vehicle. Fuel cans also need to go in your vehicle and not in camp where you have

The author with a survival teepee.

a campfire going. If you brought scuba gear, keep it secured in your vehicle.

If you are leading this legend trip, then you need to make sure everybody gets the camp set up before it gets dark. It is important to get all your gear set up, especially your tents. Around lakes in the summer, mosquitoes or other insects will drive you crazy. Make sure you have the mosquito candles ready and when the sun goes down, you need to have the bug spray ready. Rivers are different. Mosquitoes do not like flowing water and fish eat them.

Setting up a campsite is the same as a Bigfoot

113

legend trip so please review that chapter for explicit details and advice.

Now that you've got your base camp set up, it is time to scout around the area and see what's out there. In the military this is called a reconnaissance or "recon" for short. If you have a big enough group, it is great to break into teams and look in multiple areas. Get your map out and, with the team, plot where you want to look. Look for the location of sightings and make a plan based on that. If there is enough time, you should take all the teams with you when you go over the area you intend to search. It's easier than going back and explaining it on a map. Something can get lost in the translation. Make sure everybody knows what they should look for and point out where the sightings happened. If it's later in the evening and it's getting dark, wait until the next day to leave the camp, especially if you are looking for river cryptids.

Have somebody stay back at base camp and monitor the radio. Break everyone into teams and assign them what I call AORs (Areas of Responsibility). These are areas that the team is to go investigate and set up a static post, scan the lake or river and then proceed to the rally point. You can get almost a hundred percent scan of the lake or waterway with multiple teams. These AORs should be marked on the radio so the base camp can keep track of them. You should try to have a team on the water with a boat or canoe. It is best to have them where sightings have occurred. If there is a lot of boat traffic, then move them to an area where it is more quiet and secluded.

The boat team needs to stay in a certain area so if another team sees something strange from the shore, you can give directions based on where the team is located. Two good pieces of equipment to have with the boat team are a hydrophone and fish finder. Make sure

Underwater Hydrophone.

you have already acquainted yourself and team members with this equipment before the actual hunt so familiarity of use is already present.

The hydrophone is a waterproof microphone that is designed to be used underwater for recording or listening to underwater sound. If you do use this equipment, be aware that any sounds recorded should be checked against previous recordings of known fish/aquatic animals. Hydrophones can be expensive, unless you want to purchase a used one

A fish finder (sonar) is an instrument used to locate fish underwater by detecting reflected pulses of sound energy. Sonar is prone to ambiguities and artifacts and sonar graphs should be checked by experts in interpretation in that field. There are expensive fish finders and there are cheap ones. It all depends how much you want to spend on one.

Each team needs to a have a working radio with fresh or extra batteries or cellphone. I have the teams do radio checks before they move out to their AORs. I've gone over with the teams to always return to base camp if they can't get reception on the radios. In other words, if they can't pick up anybody on the radio then turn around and come back. Also if they see panther or bear tracks, then they are to radio it in and return to the rally point. I go over all of this with everybody, before each team moves out to their AOR. Depending on the size of the lake or river, each team should take water and food. Each team should take a survival kit when leaving base camp because they also have first aid items like band aids and antiseptic wipes.

115

Legend Tripping

If the lake or river covers a large area, you might consider having the teams use vehicles to go to their AORs. It's easier and quicker. Have a dependable 4x4 vehicle back at base camp in case a vehicle breaks down or something goes wrong. If a vehicle breaks down, you may have to tow it with another vehicle. Jeeps are good for that.

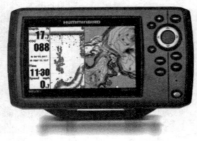

A Fish Finder.

There are occasional land sightings, so looking for drag traces is a good idea. There are actually fossilized drag traces of animals on prehistoric beaches and water beds that may have been left by plesiosaurs/sea turtles. These very much resemble the modern trails left by elephant seals and sea turtles. First and foremost, look for tracks. Look for loose soil or muddy areas where tracks are easy to see. You'll find these tracks along the banks of the lakes or rivers. You also need to look to see if there is evidence that something large came out to the water, like torn-down branches.

If you are conducting your legend trip along a river with swamplands next to it, you need to watch out for everything around you. For example, in the swamps there are cypress trees and their roots do not grow straight down but rather to the side and up. These roots, called knees, look like stalagmites and can be sharp; they are especially dangerous after dark. That is why my team and I stay on the dirt roads at night because of cautionary tales of hunters falling and becoming impaled on them. Also, there may be sinkholes, which you can't see, and you can't tell how deep they are, creating a dangerous situation. Make sure you go over all of this with your team before you enter the area.

116

During the recon, you need to choose a rally point—a designated area for everyone to meet after the hunt, which is usually on the opposite side of the lake or a certain distance down the river. Have the teams decide where to set up observation points (OPs) where a team can get a good look at the lake or river and where to place the trail cameras. Use trail markers or orange 550 cord to mark your OP (trail markers work best because you can see them at night).

Trail (game) cameras can be set up pointing at the lake or river. Unlike land-based cryptids, aquatic ones are not shy about having their picture taken. They should also be set up during the day in secure areas where the creature was sighted. Make sure you remember where you put them. Make sure you put a lock on it. Be prepared to leave your camera out for a while unless you are just doing a weekend legend trip. Set up some kind of trail marker close by so you can find them to retrieve them.

After you finish the recon, head back to camp. You need to talk with the teams about their AORs and what their plan is. This is the question and answer time. Do this now and not in the morning when they are hiding out. Make sure everyone knows the plan for the investigation. Reiterate safety procedures to everyone. Finish the evening with dinner and make sure everybody helps with the camp chores and cleans up.

At daybreak, when it is time to move out, get the teams ready, load up the boat/canoe(s), and send the teams out the their AORs. Before you head out, always double check the radios, cameras, and gear. Have all teams keep their video cameras on and recording, and then send them to their area. Each team should stay on their paths or dirt roads. When it comes to rivers, there might be quicksand along the shoreline. It is better to stay on dirt paths and roads to ensure nobody

117

Canoeing through the Green Swamp.

will get lost, and making it easier to backtrack to the rally point. Each team will move to their AOR, wait, and listen.

If after a couple of hours nothing has happened, I usually call the teams in and reassign AORs. That way they don't get bored looking at the same thing all day. Call them in when the sun goes down and it gets dark. An exception to the rule is when a team starts to see or hear things. If you or one of your teams hears something, then have everybody proceed to that AOR or see what they can observe from their AOR. Remember, always keep the video camera in record mode and keep a running commentary explaining where you are and what time it is.

When you get all the teams back, inventory all gear. If you are on a team getting back to base camp late, as a safety measure, call on the radio and let the base know you have stopped and are listening or looking for something. Give them your location as well. It only takes a couple of seconds to do this. If a team does not show up at the prescribed time, don't panic. First, call them on the radio and see where they are. On the way back, a team will see or hear something and stop to

118

investigate. If they don't answer (radio/cellphone) and it has been a while, then send only one team with a member who knows the area.

If you have done your briefing right and every team stayed in their assigned zone or road, you will reasonably know the general location of each team. If you lose radio contact due to equipment failure, call out to them and see if the missing team can hear you. Make sure only one team is calling out to them because if all the teams do this, then you won't be able to hear the lost team when they reply. If you are doing your legend trip on a river and the boat team has not arrived back, you need to make sure they know to call when they are running late or stuck for some reason.

If the worst happens and you can't find them, call 911. Fish and Wildlife officers will come out, and they often have helicopters equipped with heat detecting devices and will be able to find the lost team. When they arrive, give them the location where the team is supposed to be, which will give them an area to start their search. In the whole time I have been legend tripping, I have not lost a team. I always ensure each team has an experienced person with them, stays on the road, and has a working radio.

When all the teams are back at the rally point, then you do a quick briefing to find out what all the teams saw or heard. Make sure they know where it was they heard the noise or saw the object. That way you can return to the location and do a more thorough search of the area to find evidence. Do a sketch, because things look different in daylight and your team might not remember the exact spot in daylight.

Once back at base camp, get everyone together and go over the day's events and talk about what you saw and heard. Review all pictures and video/audio recordings. If you do have something on the picture,

119

you or a team will need to go reexamine the area and make sure that what you have in the picture is not a log or floating debris. If you or a team get a video and/or picture of the aquatic beast, my hat's off to you. You can repeat this procedure depending how many days you decide to stay out there.

Now if you want to do some nighttime operations (ops) and see if the creature comes out, you need to make sure every team knows what to do in case they get lost or are running late. I don't recommend having a boat team if you are doing night ops, it is better to have your teams equipped with either a thermal viewer and/or night vision goggles.

A thermal imager is a great tool to use when looking for all kinds of cryptids including aquatic ones. These expensive devices will scan an area and pick up heat signatures. In other words, if there is something alive and giving off heat, this device will pick it up. It works great during daytime as well as at night. Thermal imagers come in a variety of designs, but as I have pointed out before they are all expensive; usually, the thermal imagers you see on monster hunting and paranormal shows are rented. As I said, they are great for legend tripping, but they are expensive and fragile.

Night vision scopes/cameras magnify any kind of light source and you can see from quite a distance away. They go through batteries rapidly so make sure there are extra batteries on hand. Most are not waterproof so you might not want scopes assigned to the boat team unless it is a large boat.

One thing I like to do is to tie in one legend trip with another. In Astor, Florida, they have a legend of a river monster that dwells in the St. Johns River and there have been numerous Skunk Ape sightings in Ocala National Forest, which is right next to Astor. I look for the Astor Monster in the daytime and the Skunk Ape at

night. You can also find a local haunted place as well.
   Here is a quick packing list for your legend trip. A more detailed list is in Chapter 17 Equipment and Tools.

Aquatic Cryptid Legend Trip Equipment List:

- Camping gear, including tent(s), sleeping bag(s), and cooking stove
- Outdoor clothing, including snake boots
- Sunglasses
- Rain gear—Gore-Tex is great because it also keeps you warm
- Bug spray/sunblock
- Water and items to clean water
- Food
- Trash bags
- Canteens
- Knife/machete/shovel
- Flashlights/head lights/light sticks
- Batteries for all equipment devices
- Camera—one that is waterproof or waterproof camera shell
- Camera—one that has IR capabilities
- Camera stands and pods
- Temperature detector
- Fish Finder
- Hydrophone
- Binoculars/telescope with stand
- Evidence kit including print casting material
- Map of the area/GPS—this is good to use so you can mark your location
- Canoe with oars and life vests

Here is what to carry in the backpacks for day trips:

- Camera with night vision
- Survival kit
- First aid kit—include poison ivy cream, moleskin for blisters
- Foot powder (cold weather)
- Petroleum jelly (hot weather and swamps)
- Extra socks
- Canteen with cup
- Flashlight (two)—always carry a headlamp and an extra flashlight
- GPS (with extra batteries)/ Map of area
- Compass—in case the GPS stops working
- Poncho (for use in bad weather or as a shelter)
- Rain gear
- Back-up knife
- Water purifier pump
- Plaster casting kit
- Binoculars
- Trail camera
- 550 parachute cord
- Marking kit
- Bear mace
- Machete
- Food (beef jerky, trail mix, peanut butter crackers, and an MRE)
- Solar wrap used to recharge a cell phone or GPS
- Toilet paper/baby wipes (you will need them)
- Sunscreen/bug spray

Chapter 7
Haunted Sites
and the Paranormal

Ghosts, specters, apparitions of the undead; these linked supernatural terms encapsulate an area of interest that fascinates and horrifies at the same time. From haunted graveyards to haunted prisons, America's towns are filled with haunted places. Remember listening to ghost stories as a child, then covering yourself up with your blanket in bed, wondering what ghost lurks in your closet or under your bed? Some ghost stories are steeped purely in folklore and legend, and some carry somewhat more weight with them.

The next legend category I want to go into is the paranormal. This field, known today as "ghost hunting," has gained in popularity as a result of numerous paranormal television shows. A ghost hunt or paranormal investigation is a scary and exciting legend trip to go on. Another great thing is that there are many places to go ghost hunting. The hard part is finding a location where a paranormal investigation hasn't already been done. There are a few places where paranormal incidents continue to happen, but be prepared to travel to find these haunted places to do an investigation.

Note: Not every abandoned house or building is haunted, and as I have stated before, you can be charged with trespassing when entering a

structure without permission.

I discovered in my research that most lighthouses in the United States have a history of hauntings, the most famous being the **St. Augustine Lighthouse** in Florida. It was originally built in 1824 and owned by Dr. Alan Ballard. Because he was forced to sell it to the government and vowed never to leave it, legend has it, he didn't. People have reported seeing his apparition around the property. One of the keepers, Peter Rasmussen, was always seen enjoying a cigar, and today people report getting the whiff of a cigar.

When it comes to ghosts associated with the lighthouse, the story of the two young girls is the most popular. The story goes that in 1873 Hezekiah Pity, who was hired to renovate the lighthouse, had two daughters, Eliza, 13, and Mary, 15. The two girls were playing around the grounds of the lighthouse and found a cart that was used for carrying building materials from the bay to the lighthouse. Despite warnings from their father, Eliza and Mary both climbed into the cart. Suddenly it broke loose from the rope and slid down a hill and into the bay. Sadly, both girls drowned. Legend has it that the ghostly sound of the two girls laughing can be heard in the tower late at night. Also the ghostly apparition of the oldest daughter, Mary, can be seen still wearing the same blue velvet dress and blue hair bow she died in. Ghost hunting television shows have had some pretty positive results during their investigations at the lighthouse. In fact, The St. Augustine Lighthouse is considered the most haunted house in America. A couple of years ago my family went on one of the Halloween night adventures. We did in fact hear an invisible entity coming up the stairs. Again, this is one of many lighthouses that are supposedly haunted. The lighthouse is located at 100 Red Cox Drive, St. Augustine, FL

124

Cape Hatteras Lighthouse in North Carolina is considered the most popular lighthouse due to its splendor and scenic appearance, but it also has a reputation for being haunted. It is said to be haunted by Theodosius Burr, who was lost in a shipwreck off the Carolina coast in 1812. People have reported seeing his ghost called "the Grey Man" walking the shores late at night near the lighthouse, looking for his ship. Legend has it that Burr's shadowy form is seen right before a storm. The shores off Cape Hatteras are known as the "Graveyard of the Atlantic" because more than 1,000 ships have sunk in these waters since records began in 1526. The Union ironclad, *USS Monitor*, sank on 31 December 1862. Many witnesses have reported seeing "ghost ships" and hearing the eerie sounds of drowning screams for centuries. These ghostly sightings continue today.

A lot of people don't know that as well as being a maximum security island prison, Alcatraz is also a lighthouse for ships entering San Francisco Bay. Alcatraz has a long history of paranormal activity, which I will go over in the Prisons and Penitentiaries section of this chapter.

If you are interested in going on one of these ghostly tours, find out where the nearest lighthouse is and check its website. Some of the lighthouses are neat to visit but can be quite expensive, especially around Halloween. Find if they are offering any special discounts and take advantage of them. Also be prepared, it is a long way up the stairs of some lighthouses, and you need to be in pretty good shape to make it to the top.

Most lighthouses have museums right next to them, which you can visit as well. Some of the museums themselves have had some paranormal events. The people who work there are only too happy to talk about the paranormal activity going on.

125

The imposing walls of the Eastern State Penitentiary, Philadephia.

A lot of old prisons and penitentiaries have seen a resurgence in popularity as haunted places. The **Eastern State Penitentiary**, located right outside Philadelphia, Pennsylvania, is a neat place to visit. Since its closing in 1971, numerous shadowy figures have been seen roaming the cells and unexplainable sound have been heard. It is open year-round and offers nighttime tours. It has been featured in numerous television shows and movies. It is popular with paranormal groups who have conducted investigations at night and had activity. It is now also a museum you can visit. It is located at 2027 Fairmount Ave, Philadelphia, PA

Alcatraz Island started off as a military prison in the 1850s. In 1933, it was built up to be a maximum security, minimum-privilege penitentiary designed for the most incorrigible inmates. Alcatraz is known for its famous, or I should say, "infamous" prisoners like Al Capone, George "Machine Gun" Kelly, Alvin Karpis and Arthur "Doc" Barker. It started reporting paranormal activity by the guard force before it closed in 1965.

126

Later. parts of the prison were reopened by the Parks Services for daily public tours. Weird sounds have been reported in a corridor where some prisoners were shot and killed during a prison break. The area known as "the hole" has a legend of an incident that happened in the 1940s. A prisoner in Cell 14d was heard screaming that he was being attacked by something with glowing eyes. The next morning the guards found him dead from strangulation. They never did find out who killed him. From that time witnesses have reported unexplained cold spots in the cell and weird sensations. Night guards have reported seeing weird shadows moving in the hallways. Alcatraz does offer nighttime ghost tours of various parts of the island and prison. Tourists have reported seeing strange shadows and hearing screams during this tour. If you want to visit "The Rock" go to http://www.alcatrazislandtickets.com/ to get tickets.

The old ***Carbon County jail*** in the city of Jim Thorpe, Pennsylvania has a long and interesting paranormal history. The jail was built in 1869-1870 when the town was known at Mauch Chunk. The jail

Alcatraz Island.

The Old Jail in Carbon County, PA.

itself is an awesome two-story, fortresslike rusticated stone building, with a giant cliff right behind it. The place just looks like it should be haunted. The jail has thick, massive walls and a square, one-story guard turret above the main entrance. It features arched windows on the main facade and on the turret.

The building's notable claim to fame is the mysterious handprint on the wall of one of the cells. It was left by Alexander Campbell, a "Molly Maguire" who was hanged in 1878. The Molly Maguires were an Irish 19th century secret society active in Ireland, Liverpool and parts of the eastern United States. Their actions, while sometimes violent, were in defense of their jobs, and against their exploitation by the coal mine owners. The coal mine owners, especially Franklin Gowen, were attempting to control coal in all aspects—they owned the mines so they controlled production, and owned the railroads so they controlled shipping.

128

They needed to control the miners and the miners were revolting against them. Twenty suspected members were unjustly convicted as there was no evidence presented at their trials to prove their guilt of murder and other crimes, and were executed by hanging in 1877 and 1878. A number of suspected Molly Maguires were imprisoned in Carbon County jail while awaiting trial in 1875-1876.

Legend goes that to proclaim his innocence, Mr. Campbell placed his hand on the wall leaving the print that he stated would stay there forever. There is evidence in an 1884 oral history that people came to old Mauch Chunk to see the handprint of Thomas P. Fisher, so the museum now says the print is either from Mr. Campbell or Mr. Fisher. Despite many attempts to remove the handprint, including building a new wall, the mark still remains today.

Today the jail is a museum and you can go view the handprint. The Old Jail is open for daily tours (closed Wednesdays) from Memorial Day through Labor Day and on weekends in September and October. The ghost tours are only held on a couple of Saturday nights in October. People have claimed to see men dressed in period clothes in the cells and metal walkways, which many paranormal investigators think are the ghosts of the Molly Maguires. You cannot take pictures of the handprint but you can purchase them at the museum's gift shop. I have been to this museum two times. The jail is located near the downtown area of Jim Thorpe at 128 W. Broadway, which is the main road of the town.

St. Augustine in Florida is considered by many to be one of the most haunted cities in the United States, followed closely by Savannah, Georgia. Apart from the lighthouse and Flagler College, there are other locations in the city with a paranormal history.

The **Old Jail** in St. Augustine is considered one

129

of the oldest in the United States and offers both daytime and nighttime tours of the building. It is a large building, where numerous paranormal incidents have been reported. People have detected, at different times, two awful odors can loft through the building, and a sickeningly sweet smell that makes the living uncomfortable has been reported. There have been apparitions/shadows that have been reported on occasion. An apparition of a man sitting on a chair has been seen numerous times. A cowering apparition was spotted in a cell by a tour guide, but it disappeared through a wall. In one of the women's cells, an unseen presence has been known to push and trip people. During a tour, a tour guide first felt a punch in his side, and then a cold hand move down his back; but being the professional that he is, this terrified tour guide managed to finish his spiel. People have reported voices of unseen presences as well as wails, yells and moans. The sound of a little girl's voice has been heard in one of the children's bedrooms used by the sheriff warden's family. It is located in downtown St. Augustine at 167 San Marco Ave. There are signs that lead you right to it.

Also in St. Augustine is ***Ripley's Believe It or Not Odditorium***. Not only does this beautiful three story historic castle house over three hundred exhibits, some being from Robert Ripley's original collection, but it is also said to be haunted. Also referred to as Warden Castle, it was built in 1887 as the winter home of William G. Warden. He was a business partner of John D. Rockefeller and Henry Flagler.

In 1941 the castle was purchased by famed novelist Marjorie Kinnan Rawlings and her husband, wealthy hotelier Norton Baskin. They had it remodeled as a hotel. The castle then hosted many famous and prominent guests. Rawlings had an apartment put in on the top floor of the castle. In addition to its collection of unusual

130

Ripley's Believe It or Not Odditorium in St. Augustine, FL.

artifacts and stunning architecture, Warden Castle is also a focal point for ghost hunters. On April 23, 1944, two women died in a fire in this very hotel. Legend has it that these women were actually murdered, and the fire was set to cover the evidence. The women (Betty Richeson, daughter of a prominent Jacksonville family and Ruth Pickering, friend of hotel owners Baskin and Rawlings) were reportedly unknown to each other and the rumors still circulate as to how the fire began. There was an unnamed man that is now called "Mr. X" who is suspected in these murders. These two women, along with Mr. X, are said to haunt this castle today. Who was the man staying in Room 13 and what really happened on that fateful day? The hotel was also a favorite of Robert L. Ripley who tried unsuccessfully to purchase the structure. In 1949, following his death, Ripley's business associates and brother managed to

secure the estate and opened it in December of 1950 as the first permanent Ripley's Believe It or Not! Museum. Ripley's offers a nightly haunted tour of the castle and operates a "ghost train" that takes visitors on a tour of the haunted locations in St. Augustine. Among these are the Fountain of Youth Park grounds and a historic cemetery. Ripley's Believe It or Not Odditorium is located in downtown St. Augustine at 19 San Marco Ave.

Some haunted houses have been reopened as bed and breakfast hotels. For those who don't know, a bed and breakfast is a home, often old, that has been converted into a mini hotel that likely features an awesome breakfast in the morning. They are usually a little more expensive than a hotel, but they are much quieter and more peaceful. They are quite popular in the New England area of the United States. These places offer not only a really nice atmosphere to stay in but also an opportunity to conduct a paranormal investigation.

132

1. St Augustine Lighthouse, FL
   Flagler College, FL
   Ripley's Believe It or Not, FL
   St Augustine Old Jail, FL
2. Camp Hatteras Lighthouse, NC
3. Eastern State Penitentiary, PA
4. Alcatraz Island, CA
5. Carbon County Jail, PA
6. Bucksville House, PA
7. Winchester Mystery House, CA
8. Clinton Road, NJ
9. Seattle Underground, WA
10. Bird Cage Theatre, AZ
11. Bell Witch Cave, TN
12. Lizzy Borden House, MA
13. Waverly Hills Sanatorium, KY
14. Whaley House, CA
15. The Myrtles Plantation, LA
16. The Stanley Hotel, CO
17. St. Louis Cemetery, WA
18. Villisca Ax Murder House, IA
19. Linda Vista Hospital, CA
20. Bachelor's Gove cemetery, IL

When we visit Pennsylvania, my wife and I like to stay at the ***Bucksville House*** in Ottsville. This place has been featured a number of times on television for its paranormal activity. We set up our cameras at night before we went to sleep. We didn't get any apparitions, but Tracy felt something pull on her hair that night. I'm glad nothing touched me. Recently we stayed at Indian Rock Inn at Upper Black Eddy, which is located right next to the Delaware River. It is my favorite place to stay when we are in the area. The owner told us that while he does not believe in ghosts, he has allowed some local paranormal groups to conduct investigations on the premises.

The most famous bed and breakfast place also has a dark and sinister history. This beautiful three-story eight-room building located in Fall River Massachusetts is called the ***Lizzie Borden house***. In 1892 the bodies of Andrew and Abby Borden were discovered horribly killed with an axe. Mr. Borden's daughter Lizzie gave the police strange and contradictory answers about the murders. She became the prime suspect and was later charged with her parents' murders. Lizzie's trial took place in New Bedford beginning June 5, 1893. She was acquitted on June 20, 1893. Today the house where the murders happened is considered not only a five-star bed and breakfast but also a museum. There are daily tours of the home. You are allowed to take pictures, but you need permission to do sound recordings. There are no late night ghost tours offered due to it being an active bed and breakfast. You can, however, make reservations and stay in one of the rooms where the murders occurred. You can go to their website and do it online. Located just fifty miles south of Boston, minutes

133

from Providence or Newport, R.I. and the gateway to Cape Cod, this landmark home is accessible from all major highways. The house is located at 230 2nd St, Fall River, MA.

A hotel served as inspiration for one of Stephen King's best-selling books, *The Shining*. It is called the **Stanley Hotel** and is located in Estes Park, Colorado. This beautiful 140-room hotel is ten miles from the entrance to Rocky Mountain National Park and offers panoramic views of Lake Estes, the Rockies and especially Longs Peak. This hotel has a long history of paranormal activity and has been the subject of many ghost hunting shows. It is considered one of the must see places for ghost hunters. This three-star hotel offers daily ghost tours to their guests and visitors just wanting to see this historic hotel. You can make reservations to conduct a paranormal investigation. Many visitors have reported hearing and seeing strange things on the tours. The hotel is located at 333 E Wonderview Ave, Estes Park, CO. You can go to their website and make reservations to stay there or conduct a ghost hunt.

A lot of old abandoned hospitals have a history of paranormal incidents. The most famous or infamous is the **Waverly Hills Sanatorium**. Nestled in the hills of southwestern Louisville/Jefferson County, Kentucky, this place has become the Mecca of ghost hunting. Hundreds of paranormal groups have conducted investigations of this huge building with some interesting results. In the early 1900s Jefferson County was hit by an outbreak of tuberculosis (the "White Plague") which prompted the construction of this hospital. This two-story facility accommodated 40 to 50 tuberculosis patients during that time frame. It closed in 1961, when the introduction of the antibiotic streptomycin reduced the need for such a hospital. Today it is considered on the most haunted hospitals

134

The Winchester Mystery House.

in the eastern United States. It has been featured in numerous paranormal shows. In 2001 the facility was purchased by Tina and Charlie Mattingly who offer tours. They also host a haunted house attraction during Halloween, with proceeds going toward restoration of the property. They are also in the process of restoring the building. Public tours are offered on the weekends March through August. They also offer six-hour ghost hunts Friday nights 12 am to 6 am and an eight-hour one on Saturday 12 am to 8 am. You need to make reservations on their website to attend these tours. The facility is located at 4400 Parolee Ln, Louisville, KY.

The **Winchester Mystery House** is without a doubt the creepiest haunted house in Silicon Valley. It was started in 1884, and was built by Winchester gun heiress Sarah Winchester—widow of William Wirt Winchester, son of the first president of the Winchester Repeating Arms Company. For over a forty-year period, construction continued up until 1922 when Miss Winchester died. A veritable hive of 160 rooms, the

135

mega mansion is a 6-acre labyrinth of false doors and stairs that lead absolutely nowhere—ad hoc additions reportedly made by Winchester to confuse the evil spirits of people shot and killed by the firearms of her dead husband's company. There are tours offered daily and an annual ghost investigation during the month of October. The house is located at 525 S. Winchester Blvd, San Jose, CA.

Cemeteries and graveyards have a long history of paranormal activities, but as I said before, check and get permission before to going out there at night. Some cemeteries will not allow anybody out there at night, and if you are caught you will receive an expensive fine from the authorities. As I have stated all through this book, "Only go ghost hunting where you are allowed." It can turn your legend trip into an expensive lesson.

There are a number of places in the United States where incidents occur that are believed to be paranormal in nature.

Clinton Road in West Milford, New Jersey has been called "The Most Haunted Road in America." It's been covered by major media outlets and has numerous supernatural stories surrounding it. This 10-mile stretch that runs from Route 23 to Upper Greenwood Lake has spooky legends that have surrounded it for almost 100 years. It has apparently been host to ghosts, witches, unearthly animals and earthly Klansmen. One story says that two brothers stumbled across a KKK meeting on the road, near Cross Castle, and barely made it out alive. Cross Castle, which is no longer there on Clinton, served as a meeting spot for a different kind of devil worshipers. There have also been reports of the mysterious flying cryptid The Jersey Devil, and also mysterious hellhounds. One of the popular legends on Clinton Road is that of the ghost boy of Clinton Brook Bridge. There have been reports of his reflection appearing in the water but the most talked about story is that if you throw coins off the bridge into the water, he will throw them back. Clinton Road is located right outside of West Milford. You don't have to pay for

The Seattle Underground Tour.

anything other than the gas to drive out there. A word of caution—Clinton Road is a two-lane that is windy at certain parts and is really dark at night. The bridge is located next to Clinton Reservoir.

In 1965 Bill Speidel started his **Seattle Underground Tour** of the Pioneer Square area. The tour is a seventy-five minute leisurely, guided walking tour beneath Seattle's sidewalks and streets. As you roam the subterranean passages that once were the main roadways and first-floor storefronts of old downtown Seattle, guides regale you with the stories our pioneers didn't want you to hear. Ghost tours are offered into the underground by "Spooked in Seattle." This event is offered the last Friday of every month, 10pm, and runs about two hours. You'll need to bring a small flashlight, a camera, a recorder, a video recorder and an EMF detector. There have been numerous paranormal seen and recorded in the underground. The tour also includes free admission into the new Death Museum.

Bird Cage Theatre in Tombstone, Arizona has a long history of paranormal activity. It was made famous in the 1993 movie *Tombstone*. Eerie music, laughter, and shouts often echo through the building, and the spirits of cowboys and prostitutes are often seen. Legend has it that over twenty-six deaths have occurred

137

in this small theater due to either brawls or gunfights. This famous landmark of the Old West has been featured on numerous paranormal television shows. Today the theater is a museum and features ghost tours every night. Guests on the tour have reported being touched by an unseen entity. The theater is located at 535 E. Allen St, Tombstone, AZ.

Bell Witch Cave is a mysterious cave with a paranormal legend. It is located in Adams, Tennessee near where the Bell Farm once stood. The cave is approximately 490 feet long and has been associated with the famous Bell Witch haunting of 1804. It was during this period that paranormal events happened to the Bell family which some say were caused by the Bell Witch. The cave is located on property once owned by the Bell family. Many believe that when the witch departed, she fled to the sanctuary of this cave. In the particular legend in which the cave is featured, young Betsy Bell and some of her friends had gone to explore the cave. While they were there, one of the boys crawled into a hole and became stuck. A voice cried out, "I'll get him out!" The boy felt hands grasping his feet, and he was pulled out of the hole. The Bell Witch (still invisible), then gave the young explorers a lecture on reckless cave exploring. There has been no written evidence to back up this story on the cave, but ghost hunters have been conducted investigations in the cave with surprising results. One group filmed mist that mysteriously appeared out of nowhere. There is a replica of the Bell family cabin nearby where a poltergeist incident happened. The cave was featured on the popular paranormal show *Ghost Adventures*. If you want to visit this spooky place it is located on the outskirts of Adams, Tennessee at 430 Keysburg Rd.

There are some old colleges that have a reputation for being haunted. One of the more popular ones is **Flagler College** in St. Augustine. Did you know that there is a tile with railroad developer Henry Flagler's face on it at the college named after him? It is located in the United States' oldest city of St. Augustine. It's true. Constructed in 1885 as the Ponce de Leon Hotel, it was the first of its kind. With more than 500 rooms, and design features such as intricately carved solid oak pillars and hand-painted murals, the Ponce de Leon was and still is considered a magnificent work of architecture.

If you step into the lobby of the college and look carefully, you will see in one of the circular patterns near the main entrance a tile that stands out. This little

Flagler College, St. Augustine, FL.

139

red tile, no bigger than a quarter, bears a remarkable resemblance to Henry Flagler. The college staff do not know how it really got there. Some think that the tile might have been put there on purpose. Because the tiles were put down individually, it is very possible that the one with Flagler's face was placed intentionally.

There are some supernatural legends that surround the tile. One popular tale is that the face appeared shortly after Flagler's funeral, which was held in the rotunda of the hotel in 1913. A worker noticed the tile the afternoon after the ceremony and pointed it out to management. No one had seen it there before. Flagler's face on the tile, as the tale goes, showed that his spirit was trapped in his beloved hotel. Today you can go look at the tile and it's free. It is located in the ringed tile formation to the left when you walk into the main lobby. It is not very big so it might take you a while to find it. Anybody working there will show you the tile and you can even take a picture of it.

Mr. Flagler's ghost has been seen numerous times by not only the collage staff, but by students attending the collage. The huge building facility is located in downtown St. Augustine, not far from the old Spanish fort, which also supposed to be haunted. The collage is located at 74 King Street and you'll see it once you come into the city. Next to Sarasota, St. Augustine is one of the most haunted cities in the United States.

These are but a few of the many haunted places located in the United States. The next chapter tells how to actually conduct a paranormal legend trip or ghost hunt. You just need to check around and find a haunted place. Be prepared to be both frightened and excited.

Chapter 8
Paranormal Legend Trip

It's midnight as the moon casts its shadow through the window. As you slowly walk around the small concrete cage lined room, you can try to image what this place was like when it was open. You look down at the only light, coming from your EKG meter. You watch the dial closely in case it moves for any kind of noise. You have come here to this old jail to conduct a ghost hunt. This now-abandoned building has a long history of being haunted. The owners have allowed you and your team to stay the night and see if the stories are true. Suddenly you hear a noise. You look back out the door, and down the hall you see a shadow move from one side to the other. A shiver runs down your spine. Welcome to paranormal legend trips!

Paranormal legend trips, usually referred to as ghost hunts, are much different from cryptid monster hunts. To begin with, you have to approach ghosting with an entirely different attitude. You're looking for something which might not be visible to the negative eye. You have to learn to be extremely quiet and patient.

I remember going on my first paranormal legend trip back in 1980. As a teenager growing up in Kansas, I talked a couple of my friends into going to these railroad tracks outside of town and check out a ghost light. Now the ghost light, as legend had it, would be seen late at night moving down the railroad tracks. It was supposed to be of a headless train conductor, who lost his head during a train accident. He was now doomed to walk

141

the tracks eternally, with his lantern to search for his lost head. If you approached the light it would disappear, only to reappear after you walked away or further down the tracks.

The Headless Conductor.

Most of the time, we would not see anything, so we would wait for about two hours and then leave. One night though, our patience paid off and we finally saw the light. We arrived shortly after midnight as we decided to go after we finished work. The location where you're supposed to see the light is in a state park; in Kansas, the state parks are not closed at night, or I should say this one wasn't. This park was a popular venue for date night with secluded parking spots where couples could fog up the windows with little to interrupt.

There used to be a train station with some warehouses at the site. But it had long ago fallen into disrepair and was later destroyed, leaving an open field with railroad tracks going east to west. Now these tracks were no longer used so there was grass growing between the rails and ties.

At certain times, there would be other cars out there with people all waiting to see the ghost light; on this night, we were the only car there. It was autumn and starting to cool off at night so we all had to put jackets on, particularly because of the wind. Remember Kansas is a flat state so there is a lot of wind, especially at night. We all walked up to the train tracks and looked around. It was quiet except for us and the wind. We looked down the tracks and waited. Now legend had it the ghost light would come in an easterly direction so we concentrated our attention in that direction. As

142

you can guess, as all scary stories go, we didn't see anything. There was never any noise associated with the ghost light so we weren't sure if we were to listen as well. I guess maybe we thought we'd hear a train coming down the tracks, but again, nothing. We talked about the light and exchanged stories we heard from other teenagers who claimed to have witnessed the ghostly light. And still we waited.

I remember thinking it wasn't going to happen this night, when my friend Phil pointed down the tracks and said, "What is it?" We all turned to see. At first I didn't see anything, but then I saw it. I remember thinking it looked like somebody walking with a flashlight on the tracks. We all stared and listened. If it was a person with a flashlight, we would have been able to hear them walking on the gravel, as sound travels further at night. All we heard was the wind as the light was coming toward us. I tried hard to look closely at it and make some logical sense. "It couldn't really be a phantom train conductor looking for his head," I thought. When the light came about a hundred feet from us, my friend Phil yelled, "Who is with the light?" The floating specter light continued to come down the tracks. I finally mustered up the courage and walked toward it. My friends followed. When we were about twenty feet from the light it suddenly went out. We all stopped in our tracks and looked around. The light had vanished. I then pulled out my flashlight, turned it on and scanned the area. There was nobody out there except us. Finally Phil spoke: "What do you think that was?" I didn't answer as I continued to scan the area with the beam from my flashlight. The silence was broken as Robert yelled as he pointed, "There it is!"

The ghost light had reappeared further down the railroad track heading west. We watched as it slowly got smaller as it moved away and we could barely see it

143

down the tracks. We then started going on about seeing a real ghost light while we walked back to the car, always looking over our shoulders to make sure the light didn't reappear. As we approached the car, Phil was the first to unlock it and open up the driver's side door. I reached for the passenger door, but suddenly I saw a large figure edstanding next our car. A figure without a head. I don't know who screamed louder, me or Rob, but Phil jumped back out of the car to see what we were looking at. The figure didn't move, it just stood there. Suddenly it made a sound: "What are you doing out here, the park's closed." The headless figure bent over to reveal a head of a man with a large gray mustache and with a large ranger hat.

Relieved we were not going to be spirited away, we all started laughing. We then told the park ranger our story, and he stated we were at the wrong place. In fact we were in the wrong state. The legend of the headless railroad phantom was in Missouri, about a hundred miles from where we were at. Well, that was the end of that legend trip. On a side note, while researching the legend of the headless railroad phantom, I found out there are three other states besides Missouri which have same legend. Texas, Ohio, and North Carolina all have headless phantoms associated with ghost lights.

Numerous books have been written on the subject of setting up and doing a ghost hunt. If you have your heart set on doing paranormal research, contact a local paranormal investigation group and ask if you can accompany them on their next ghost hunt. There are a lot of them out there and they usually have a website and are regularly looking for new members. Good paranormal groups take the investigation seriously and you can learn a lot from them. Plus, they know where the local haunted sites are. I recommend if you go with them on a ghost hunt, do not make any commitment

144

to join. Tell them you want to see how a paranormal investigation is done by professionals. That will boost their egos. Ghost hunters love to show off what they do. While most paranormal groups are in it for the science and curiosity, some keep their finds private and will ask you to commit to their club rules. I will give you an example. My wife, Tracy, found out the second floor of the Bartow, Florida jail was supposed to be haunted. We asked around, and I talked to a couple of the guards, who related the place was in fact haunted and they had video evidence to back it up. We then asked if we could go up and do a paranormal investigation. They replied "No" and went on to say their paranormal group, which consisted of just the three guards, was still conducting an active investigation on the jail and they were making plans with a television show to come film their investigation. In other words, it was their haunting and they were not sharing it because this one could launch their television careers. That's why I suggested you not commit yourself to join until you know your local group well.

Now if you don't want to deal with these paranormal groups and want to do a ghost hunt on your own, I will show you how to conduct one. Some places that are reputed to be haunted will charge a fee for groups to conduct an investigation. For some people, it is all about the money. It is becoming increasingly hard to find a haunting somebody hasn't already investigated, especially a lighthouse. Most lighthouses will make you pay to do an investigation, but I will say this: we have a great time when we go to lighthouses.

Also, on a side note, my wife has a policy to not allow young children on a paranormal investigation. This kind of thing can really scare a child, who can develop lasting fears. You never know what you are going to see in a supposedly haunted house, and there

145

have been cases where a child becomes the center of the paranormal activity. I saw a TV show in which a woman took her young son with her on a ghost hunt. He supposedly got possessed by the ghost or evil spirit. This can happen to young family members if you bring them on paranormal investigations. Monster hunts are different, because when you leave the woods, the monsters stay in the woods. Ghosts can supposedly follow you home.

The best place to start off is a graveyard or cemetery. Most paranormal groups like to stake out cemeteries if they can't find a place to investigate. There is nothing wrong with this, and it can in fact be fun and a lot less dangerous than searching a building. Just remember, not every graveyard or cemetery is haunted. If you are just starting off and you want to do investigations with just your family, then a cemetery is the best place to start. There is always a cemetery in the area. If you decide to take this course of action, you need to contact the local law enforcement office and notify them you and your family will be out there so you don't get in trouble. Most people don't know you have to ask permission to go into a cemetery after hours; in some states it is illegal to be in a cemetery after dark, so check your local ordinances. There have been some cases of vandalism, so the police are very cautious when they see people roaming around a graveyard at night. Also, some satanic religious groups have been known to do their rituals at night in cemeteries. Most law enforcement agencies will allow you to do a ghost hunt, if it is a county cemetery; they just want to be told who is out there.

146

Privately owned cemeteries will not allow you to do an investigation, because it is an insurance liability. If you do go there at night, you can and will be charged with trespassing.

Some law enforcement agencies do not pass the word of your nighttime adventure and you will have some patrol car roll up and ask what you are doing. Don't panic or get upset, just explain to them what you are doing and relay you have permission to be out there. The patrolman will radio it in and all will be well. They may also comment you are wasting your time. Don't let this faze or deter you. Whenever you are investigating the unknown, you are always going to run into the closed-minded. It happens all the time with my family and me.

When you find a cemetery to investigate and you get permission, you need to do a daytime recon of the location. Check it out and look for where you want to set up and walk around. Most cemeteries have small paths for visitors to drive, so it won't be hard to pick different routes for the teams. If a headstone is a large figure, it does not necessarily mean there is a ghost or entity around it. It just means the dearly departed's family is rich. My wife likes to look for the really old tombstones. She feels this is where you will get the most activity. Make a sketch with references to the areas where you want to conduct your ghost hunt. Sometimes really large cemeteries will have maps they give out, which you can mark and use.

Once you have planned out which area you want to hit that night, go home and sit down with the family or group and decide who is going to go where. Again, I don't recommend this kind of legend trip for some children. If you decide to go this avenue, I recommend you keep them at base camp and let them run the main radio, or if you set up a camera, let them keep an eye on it. You also want to find an area away from the main streets. Car lights can affect your cameras and listening devices. Like a Bigfoot/cryptid hunt, you need to check out the cemetery/building in the daytime and plan where you want to conduct the investigation and find what you think will be "hot spots." Hot spots are areas where you think there will be, or have been told there is, paranormal activity. Draw a sketch of the area. If you are doing a paranormal investigation in a residence, a high-powered laser is a great tool to have. This device emits a grid of green dots useful for detecting shadows or general visual disturbances. If you have a hot spot in a room, set a running camera in front of it to catch potential evidence. Most cemeteries are not big, so it shouldn't be difficult to do. Mark the area with some kind of marking, but make sure the marking is not permanent.

When it comes to a paranormal investigation, you want to try to get video proof. You do this by placing cameras at strategic points in the area or the residence where you are conducting your investigation. In order to be thorough, you will need more than one camera, possibly three, depending on the size of the place. You need to set them up in areas where nobody can disturb them, other than the ghost(s). Some professional investigators set up night vision cameras which are all tied into a main computer recording all cameras at once. This is great if you can afford these systems and you are serious.

Most investigators carry a camera with them when they do a walk-through of the place. It is probably the most exciting part of the investigation. You are walking around a place

Camera with Night Vision.

in complete darkness, other than the light from the camera, knowing some unknown entity haunts this location. You should also place audio recorders around different locations. Paranormal investigators have gotten some of their best proof with these.

After the investigation is over, retrieve the cameras and load the recordings into the computer and listen. It is really exciting to hear a faint voice and then bring up the volume to hear what the voice is saying. Just be careful to rule out any outside source before you present your evidence. Some old, abandoned residences make great homes for stray cats and they are often the culprits in paranormal recordings.

Unlike a monster hunt where you should break up into teams, you can either break into groups or stay as one big group. Just make sure you go over what the game plan is with each team member. It makes everybody feel a little safer if something should happen. Also, assign a certain piece of equipment to each team member so you don't carry it all yourself and end up forgetting something. It makes everybody feel part of the team and the investigation. Have one member be responsible for carrying and setting up the video cameras while another will carry and use the EVP monitor. I usually carry the night vision device. Because my wife knows what to look for, I have her lead the investigations and choose who's carrying what piece of equipment. My wife takes the investigations seriously, and every team member enjoys each outing.

When you start your ghost hunt, it is good to walk around and wait till you get a hit on your EVP. Then have one person, and one person only, attempt to talk to the ghost during what is called the contact session. My wife usually does this, because she knows what to say. Be careful when letting the younger kids do this. They might think it silly and start asking stupid

149

questions. If there is an entity or ghost, it might not like what is being said. This is why Tracy insists she do all the talking. It's important nobody else talks during the contact session. Whoever is holding the listening device needs to ensure the device is turned on. Always bring extra batteries. You can mount your camera on a stand or tripod, but it is a lot better to just carry it around. Both of my cameras have night vision capabilities.

If you do not get any EVP readings, then walk to another area you want to investigate. First look around and take in your surroundings. Then have one person conduct the contact session and listen. This person has to be serious about it. If they don't believe in what they are doing, then nothing is going to happen. If nothing happens—and it usually does—first of all, do not get disappointed, but just move on to another location. You can leave a listening device or a trail camera at the area, but don't forget where you left it. These devices can be expensive. Mark it on your sketch and move on to the next location. When you get a hit, then the excitement begins. Be prepared to see something, and if you or your family does, don't get scared and run. You need to talk to your family and make a plan in case something does happen. Most of the time you won't hear anything except squirrels, raccoons and armadillos.

When teams make their walk-around, it is good to have "trigger objects." Ghost hunters use trigger objects to draw or lure spirits out. A trigger object gives the spirit a way to show it is there, by making the trigger object move. To lure spirit children, a ball can be put down for them to play with. Some paranormal investigators do not like balls as trigger objects because they easily move on their own. They do, however, attract spirit children. It is best not to use an object which might fall over easily, such as a stuffed animal. The general consensus is, once you have an object that won't move

150

on its own, place it within a circle or on a piece of paper and draw a line next to it. A variation on this method is to place an object on a layer of flour. Then put it somewhere your group will not disturb it and aim a camera at it. Also, place a meter next to it and see if your camera picks up any fluctuations on the meter when the object moves. It is best to use small trigger objects, but not too small to see on a camera.

When you have made it to your last hot spot and you are finished, then you need to turn around and go back and retrieve your listening devices and trail cameras. Don't leave them overnight in a cemetery; a building is one thing, but out in the open is another. You can do another sweep of the hot spot if you want, and again see if anything happens. Some people believe nothing will happen till after midnight. I don't know why they think this, but you can give it a try. If you have young teenagers, they will get tired by then. Again, try to keep everybody excited and motivated so they don't become disappointed if nothing happens.

When you finish and you've retrieved all your listening devices and cameras, then it is time to head home and go over the videos and sounds. This takes time, and I recommend you do it after a good night's sleep. You need to get the whole family or team involved in going over the evidence. Each person gets a sound device to listen to or a video to watch. This is the boring part of the investigation, yet one of the most important parts as this is where your investigation pays off. If you find yourself falling asleep while you are watching the video or listening to the recording, turn off the recording device and take a break. You could miss something important if you were to fall asleep.

If you do see something odd or paranormal, then you need to watch it a couple of times. You need to say to yourself, "What could this normally be?" If you see

151

an object move, ask yourself if somebody off camera made it move. I hate to say it, but ninety percent of the time a person accidentally moved a table or rug, causing the object in question to move. A popular television show was questioned on the integrity of an object seen moving on the show. A lot of people think it was hoaxed in the interest of ratings. Think about it: how many people are going to watch a show where the ghost investigators never find anything? If you even suspect the object moving was an accident, then let it go and move on to another. If an object moves by paranormal means, then it will most likely move again.

If you see something that looks like an apparition, again, look at what it could be normally. A car driving by can cast weird lights on a wall. Also look and see where everybody else on the investigation was during the apparition sighting. I'm not trying to discourage you about seeing things. It is just you need to know you have considered every possible explanation for the apparition before reaching a conclusion of a haunting. If you say it is a ghost and it turns out to have a logical explanation, you will lose some credibility as a paranormal investigator. I go into every investigation with an open mind, but I also keep a logical mind as well. Being a military policeman for more than twenty-one years taught me that.

With that being said, if you find something nobody can explain then you have had a successful investigation. If you are ghost hunting in a building, you have to get your proof together and present it to the owners or the people in charge of the building. I have found most of them already believe they have a haunting, so when you tell them you didn't find anything, they might not take the conclusion very well. Others might be thankful for not having a haunted residence. If you have proof, or what you believe to be

152

proof, give the owners the privilege of deciding how or if they want the results shown to the public as they may not want them shown. It probably won't happen, but you have to provide them the courtesy.

Many paranormal groups have their own website, which is where they like to show their investigation results and videos. As I have stated before, do not expect to become a wealthy person with ghost pictures. To date, all photographs have come under scrutiny and most people think they are hoaxes. If you go ghost hunting and you get some really good evidence, then enjoy it and show it off, but don't expect some big television company will want to have you on a show. I have seen many good supposed ghost photos, and the people who took them really believed in their hearts the photo was genuine and they left it at that. They don't care what anybody thinks. If you are ghost hunting to enjoy it with your family and you get some really good evidence, then enjoy it as a family. Some people like the idea of ghosts because if there are ghosts then there is life after death, which means there is a heaven and hell. They believe ghosts are stuck in purgatory.

Ghost hunting offers hours of excitement and a lifetime of stories to be told from generation to generation. On the flip side, it can also be boring. It is rare something happens right away during an investigation. Unfortunately, there are times when nothing happens. You need to stress to your family ghosts do not just appear at the drop of a dime. There are different kinds of hauntings, and some only happen during a certain part of the year. You may set up your equipment in the wrong room or location. It is important during an investigation you don't just sit around and wait. You need to be mobile and walk around which is when you find the cold spots and feel something touch you. I'm not saying you can't sit around at all; just don't stay in one place all night as you will end up falling asleep. If your team falls asleep, they will lose interest in ghost hunting.

I encourage you to allow all team members to use some of the equipment. In fact, encourage them to use all the equipment at different points during your investigation. It will stop them from getting bored. Young team members love using the Bionic Ear. It also keeps them interested in the investigation. I wish I had more than one, because all of them want to use it. Just remind them they will hear everything including small animals roaming around the property. If they hear or see something, do not be quick to doubt them; remember, the location is supposed to be haunted. Listen to what they say and ask questions, but in the end don't say, "It was probably a stray cat." Ask them what they think it might be. When my kids say they heard something, I ask where and we go see what made the noise. You have to be positive when you are looking for something like cryptids and ghosts. People gravitate to a person with a positive attitude.

When you end the ghost hunt, your group needs to retrieve your equipment. If you make a mess, be sure to clean it up. A rule of thumb in the military is to give it back better than the way you got it, and this includes a home. If the home is trashed at the beginning, then do not conduct the ghost hunt. You don't want your family getting sick. We have had that happen before. We made an excuse that we couldn't conduct the investigation for some reason, and we left. If a witness is serious about having an investigation done, then they will have a clean house. Also, it might be a good idea to conduct a walk-through with a member of the home and make sure everything is good with both parties.

If it is late when you finish, have your team get some rest, including yourself. When you get up in the morning, assign each member a listening or viewing device to review possible evidence. For example, one member could view one of the videos, another member could view the other video, and another could listen to the recordings. Have them do this for maybe thirty minutes, and then change over. What happens is, you get tired of watching the screen and you end up falling asleep, and the same thing happens with listening devices. Also, have them take breaks on their own. You or somebody needs to keep an eye on them and make sure they don't fall asleep. They might miss something on the video or audio.

This is a simple ghost hunting kit to take with you. Chapter 17 on equipment lists more items you can add.

Ghost Legend Trip
- Camera—one that has IR capabilities
- Camera stands and pods
- EVP (electronic voice phenomenon) detector
- Temperature detector
- Flashlights/head lights/light sticks
- Batteries for all equipment devices
- Game cameras—it is better to have more than one so you can put them in multiple places
- Cold weather clothes
- Sound recorder

Legend Tripping

EMF Detector.

EMF Detector.

Temperature Reader.

Chapter 9
UFO Sites and Ghost Lights

On July 8, 1947, an explosive headline dominated the cover of the *Roswell Daily Record*: "RAFF Captures Flying Saucer on Ranch in Roswell Region." Less than two weeks earlier, a private pilot, Kenneth Arnold, reported seeing from his aircraft a string of nine shiny unidentified flying objects cruising past Mount Rainier. To everyone, it confirmed Earth was being visited by aliens from another planet.

Just as quickly as the word spread, the Air Force retracted the Roswell news statement, saying it was just a weather balloon. But the story didn't die. People started coming forward saying the Air Force had lied and a flying saucer did in fact crash in the desert, but it was quickly recovered by the military and taken into hiding. Witnesses said they saw the bodies of dead alien beings taken away by military officials. The story has become a legend in UFO lore and today if you ask anybody about Roswell, they'll say, "It is where the flying saucer crashed back in the 40s."

In 1988, a friend took me out to Roswell, New Mexico, to visit the site where a flying saucer allegedly crashed. While there are three different crash sites popularized in the famed 1947 Roswell UFO event, the plot of land on the outskirts of Corona is said to have been the final resting place of the alien ship. This is the most popular location to visit. The site is located about 30 minutes north of Corona on Hwy 285 (aka Main Street), between mile markers 132 and 133. UFO researchers believe the craft probably "skipped" near Roswell, leaving debris, but regained altitude and finally crashied in Corona.

Legend Tripping

The "official" entrance to the dirt road leading to the crash site is located on private property and is closed. Good news is, there is an alternate route through public land. Bad news is, for this particular path you

Sign at the Roswell crash site.

will need a 4X4 vehicle. Breaking down in the middle of the desert, without cell phone service, is another concern for observers. Another safety consideration is this area is full of rattlesnakes, so keep a watchful eye for them. Around a mile down this rough, dirt path, a rusted-out truck and a shed can be seen, meaning you're now at the debris field left by the craft's landing.

Two large red monoliths point toward the landing path of the aircraft, and a short walk will lead you to a stone marker placed at a location where the alien spacecraft allegedly came to rest. The inscription reads:

WE DON'T KNOW WHO THEY WERE, WE DON'T KNOW WHY THEY CAME, WE ONLY KNOW, THEY CHANGED OUR VIEW OF THE UNIVERSE. THIS UNIVERSAL SACRED SITE IS DEDICATED JULY 1997, TO THE BEINGS WHO MET THEIR DESTINIES NEAR ROSWELL NEW MEXICO JULY 1947.

It's not hard to imagine what it was like back then when a strange aircraft crashed, and small deceased aliens lay scattered next to their mangled aircraft. Though the government has tried to explain this event, the legend refuses to die.

158

When it comes to extraterrestrials and UFOs, there have been sightings of alien-like beings in almost every part of the US. Some of these supposed UFO landing sites, you can still visit. When it comes to UFO sightings, this occurs almost on a daily basis. Florida was once a hotbed of UFO sightings, but that is not the case anymore. MUFON keeps an up-to-date database on UFO sightings.

This chapter is a brief overview of some of the neat legends and locations where extraterrestrials not only visited us but landed their craft. For this chapter, I referenced Jerome Clark's 1997 book *The UFO Book: Encyclopedia of the Extraterrestrial.*

Would you believe there is a gravesite for an extraterrestrial whose ship crashed in 1897? If you go to the cemetery in Aurora, Texas, you can see the grave. On April 19, 1897 the *Dallas Morning News* ran a story saying an alleged UFO hit a windmill on the property of Judge J.S. Proctor two days earlier, at around 6 am central time, resulting in the total destruction of the craft. The pilot, who was reported to be "not of this world," did not survive the crash, and was buried by the citizens of Aurora "with Christian rites" at the cemetery.

It goes on to say the wreckage from the crash site was dumped into a nearby well located under the damaged windmill, while some ended up with the alien in the grave. The cemetery contains a Texas Historical Commission marker mentioning the incident. Now if you want to go visit the gravesite, you will have to get permission from the Aurora sheriff's department before going out there. There have been reports of theft and vandalism to the grave, so the town is very strict about who they allow. The original headstone for the visitor's grave was stolen in 1970, but a new one with a flying saucer on it was put in its place in 2008.

Legend Tripping

There is no cost to visit the cemetery, located on the outskirts of Aurora, a very nice and peaceful town. There have been reports the whole story was a hoax to stop the town from dying, but whatever the case, it is

The marker at Aurora, Texas.

still considered a famous legend in the UFO case files.

Another place where a strange object crashed and was spirited quickly off by the military is Kecksburg, Pennsylvania. On December 9, 1965, a large, brilliant fireball was seen by thousands in at least six US states and Ontario, Canada. It streaked over the Detroit, Michigan/Windsor, Ontario area, and reportedly dropped hot metal debris over Michigan and northern Ohio, starting some grass fires, and caused sonic booms in western Pennsylvania. Eyewitnesses claimed something crashed in the woods and reported finding an object in the shape of a large acorn about as large as a small vehicle. Witnesses further reported an intense military presence closed off the area and removed the object on a flatbed truck. Later the military claimed they searched the woods and found "absolutely nothing." When you visit the crash site there is nothing really to see. In front of the woods is a life-size replica of the object, as described by witnesses. It is painted brown and decorated around its brim with some type of writing. It is elevated on a platform about 10 feet high in the air.

In 1967, in Nova Scotia, Canada an unidentified object crashed into Shag Harbour. An investigation was conducted by the Canadian Navy. The incident was later classified as unsolved by the Canadian Department of National Defense when a clear conclusion could

160

not be reached. There is a marker near the harbor commemorating the incident.

As recently as July 2011, residents reported seeing a bright light and noise as a large glowing UFO/USO-like object crashed into the ocean at Flagler Beach, Florida.

When it comes to alien abductions, the story of Betty and Barney Hill is considered the most famous. In September 1961, Barney and Betty Hill of Portsmouth, New Hampshire reported they had been kidnapped by aliens. According to their statements, they had been followed by a flying saucer while driving in their car, abducted and then subjected to intimate physical examinations. Under hypnosis, the Hills maintained their story which aroused massive interest and publicity. Though Betty and Barney are no longer with us, their story lives on. There is a road marker outside of Portsmouth to mark where the incident occurred.

If you do go to investigate these UFO crash/landing sites, I caution you, watch out for the Men in Black.

Have you ever heard of ghost lights? Sometimes called spook lights, they are defined as mysterious lights which appear at locations without any explanation or identifiable source. A neat thing is there are locations all over the United States where these unexplained

lights are seen with regularity. And the most awesome thing is they are free to go see. Most of these lights have been observed for centuries, first being reported by the Native Americans in the region. There are some really cool legends to go

Official sign about the Hill abduction.

with each spook light. In this chapter I will briefly go over some of the most famous of the spook lights and their legends. I included ghost lights in this chapter because some witnesses claim to also see UFOs accompanying these strange phenomena.

Are they extraterrestrial? Paranormal? Nobody knows.

Probably the most famous ghost lights are the Marfa Lights which are seen from Route 67, near the town of Marfa in Texas. Nobody in Marfa seems to know for sure what the lights are—but thousands of people have seen the many lights which come and go, break up into two or three different lights and then disappear, only to reappear again a short time later. There seems to be no way to predict when the lights will appear; they're seen in various weather conditions, almost every night of the year.

According to the Texas State Historical Association, the first mention of the lights comes from 1883, when cowhand Robert Reed Ellison claimed to have seen flickering lights one evening while driving a herd of cattle near Mitchell Flat. He assumed the lights were from Apache campfires. On the flip side, the Native Americans who also saw the mysterious lights thought they were fallen stars, struggling on the ground. Ellison was told by area settlers they often saw the lights, too, but upon investigation, they found no ashes or other evidence of a campfire.

During World War II, pilots from nearby Midland Army Air Field tried to locate the source of the mysterious lights, but were unable to discover anything.

Marfa Lights plaque.

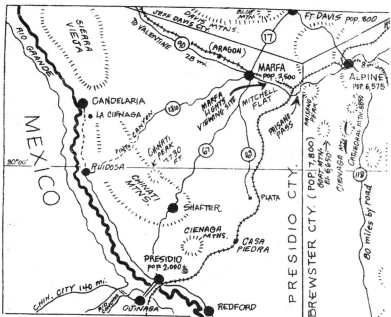

There is even an observation area on the roadside of Route 67 (also called Route 90 in this area) where you can stop and watch for the lights. There have been various studies on these lights and most conclude it is nothing more than a mirage of lights from other vehicles in the area. But since the lights have been seen before lighted vehicles existed, this seems like a strange explanation. In 1987, while stationed at Fort Bliss, Texas, I journeyed to Marfa to see the lights. When I got to the observation area, there were other people already sitting on their vehicles waiting for the show to begin. As the sun went down behind the mountains, I looked toward the base of the mountains. At first I didn't see anything, but then I could see the lights appear. In fact, I was the first to see them. I pointed and said to my

163

friend who went with me, "There they are." He had been there and seen them before and responded, "That's the ghost lights." It was a really neat experience.

There are two famous ghost lights coming from North Carolina. The first is the Maco Light. It has been seen between the late 19th century and 1977 along a section of railroad tracks outside of Maco, North Carolina. Sightings have continued into the 21st century even though the tracks were removed in 1977. The light is said to resemble the glow from a railroad lantern and is associated with a legend describing a fatal accident, which may have inspired tales of a similar type around the country.

The legend is of a train conductor by the name of Joe Baldwin; he was the sole occupant of the rear car of a train on a rainy night in 1867. As the train neared Maco, Baldwin realized the car had become detached from the rest of the train and he was aware that another train was following, so he ran to the rear platform and began waving his lantern in frantic attempts to signal the oncoming train. But the engineer failed to see the stranded railroad car in time, and Baldwin was decapitated in the collision. Shortly after the tragic death, the residents of town and railroad employees reported sightings of a white light along a section of railroad track through the swamps west of Maco station, and word spread Joe Baldwin had returned to search for his missing head. The light was said to appear in the distance, before approaching along the tracks facing east, bobbing at a height of about 5 feet, and either flying to the side of the track in an arc or receding from the viewer. Similar "headless brakeman" stories have been associated with other ghost lights in the United States.

The next North Carolina spook light I want to talk about is the Brown Mountain Lights. These mysterious orbs of light are reported near Brown Mountain in North Carolina. Brown Mountain is a long, low-lying ridge on the border of Burke and Caldwell counties in western North Carolina and is part of the Blue Ridge Mountains. Most of it belongs to the Pisgah National Forest. For perhaps 800 years or more, ghostly lights have been seen flaring and creeping along,

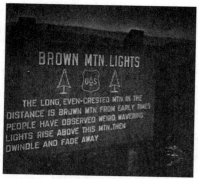

Sign for the Brown Mtn Lights.

and below, the ridge at night. Cherokee and Catawba Indians are said to have reports dating back to 1200 for the lights, and local lore tells of a fierce battle between the two tribes where most of the tribes' warriors were killed in a clash. The night after the battle, maidens lit torches and searched the mountain for their slain warriors, permeating the land with their grief which manifests itself as the glowing orbs still seen to this day. There are also stories of UFOs being seen near Brown Mountain as well as sightings of Bigfoot creatures, fairies and other strange beings.

Author Manly Wade Wellman grew up hearing these strange tales, and wrote about his fictional hero Silver John's travels and frequent encounters with strange creatures and superstitions emanating from the legends and superstitions of the Blue Ridge Mountains.

The first documented report of these lights was in September 1913 when a fisherman reported "mysterious lights seen just above the horizon every night," red in color, with a pronounced circular shape. From that time on, people have been seeing these strange lights.

Thousands have witnessed the ongoing spectacle. The lights have been investigated three times by the

165

United States government, and countless times by private groups. You can view these lights from different locations which are all marked with signs for your convenience: Blue Ridge Parkway at milepost 310, Highway 181 between Morganton, NC and Linville, NC. Additionally, good sightings of the lights have been reported from the top of Table Rock, outside of Morganton. One of the best vantage points, Wiseman's View, is about four miles from Linville Falls. The city of Morganton recently improved a Brown Mountain Overlook on Highway 181 for the purpose of attracting those who visit the area to see the lights. The best time of year to see them is reportedly September through early November.

I had the opportunity to visit the Brown Mountains during a trip to Kentucky. I had heard about the lights and decided to go check them out with my family. I stopped at one of the signs on the Blue Ridge Parkway (this was the easiest one to find) and waited for the lights. My son Sean was the first to see them. The lights seem to almost dance around. I thought they were pretty much white in color. We watched them for about an hour but as the children lost interest, we departed.

The next spook light is the Hornet Spook Light, also called the Hollis Light and the Joplin Spook Light. It appears in an area known as the Devil's Promenade on the border between southwestern Missouri and Oklahoma. This mysterious ball of fire has been seen for almost one hundred forty years.

The first report has it seen twelve miles outside the town of Hornet, around 1866. In 1946, the Army Corps of Engineers conducted an investigation into the mystery and concluded it was "a light of unknown origin." It is reported to spin down the center of a gravel road at great speed and then rise up, bob around and weave from right to left. The light seems to retreat when

166

TRI-STATE
SPOOK LIGHT AREA

(11 miles SW of Joplin, Mo.)

Located just 4 miles south of the East Toll Gate (terminus) of the Will Rogers Turnpike on the Oklahoma-Missouri state line road. Follow State Line Road until you cross the second small branch. Drive slowly ½ mile further to the free viewing platform. Park near platform and turn off car lights. Walk to platform and look west—GHOST LIGHTS WILL APPEAR. To be fully informed about the "lighted" UFOs, visit the Spooksville Community Building and Museum. There is no charge.

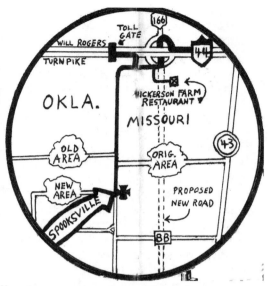

it is pursued, never allowing anyone to get too close.

A number of legends have sprung up to explain the phenomenon. One legend tells of the spirit of two young Quapaw Indian warriors, and another legend relates the light is from a headless Osage Indian chief searching for his missing head with a torch. Another legend tells the light is a lantern of a miner whose children were abducted by Indians.

The next mysterious light is called the Gurdon Spook Light and is located near railroad tracks outside the town of Gurdon, Arkansas. The location is still in use by the railroad and is a popular Halloween attraction in the area. Like other lights it has been described as appearing in various colors and has been reported to bob up and down and around. According to legend, the light is associated with William McClain, a railroad worker who was killed when he fell into the path of a

167

train. His head was separated from his body and was never found and the light is from his lantern as he searches.

The Paulding Light (also called the Light of Paulding or the Dog Meadow Light) is a light which appears in a valley outside of Paulding, Michigan. Reports of the light have appeared since the 1960s, with popular folklore providing such explanations as the paranormal, geologic activity, swamp gas, or optical illusion. The first recorded sighting of the Paulding Light came in 1966 when a group of teenagers reported the light to a local sheriff. Since then, a number of other individuals have reported seeing the mysterious light, which is said to appear nearly every night at the site.

Although stories of the light vary, the most popular legend involves the death of a railroad brakeman. The legend states the valley once contained railroad tracks and the light is the lantern of the brakeman who was killed while attempting to stop an oncoming train from colliding with railway cars stopped on the tracks. Another story claims the light is the ghost of a slain mail courier, while another says it is the ghost of an Indian dancing on the power lines run through the valley. In 2010, the Paulding Light was featured on the SyFy television show *Fact or Faked: Paranormal Files*. The investigators were depicted trying several experiments in an unsuccessful attempt to recreate the light, including using car headlights from a north-south section of US 45 and a flyover by an airplane with a spotlight. After failing to copy the lights, the investigators

168

concluded the phenomenon is unexplainable.

The last light I want to talk about is the St. Louis Light appearing in Saskatchewan, Canada. This mysterious phenomenon involves a strange light moving up and down along an old abandoned rail line at night,

Official sign for the Paulding Light.

changing colors and brightness. It is reported to be seen south of Prince Albert and north of St. Louis. Even when the track was removed along that section, the light was still being seen. As is typical with ghost lights near railroad tracks, the local legends relate it to some phantom ghost train or the ghost of a railroad worker looking for his head after a grisly death. In 2014 the Canadian Post issued a stamp, part of a series of five depicting of famous Canadian ghost stories, depicting the St. Louis ghost train.

As you can see there are numerous areas around the United States and Canada that have this strange phenomenon of ghost lights. Are they extraterrestrial or paranormal in origin? Or are they simply car lights? One thing is for sure—the lights still appear to this very day. You can go to one these places and watch them, and the best part is it's free.

UFO Legend Trip

- Camera—one that has IR capabilities
- Camera stands and pods
- GPS—this is good to use so you can mark your location
- Bionic ear device
- Camping gear including tent(s), sleeping bag(s)

169

lanterns and cooking stove
- Fuel for cooking stove
- Water and items to clean water
- Flashlights/head lights/light sticks
- Rain gear—Gore-Tex is great because it also keeps you warm
- Binoculars/telescope with stand
- Evidence kit including casting material
- Cold weather clothes

Chapter 10:
Extraterrestrial Legend Trip

The night sky is peppered with constellations, planets, and occasional meteors. Every so often something else appears like a bright light, or flashing multicolored lights, moving in strange, unfamiliar patterns. Have you ever looked up at the night sky and wondered who else could be out there? Are there races of aliens visiting this planet in strange crafts? Among legend trips, a search for extraterrestrials is different but just as exciting. With extraterrestrial or UFO legend trips, the primary focus is the sky as you're looking for something to appear in the heavens. With this you have to learn to be extremely quiet and to exercise patience.

I remember in the 70s, during the UFO craze, I read in the newspaper where Charles Hickson and Calvin Parker claimed they were abducted by aliens while fishing near Pascagoula, Mississippi. Even though the men were questioned heavily by authorities and naysayers, both men passed lie detector tests. This incident later became known as the 1973 Pascagoula Abduction. Their tale had everybody looking at the night sky searching for something out of the ordinary. I was one of those heading outside at night with my binoculars to look for UFOs. My fascination with UFOs would later be strengthened when I saw the 1970 movie *Close Encounters of the Third Kind*.

I refer to the excursion described here as a UFO Legend Trip, that is spotting UFOs, usually in the night sky, and taking pictures or recordings to capture their activity. With this legend trip, you can either do an all-nighter or make it a day legend trip. For UFO crash

171

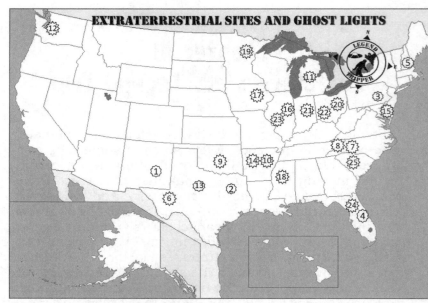

sites, I recommend a day legend trip (Chapter 14). There is a list of equipment at the end of this chapter. You can add more equipment or take some away. It's up to you. This is just a basic guideline when you're out looking for UFO's.

The first thing you need is to find out where in your area there have been UFO sightings, or better yet, a UFO hot spot. UFO hot spots are areas with the highest concentration of UFO sightings. Strange aircraft, like Bigfoot and ghosts, don't always reappear where they were originally seen. But there are areas where they are seen more than once. Of course this is no guarantee you'll see something, but you have to start somewhere. With all legends, persistence will pay off. If there is not a UFO hot spot in your area, find the closest and plan a legend trip. This legend trip generally does require you to stay out all night and maybe camp out. You can stay at a hotel, but that can be expensive.

172

1. Roswell UFO Crash site, NM
2. Aurora Alien Grave site, TX
3. Kecksburg UFO Crash site, PA
4. Flagger Beach UFO Crash site, FL
5. Betty and Barney Hill Abduction site, NH
6. Marfa Lights, TX
7. Maco Lights, NC
8. Brown Mountain Lights, NC
9. Hornet Spook Light, OK
10. Gurdon Spook Light, AR
11. Paulding Light , MI
12. Yakima Lights , WA
13. Anson Light, TX
14. Dover Light, AR
15. Hebron Light, MD
16. Jacob's Lantern, IL
17. St Mary's Light, IA
18. The Black Jack Lights, MS
19. Old Brewery Hill Spook Lights, MN
20. Elmore Rider Light, OH
21. The Moody Light, IN
22. The Oxford Light, OH
23. Maple Lake Lights, IL
24. Greenbriar Road Light, FL
25. Bingham Light, SC

Extraterrestrial Legend Trip

Here in Florida, the hot spot use to be in the Gulf Breeze area, but now it seems to be all over Florida. A lot of witnesses reported sightings next to NASA near Titusville. Also military bases seem to attract UFOs.

A number of UFO websites have online databases listing sightings by state, date, and shape so you can find out the latest sightings in your area. You can get sign up for their newsletters online that also feature current UFO sightings. You can also learn a lot by reading through others' reports. These UFO sightings groups are:

- National UFO Reporting Center
- MUFON (Mutual UFO Network)
- UFOdb

Once you find a UFO hot spot you want to check out, you need to gather as much up-to-date information as possible. This information will be pertinent to where you will be conducting an exciting legend trip. If you know somebody who saw the UFO, interview him or her. Also get their permission before contacting others. Try to locate any witnesses who are involved with the location and the sightings including residents, employees, and owners— whoever might have knowledge of potential activity.

Also you have to familiarize yourself with the constellations and planets. If not, you're bound to mistake a star for a UFO. You can get an app for your cell phone called Star Gazer that allows you to point your phone up in the sky and it will tell you all the stars, constellations, and planets in that section of the night sky. This is great to have and you won't end up

173

getting overexcited when you see blue and red lights twinkling in the sky, and shout out to the team an invasion is coming. Also go to a place that doesn't have a lot of air traffic, so you don't mistake human aircraft for UFOs

After you have all the information about the area or hot spot, it's time to plan the UFO legend trip. If the area is in a different city or state, you'll need to make travel arrangements. You'll need to decide how many vehicles you'll need and what kind of extra equipment you'll need. Make a call out to your friends and invite them on your extraterrestrial adventure. Once you have your team of legend trippers together move out.

When you arrive to the UFO hot spot, the first thing you need to do take into consideration where to set up your base of operations. I like to find campgrounds close to the sightings area. With UFO sightings this may not be easy to do. You may have to find a camp-site close to the area or you might be able to get per-mission from the landowners to camp out there. It's good to go to an area nice to look at even if you don't see a UFO. If you have to hike a considerable way to the hot spot, never go rucking or hiking by yourself. If you can't find anybody to go with you, then wait until someone is available. I cannot stress this point enough. Some sightings take place over lakes and there usually are trails around lakes. Some reports, like the ones in Puerto Rico, describe a UFO actually descending into lakes.

For Scout Masters and Venturing Crew guides, you need to see if there is a Boy Scout or Girl Scout camp near the lake and maybe incorporate a UFO legend trip into your weekend outing. It adds to the excitement of the trip. It gives you and your troop something to look for when they are hiking.

Setting up a base camp is pretty much the same as

174

doing a Bigfoot legend trip. I always make a checklist to make sure I set up everything we need. Again, you can do it the way you want, because everybody is different. This checklist has worked for me, and I've been doing this for years.

First, I pick an area for my base camp close to the UFO hot spot, if possible. Plan on different locations in case someone is already camped at your chosen spot or if you have a larger team. You also need to plan on coming back to this spot multiple times over the course of months or even years. Furthermore, if your chosen spot is full of campers, it might be a good idea not to tell everybody what you're doing other than camping.

When you arrive at your actual campsite, the first thing to do is unload your camping gear to get base camp set up. If you brought water gear, put your boat or canoe in a secure location. Fuel cans need to go in your vehicle and not in camp where you have a campfire going.

If you are leading this UFO legend trip, assign jobs or assignments and then make sure everybody gets the camp set up before it gets dark. It is important to get all your gear set up, especially your tents. If your camp is near a lake during the summer, mosquitoes or other insects will drive you crazy. Make sure you have the mosquito candles ready. When the sun goes down, you need to have the bug spray ready. Rivers are different. Mosquitoes do not like flowing water and fish eat them.

For more in-depth details on creating a safe and secure campsite, please refer to Chapter 4.

Once you have your base camp set up, it is time to scout around the area where you want to do your UFO investigation to see what's out there. If you have a large area to investigate break into teams and check out multiple areas. Get your map out and, with the team, show them where the UFO sightings took place and then plot where you want the teams to set up.

175

Legend Tripping

If there is enough time, you should take all the teams with you when you identify the area you intend to observe in the sky. It's easier than going back and explaining it on a map. It is best to do this during daylight hours with the team, allowing review and answering questions about what is going to happen as something can get lost in translation over radio. Make sure everybody knows what they should look for and point out where the sightings happened. It is OK to go to the areas in the evening, but it's easier to do it during the day, so everyone can get familiar with the area and nobody will get lost. You want to find areas which give you or your team a full panoramic view of the sky, with nothing blocking it like trees or buildings.

Always have somebody stay back at base camp and monitor the radio. After breaking everyone into teams, assign them AORs (Area of Responsibility). These are areas the team is to go investigate and set up a static post, scan the sky and the horizon. You can get almost of hundred percent scan of the sky with multiple teams. These AORs should be marked on a map so the base camp can keep track of them. Also, if somebody gets hurt, the person at base camp can call for medical aid and have it come to the base camp. If your area is large, you might consider having the teams use vehicles to go to their AORs making movement easier and quicker. Have a dependable 4x4 vehicle back at base camp in case a vehicle breaks down or something goes wrong. If another vehicle breaks down, you may have to tow it.

Each team needs to a have a working radio with fresh or extra batteries or a cell phone. I have the teams do radio checks before they move out to their AORs. If a team loses contact, they should return to base camp immediately and either get a new radio or a member with a working cell phone. If they do see a wild animal like a panther or bear tracks, then they are to radio it in and return to the rally point or base camp. Go over all of this with everybody before each team moves out to their AORs. Depending on the size of the investigation area each team should take water and food. Always take a survival kit because they also have first aid items like band aids and antiseptic wipes.

UFOs can be seen day or night. Your regular nighttime UFOs are called nocturnal lights, while daytime UFOs are called daylight discs. Most nocturnal lights are self-illuminating while most daylight discs are metallic in color. So while you're walking down the street, look up at the clouds. You may just spot a sparkling daylight disc zipping across the sky. There are occasional UFO landings, so be on the lookout for large burn areas where there shouldn't be any, usually in large fields. Thermal imagers are good for checking out fields as they pick up heat signatures.

If you're conducting your UFO legend trip near water, watch out for everything around you. For example, if a team needs to move through the swamps to get to their AOR, they need to watch out for hidden dangers like cypress trees. Additionally, there are sinkholes, which you can't see, and you can't tell how deep they are, creating a potentially dangerous situation. Make sure you go over all of this with your team before you enter the area.

During the recon, you need to choose a rally point especially if using vehicles. A rally point is a designated area for everyone to meet back up again after the investigation, which is usually in the middle of the AORs or could be base camp.

Equipment
Many people have claimed to have seen a UFO while some have even reported being abducted. Unfortunately no one has been able to provide definitive

proof. It's imperative if you are serious about seeing and recording a UFO sighting that you have serious equipment for getting concrete data. When it comes to cameras, have a camera that takes excellent pictures at night. You'll need a special lens to capture the faint lights and patterns created by the UFOs.

You should have a camera on a tripod or stand pointing where the sighting occurred. Also keep the locks on the pod off, in case you need to reposition the camera in a different location. UFOs usually reappear in the same place over and over again. Just be ready to reposition your camera in case the UFO appears in a different location nearby. A video camera is also useful to have. The more ways you have to document the UFOs, the better. Always make sure somebody is with your equipment at all times.

Telescopes are good to have but they can be difficult to use when you see a UFO. The lens is focused on one small area and can be difficult to move where the UFO is, and if the UFO is moving it's more difficult to keep track of it with a telescope. I prefer binoculars as they are easy to use and most are pretty durable and less expensive than a telescope.

A thermal imager is a great tool to use. These expensive devices will scan an area and pick up heat signatures. In other words, if there is something in the sky giving off heat, this device will pick it up. It works great both during daytime and at night. Thermal imagers come in a variety of designs, but they are all expensive. As I said, they are great for legend tripping, but they are costly and fragile.

Night vision scopes/cameras magnify any kind of light source and you can see from quite a distance away. They go through batteries pretty quick so make sure you have extras on hand.

After the recon is complete, head back to camp to

178

review with the teams their AORs and what their plan is. This is the question and answer time. Do this now and not in the morning when they are hiding out. Make sure everyone knows the plan for the investigation and reiterate safety procedures to everyone. Then finish off the evening with dinner and move the teams out to their AOR.

The person at base camp needs to keep a record of the details of your legend trip and sightings. Each team should have a notebook and writing instrument ready at all times to jot down all necessary information right when it happens. Voice recorders are handheld devices which allow teams to record their observations without having to stop and write them down. Later, when you get to base camp record the information in a log on your computer.

Make sure every team knows what to do if they spot a UFO. First they need to radio it in to base camp. Even if you aren't sure what you saw was indeed a UFO, you need to write down the following information:

- The date and time of the sighting
- The location of the sighting
- The shape, size, and color of the UFO
- Whether there were additional witnesses

Also find out whether what you're seeing may have an explanation; for example, if you're looking for UFOs near an Air Force Base, you might be seeing human-made aircraft, even if they look unfamiliar.

UFO experts will tell you after you've hunted for UFOs for a while, you'll start to notice patterns. UFOs may have the following characteristics:

- Most UFOs don't move in a straight line, but rather up and down or in zigzags. They may not

179

move in regular patterns at all.

- UFOs don't blink, like known aircraft would; they may be shaped like discs, triangles, or something else entirely.

Before you and the teams head out to the AORs, always double-check the radios, cameras, and gear. Have all teams keep video cameras on and recording. You never know when something will happen, and when it does, it happens quickly, and by the time you have your camera up and running, it is gone. If you don't get anything, erase the recording. Each team should stay on paths or dirt roads. Make sure everyone has the right clothing for the expected weather. It might get cold at night and the weather might take a turn for the worse and you and your team will need raingear. Each team will move to their AOR and set up and look and listen.

After a couple of hours, if nothing has happened I usually call the teams in and reassign AORs. Teams won't get bored looking at the same thing all night if their locations are moved. Have the teams call base camp when they first get set up and then every couple of hours. They can also call you at a designated time or when they see something. At least one member of the team should always be awake and watching. If you or one of your teams hears something, then have everybody proceed to that AOR or see if they can see it from their AOR. Remember, always keep the video camera in record mode. You can talk and explain where you are and what time it is.

Now you might have the teams staying in their AOR till a certain time. If they are staying all night, they will need to bring a tent and sleeping bag. If that's the case, I recommend you have a roving team who will either walk or drive around to the various teams and check

180

on them.

Once all teams have returned to base camp at the end of the investigation, inventory all gear. Any team unable to make it back to base camp on time should call on the radio/cell phone and let the base know your location and reason for being stopped. It only takes a couple of seconds to do this. If a team does not show up at the prescribed time, don't panic. First, call them on the radio to determine their location. On the way back, a team may see something and stop to watch. If there is no answer (radio/cell phone) and it has been a while, send only one team who knows the area.

Daytime operations (ops) to see if a UFO appears are pretty much the same as night except teams might want to find a shaded area rather than sitting in the hot sun. It is also sometimes harder to see UFOs during sunny days. NEVER aim your binoculars at the sun.

If a team or team member gets lost, first check what AOR they were assigned. If you have communications with them, have them describe where they are and at what point they knew they were lost. If you have done your briefing right and every team stayed in their assigned zone or road, then you will pretty much know where they are. The missing team will probably be close to the area. Once you get to the lost members' AOR, call out to them and see if they can hear you. Sound travels better at night. Make sure only one team is calling out to them. If all the teams do this, you won't be able to hear the lost team when they reply.

If the worst happens and you can't find them, call 911. Fish and Wildlife officers will come out, and they often have helicopters equipped with heat detecting devices and will be able to find the lost team. When they arrive, give them the location where the team is supposed to be, which will give them an area to start their search. In the whole time I have been legend

181

tripping, I have not lost a team. I always ensure each team has an experienced person with them, stays on the road, and has a working radio.

When all the teams are back at the rally point, do a quick briefing to find out what all the teams saw or heard. Make sure they know where it was they heard the noise or saw the object and return to the location for a more thorough search. The UFO might return. Talk about what was seen and heard. Review all pictures and recordings. If your team took videos or pictures, look them over. If you do have something on a picture, you or a team will need to go recheck the area; also make sure what you have in the picture is not a plane or balloon. Repeat this procedure depending how many days you decide to stay out. If you spot a UFO, report it. You'll be contributing to the UFO community at large.

UFO Legend Trip

- Camera—one that has IR capabilities
- Camera stands and pods
- GPS—this is good to use so you can mark your location
- Bionic ear device
- Camping gear including tent(s), sleeping bag(s) lanterns
- Thermal imager
- Water and items to clean water
- Flashlights/head lights/light sticks
- Rain gear—Gore-Tex is great because it also keeps you warm
- Binoculars/telescope with stand
- Evidence kit including casting material
- Cold weather clothes

Chapter 11
Treasure Legends

As children, we were soaked in literature and pop culture where pirates bury treasure and adventurers search for their fortunes by solving vague riddles, using questionable maps with the elusive "X marks the spot." Today, there are still several legends of buried treasure. These lost caches of immense wealth are out there, just waiting for someone to find them. Treasure hunters are still out there actively tracking each clue and legend. These legendary treasures are said to be pirate gold, confederate payload, outlaw loot and some are just hidden gold, waiting to be recovered at a later time.

The most famous legendary treasure is the Lost Dutchman Mine. This is a legend of a huge gold vein located somewhere in the Superstition Mountains of Arizona. Countless people have searched for it, to no avail. The good thing is the gold is still out there; the bad thing is the area where it is supposed to be buried is the most inhospitable area of Arizona you can find with oven hot summers and frigid winters. If you do go out there, bring plenty of water.

My favorite legend of buried treasure is based on a place in Nova Scotia named Oak Island. Nicknamed the "Money Pit," treasure hunters have spent millions looking for an unknown treasure in this mysterious ancient shaft, only to come up empty-handed. Each hunter has a different theory as to what the treasure is. Everything from the Holy Grail to the crown jewels of France has been suggested; some even think it is pirate treasure. In the late 1600s, the famous pirate Captain Kidd was known to prowl the region, and one legend

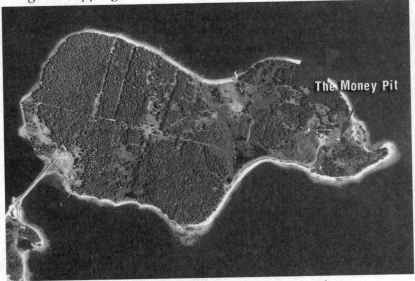

The Money Pit

An aerial photo of Oak Island, Nova Scotia.

has it he buried his treasure on Oak Island. But most historical researchers believe Kidd actually buried it on Gardiners Island, off Long Island, New York, before he was hanged. Today, Oak Island is privately owned, but they do offer tours. A lot of the areas are roped off and off-limits as the landscape is dotted with mine shafts from previous attempts to find the treasure. There is also a small museum where you can learn about the history of the island and all the efforts that have been made to find the treasure. If you visit this beautiful region of Canada, you may consider the breathtaking landscape a natural treasure.

There are famous outlaws whose buried loot was never recovered. The renowned outlaw Butch Cassidy is supposed to have hidden stolen money somewhere in Arizona. He was such an outlaw he even formed an outlaw group, called the Wild Bunch, to travel with

184

him, robbing locals and travelers with seeming impunity. Before the law was hot on his trail, Cassidy and the Wild Bunch actually buried $20,000 somewhere in Irish Canyon, located in the northwestern part of Colorado in Moffat County.

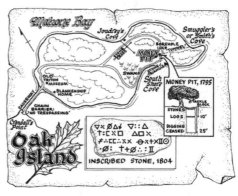

Outlaw Jesse James and his gang robbed trains loaded with gold being transported back east from the Gold Rush out west. Jesse's gang would rob a train and then make their escape up Blacksnake Creek, located on the east side of Wyeth Hill. Jesse's gang hid their gold in caves they had dug in the thick clay soil. Legend has it that Jesse died before he was able to retrieve the final gold shipment. Wyeth Hill runs along the top of the Missouri River Bluffs in northwest St. Joseph, Missouri.

Famous gangster John Dillinger's loot was never recovered. In April 1943, FBI agents found Dillinger hiding out with a few of his outlaw buddies in the Little Bohemia Lodge in Mercer, Wisconsin. The FBI raided the building, killing three civilian men. Amid all the confusion, the gangsters were able to escape out a back entrance. It is said Dillinger ran a few hundred yards north of the roadhouse where he buried $200,000 in small bills inside a suitcase.

You can also go look for the long-lost ransom D.B. Cooper took when he hijacked a plane near Portland, Oregon on November 24, 1971. He parachuted into a forest near Mount St. Helens, Washington. To this day, nobody has seen D.B. Cooper or the ransom money. The area is also popular for hiking and camping, making it

185

easy for treasure hunters who have taken up the hunt. The area is so dense and thick, it's a challenge to avoid getting lost, let alone find the money.

WANTED

D. B. Cooper

$15,000 REWARD

The man who hijacked Northwest Airlines flight 305 on November 24, 1971 and extorted the Airline out of $200,000. The identity of this individual remains unknown, but he purchased his ticket under the name of Dan Cooper. He has subsequently become better known as

If you have information regarding the identity or whereabouts of this individual, please contact the F.B.I. office in your area, the location and telephone number of which can be found in the front of your telephone directory.

This individual should be considered armed and dangerous. Under no circumstances should he be approached or capture attempted by anyone besides law enforcement officials.

Somewhere, there is $100,000 in gold currency buried when Confederate soldiers robbed two wagon trains from a Union bank in 1865 at Chennault Crossroads in Lincoln County, Georgia. Legend has it the gold was hastily buried on the original grounds of Chennault Plantation in Washington, Georgia, and remains there today. The plantation is under private ownership, and permission is required to hunt for the treasure.

There is also supposed to be gold buried near the site where General George Custer met his end at Little Bighorn, Montana. The way the story goes is a boat loaded with gold came up the Bighorn River to meet up with the soldiers in Bismarck, North Dakota. But the captain found out about Custer's Last Stand and decided to bury the gold near where the massacre happened, and it is supposed to still be there. This historical region is now a National Park, so if you find it, the government gets it.

Many tales of treasure buried in caves originated during the Gold Rush of 1849. Samuel Clemens himself spent many hours searching for treasure in the caves, probably having heard the legends of returning forty-niners burying gold there. This treasure hunting most likely inspired him to write *Tom Sawyer*, using the pen name Mark Twain.

Have you ever seen the movie *National Treasure*? For those of you who have never seen it, this 2004

186

Disney movie follows the adventures of treasure hunter Ben Gates, on his quest for a fantastic treasure collected by the Knights Templar and then hidden by the Freemasons, somewhere in the United States. He discovers clues left by them to the location of the treasure. While watching, I couldn't help but wonder, "Where did the writers get the idea for this movie?" Was there a real national treasure out there? The answer is "Yes" and legend has it that it still hasn't been found. The treasure is called the Beale Treasure.

This exciting treasure legend began in 1817 when a gentleman by the name of Thomas J. Beale, and his team of thirty adventurers, traveled to New Mexico for buffalo hunting. Towards the end of their excursion, they stumbled upon a huge treasure of gold and silver. This is where the story diverges in two conflicting directions. One version says they found a cache of gold, silver and gems in a cave. The other, more plausible version, is they found a vein of gold and silver in the mountains and mined it out from 1819 to 1821. Anyway, the story continues on to say Beale and party realized the growing treasure was too large and too dangerous for them to keep in camp as they were located in a precarious mountain region full of bandits. So, they secretly transported the treasure across the United States and buried it in a cave in the Blue Ridge Mountains near Buford's Tavern, which all the men frequented.

Before setting out across the plains with a load of treasure, it was suggested that, in case anything should happen to the party, there should be a plan in place so the treasure would not be lost to the rightful heirs. Thomas Beale was instructed to select some person who could be confided in to carry out the wishes of the party in this regard. Subsequently Beale took up winter quarters at the house of Mr. Robert Morris in

187

Legend Tripping

Lynchburg, Virginia. Robert Morris was the trusted person Thomas J. Beale selected to be his confidential agent. Thomas Beale returned to the mine in the spring of 1820 and found the work still progressing favorably.

In 1821, Beale returned east with an increased supply of gold and silver, which came through safely together with $13,000 in jewels purchased in St. Louis with silver. He deposited it with the other treasure in the same Virginia treasure site. Before returning to the mine in 1822, Thomas Beale prepared three encoded messages or papers (known as the Beale Codes or the Beale Ciphers) and two letters explaining his enterprise, which he placed in a locked box. He then went to Lynchburg, Virginia and met with Robert Morris at Buford's Tavern. Beale explained to Morris about the strongbox, advising him if he (Beale) did not return after ten years, to open it. Beale then departed and Morris never saw him again.

After more than ten years, Morris reluctantly opened the strongbox and in it he found a letter and some number-filled pages, presumably some sort of cipher or code. Morris was unable to understand the meaning of these pages. Also the story goes Beale had arranged for a letter from St. Louis to be delivered at this time, a letter containing the "key" to the ciphers, without which the treasure could not be found. For unknown reasons, this letter was not delivered and Morris was not able to learn what the ciphers said.

In 1862, Morris told an anonymous friend the story of the ciphers and the treasure they guarded. The anonymous friend succeeded in deciphering paper number two and it reads as follows:

I have deposited in the county of Bedford about four miles from Buford's in an excavation or vault six feet below the surface of the ground

188

the following articles...

The first deposit consisted of 1,014 pounds of gold and 3,812 pounds of silver, deposited November 1819. The second was made Dec. 1821 and consisted of 1,907 pounds of gold and 1,288 of silver; also jewels obtained in St. Louis in exchange to save transportation and valued at $13,000...

But, after twenty years of effort, the friend could not solve the other two pages. During this time the friend supposedly had spent so much time with the other two pages he neglected his business, which suffered. In 1885, he stopped trying to decode the ciphers and published a pamphlet revealing this story to the world.

One of the strangest treasure legends is about a stranded ship 100 miles inland from the Pacific Ocean, in California's Salton Sea basin, toward the southern end of the Mojave Desert. This legend has persisted for centuries in reports from Indian peoples, Spanish explorers, prospectors, migrants and treasure hunters. The lost ship is said to have had millions of dollars' worth of pearls from a trading expedition on board when it disappeared.

Experts believe a large tide from the Gulf of California collided with runoff from the Colorado River. Water runoff enveloped the ship and carried it into the Salton Sea. The flood would have then retreated, leaving the vessel stranded. The ship would have been forgotten forever if it weren't for the abundance of pearls on board. The ship is assumed to be Spanish but varying legends say it might be a craft from the navy of King Solomon, the ten lost tribes of Israel, a warring people from the Indian Ocean, or even a band of pirates.

In 1870, treasure hunter Charlie Clusker claimed to have gone in search of the ship and found it and the

189

treasure. The story says Clusker journeyed back out to the ship, but never returned, leading many people to believe the ship and its cargo of pearls could still be out there.

If you check the Internet, you will find a legend of buried treasure in your area to go look for. These legendary treasures are located all over the United States. Treasurecache.net is my favorite. It is the most up-to-date site on buried treasure. Be careful, because you might be going on private or public land. And if by chance you do find the treasure, you will have to give it to whoever owns the property, or to the State. Mel Fisher had a lengthy court battle with the State of Florida over the treasure he found in a sunken ship.

So you see, there is no shortage of hidden treasure to search for. If you do decide to go look for a lost treasure, make sure your legend tripping team knows the story behind it. That makes the whole experience a lot more exciting.

Chapter 12:
Treasure Legend Trip

Ever since I saw the movie *Raiders of the Lost Ark*, I wanted to look for lost treasure. I always dreamed of one day discovering some long-lost treasure like the Lost Dutchman Mine. When I was in school I read an article about the Oak Island Money Pit located off the coast of Nova Scotia. I dreamed of being the one to discover what was buried out there. As a kid I read a lot of books about buried treasure and found there is still a lot of undiscovered treasure out there.

When I retired to Florida, I took my wife treasure hunting on the Suwannee River. The Suwannee starts at the Okefenokee Swamp and flows for over 246 miles southwesterly down from Georgia through Florida to empty into the Gulf of Mexico. A Bigfoot attack reported in the Okefenokee Swamp is related earlier in the Bigfoot chapter. This tributary is not only popular because of the Stephen Foster song "Old Folks at Home," but also for the legends surrounding it. There are numerous stories of pirates hiding millions of dollars of treasure in or near the river. In 1820 a schooner ran into a reef at the mouth of the Suwannee. This vessel was transporting $3,000,000 in gold coins destined for Spain by way of Havana. The schooner was said to have encountered a fierce storm and began taking on water. In an effort to save his the ship, the captain headed for shore. Unfortunately, the vessel sank in 30 feet of water. Today there are stories of gold coins recovered along the banks of the river.

There are stories about pirates Lafitte and Gasparilla hiding treasure along the banks of the Suwannee River.

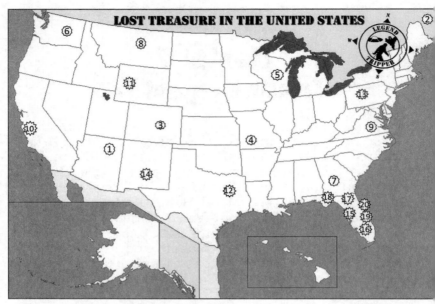

Tampa, Florida has a parade and festival to celebrate Gasparilla and the pirate invasion. In November 1953, a hotel operator out of Lakeland, Florida, Bill Sneed, located 4,500 gold coins and 3,500 of silver when he found a trove chest he located with an "electronic device" in 16 feet of water.

So, after telling my wife these exciting treasure legends, we decided on a weekend to go treasure legend tripping. When we arrived at the Suwannee, after scouting for about an hour, we found a spot on the other side of the river from Fowler's Bluff where legend has it French privateer Jean Lafitte buried his treasure hoard. As the alleged location is on private property, we kept to the public land across the river. The wife and I walked along the banks of the Suwannee for hours with her metal detector, looking for lost treasure. We went in November so the temperature was pleasant, but unfortunately the mosquitos were still out making the trek a little miserable. We combed

192

1. Lost Dutchman's Mine, AZ
2. Oak Island Money Pit, CAN
3. Butch Cassidy lost cache, CO
4. Jesse James buried gold, MO
5. Dillinger's lost loot, WI
6. DB Cooper's Lost Ransom, WA
7. Confederate Gold, GA
8. Little Bighorn lost gold, MT
9. Beale Treasure, VA
10. Salton Sea Treasure Ship, CA
11. Fenn's Buried Treasure, WY
12. Lost Treasure of the Alamo, TX
13. Dutch Schultz's Treasure, NY
14. Victoria's Peak Treasure, NM
15. Gasparilla's Treasure, FL
16. Jack Rackham's Treasure, FL
17. Confederate Gold, FL
18. Billy Bowlegs' hoard, FL
19. Ashley Gang's Loot, FL
20. Don Felipe's Treasure, FL

over two miles of the limited public river's edge, but found nothing of monetary value. We did find some rusty nails and an old butane lighter, but no gold or silver. We did however have a great time looking. I brought some food and water so we stopped at noon and ate lunch by the river. We continued our hunt until the sun started to descend behind the palm trees, when we called it a day and headed back to the vehicle. It was exciting thinking we might find something. We stopped at a local restaurant and the owner entranced us with more stories about Civil War gold also lost in the Suwannee. I asked her, "Just how much gold is supposedly out there?" She didn't hesitate. "$15,000,000.00," she answered back.

There are actually several kinds of treasure hunters. Wreck treasure hunters go looking for treasure in sunken wrecks using expensive gear and equipment. Relic hunters are looking for items with historical value like the Ark of the Covenant or the Holy Grail. Treasure legend trippers are called cache hunters. A cache hunter is somebody who looks for treasure left behind by different groups such as outlaws, pirates, or the Spanish. In this chapter I will simply refer this adventure hunting as treasure legend tripping.

Most people think treasure hunting is searching for treasure on a sunken ship. This is treasure hunting but it is the most expensive and dangerous form. The hunts require expensive government permits and if anything is found, the government gets their share. Sunken treasure hunts can be done without the expensive gear and permits. Shallow waters can easily be searched with an underwater metal detector, and hunters have found valuable objects from sunken ships pushed closer to shore by storms. This is referred to as

193

beachcombing.

The best time to beachcomb is just hours after the main body of a hurricane has passed through, while it's still raining. Some beachcombers have found silver and gold coins and even gold jewelry from the old Spanish wrecks sunk in shallow waters just off the US coast.

When it comes to treasure hunting, research and planning are essential. I found this interesting information in an article, "All Kinds of Buried Treasure," on the website oldandsold.com:

> Check your information, your legends, and your maps as carefully as you can. You cannot do too much research before you dig. Every iota of fact you gain before you start using your spade is getting you much closer to the treasure. There are laws governing the searching for—and the finding of—lost treasure. Know your laws before you dig. Always check with the territorial or state authorities in the area in which you wish to go treasure hunting. There are state laws and federal laws regarding both the finding and keeping of lost treasure.
>
> Information of all types has to be checked. Even maps that may have been in your own family for generations may need further elucidation. Remember the map you have may be a genuine pirate or lost mine map, but the man who had the treasure or knew where the mine was may not have plainly written down its location. He made the map in the first place because he didn't want anyone else to know where it was. Many times even authentic maps are backwards or even in code. "Step ten paces north" may mean step ten paces south. "Pass three rocks" may not mean rocks at all but

trees—trees which may have come down since the day the original treasure was buried. But if you have an authentic map and have the determination and the money, you might find treasure. Or you might find it accidentally. It has been done before.

You might find your treasure—provided, that is, that you have properly checked into the laws of the state in which you are going to search.

Some states, as noted above, have their own regulations concerning the digging for treasure. In Florida, for example, the treasure hunter has to have a permit costing around a hundred dollars before he can even begin to hunt for his treasure. He gets it from the land agent in Tallahassee, and after the treasure is located, the state of Florida automatically gets 12 percent of anything found within the territorial jurisdiction of the state. There is also income tax! Yes, folks, you have to pay tax on found treasure. It is the law. Can you imagine what the income tax would be on Blackbeard's hoards or Jean Lafitte's treasure?

You should research, by either the Internet or correspond to the Chamber of Commerce in the closest city to your treasure spot, to find out the various rules, laws, and regulations concerning both buried treasure and sunken treasure. You need to find out about them before you start to dig or dive. Also write to the Federal Government in Washington or check out their website on the subject of treasure hunting.

Before embarking on a treasure legend trip, research the chosen treasure legend well. The treasure may have already been discovered. Additionally, when going on

195

a treasure hunt, consider if the area is on private or public land. An example would be Oak Island in Nova Scotia, where the treasure still has not been found. The island is owned by a private firm. While they do allow tours of the island, they do not allow you to look for the treasure alone.

If the Lost Dutchman Mine is the chosen trip, remember the Superstition Mountains comprise a large area covering hundreds of miles in the desert. Hundreds of people have tried to locate it to no avail. Furthermore, treasure hunters go missing, so be careful looking for treasure.

Some treasures belong to the government, meaning finders are not necessarily keepers, for legal reasons. An example would be if D.B. Cooper's cache of money was found. This was ransom money originally belonging to the government, meaning it would have to be returned. The good news is, there is a finder's fee. It's not much but history books will always know who found the cache.

With all this said, if this exciting legend trip still seems like a great idea, then start the planning phase. Check locally and see what lost treasure is still out there and what is needed to go look for it. Check and make sure it's not on private property and get permission from the state. Now you're probably thinking, "I'll go look for the treasure and then if I find it, I'll get a permit." Wrong answer; those caught looking for a treasure without a permit by authorities will get fined. Most treasures require some excavating (digging). This is usually how hunters get caught. So get a permit if needed before the gear gets loaded.

Unless you're lucky enough to have a buried treasure in the backyard, planning a legend trip requires camping out, especially if the target area is a considerable distance away. When my wife and I went

196

up to the Suwannee River, we camped out at a local campsite. I also did a Bigfoot hunt that night, so I got to look for two legends. There are also ghost sightings along the Suwannee River.

Once the treasure target area has been determined, and you've gotten permission if needed, it's time to load up the camping and legend tripping gear and move out. Like all the chapters on conducting a legend trip, I have compiled a list of items needed for this adventure at the end of this chapter. Locate campgrounds or a hotel close to the target area. If camping, I'll go over some of what you need to do.

Find campgrounds that are close to the treasure target area and locate a campsite close to the area, or maybe get permission from the landowners to camp out there. With this kind of legend trip, there is usually only one area to look. If it's a considerable distance to hike to the target spot, never go rucking or hiking alone. If finding a partner is difficult, wait until someone is available. Most of the stories of lost treasures locate the caches in the woods and sometimes around a body of water like a lake or river.

Setting up a base camp is pretty much the same as doing all outdoor legend trips. Make a checklist of everything needed for the trip. More detailed advice is found in Chapter 4 under the "Base Camp" heading. Make variations on the equipment list based on the environment and weather expected during the hunt.

Once base camp is set up and it's still daylight, scout around the target area. If using a treasure map or code, it's best to do it during daylight hours. Compare the treasure map with an updated map of the area. It is also great to have a GPS—and most cell phones have one on them. Rivers are known to change over time. The Mississippi is a great example of this.

If there is enough time, take the team to the target

197

area. It's easier than going back and explaining it on a map. Again it is best to do this during daylight hours as something can get lost in the translation. Make sure everybody knows what they should look for and point out where the treasure is supposed to be.

Whenever leaving the campsite, always have somebody stay back to keep an eye on the gear. Now if this treasure it located in a broad area, and there are enough team members, consider breaking into teams to cover a bigger search area. Have the team's AORs marked on a map so the base camp can keep track of them. Also if somebody gets hurt, the person at base camp can call for medical aid and have it come to the base camp. Have the team move around on foot versus using vehicles. They might miss some clues just riding around. They can have a vehicle parked at the AOR, to use to come back to base camp.

Each team needs to a have a working radio with fresh or extra batteries or a cell phone. Have the teams do radio checks before they move out to their AORs. If a team loses contact, they should return to base camp immediately and either get a new radio or a member with a working cell phone. Have them report any wild animal like a panther or bear tracks, or human activity. You might not be the only ones looking for the treasure. Also some treasure hunters are not too keen on having other people out there, so be careful. Go over all of this with everybody, before each team moves out to their AORs. Depending on the size of the investigation area each team should take water and food. Always take a survival kit because they will be hiking around the AORs, and also these kits have first aid items like band-aids and antiseptic wipes.

If conducting the treasure legend trip near water, watch out for everything around. For example, if a team needs to move through the swamps to get to their AOR, they need to watch out for hidden dangers like cypress trees. Their roots do not grow straight down but rather to the side and up. They look like stalagmites and can be sharp. These are especially dangerous at night. It is best to keep the teams on dirt roads at night. Also, there are sinkholes, which presents a dangerous situation. Make sure you go over all of this with the team before you enter the area.

During the first walk-around or recon, choose a rally point, especially if using vehicles. A rally point is a designated area for everyone to meet back up again after the investigation, which is usually near a main road and in the middle of all the AORs. Once it starts to get dark, return to the campsite and have the teams do the same. Go over what the teams saw. Sometimes based on the recon, changing AORs could be a good plan of action. Then get a good night's sleep to get ready for the next day's adventure.

The next morning, when it is time to move out, have the teams load up the vehicles and boat/canoe(s), and proceed to their AORs. Have them double check their radios, cameras, and gear, before they leave. Each team should have a metal detector, if you're serious about finding this treasure.

EQUIPMENT
Metal Detector
For treasure legend tripping this is a key piece of equipment. This electronic device gives an audible or other signal when it is close to metal. They are not the ones used by law enforcement personnel to detect hidden weapons. The ones I'm talking about are the handheld units with a sensor probe which can be swept over the ground or other objects to detect buried metal objects like gold or silver. The first ones developed were for the military to find land mines in World War I.

199

Legend Tripping

Today these devices come in a wide range of sizes and prices. They can be found in toy stores and sporting goods stores. Most metal detectors are "all-purpose" detectors that will find everything from coins to jewelry, metal relics and gold. If looking for a buried treasure cache, a deeper seeking detector is needed which costs about $600.00, but it does send a signal down further than an all-purpose. If new to this kind of legend trip, go with an all-purpose detector and see how it goes. The best advice is don't buy all the equipment right away, but wait until legend tripping is a preferred path. Purchase a used, good quality metal detector. Good quality devices can be found on Internet auction sites.

Shovel

Believe it or not, this is one piece of equipment people seem to forget about. They remember the metal detector but when they go out to do a search and find something, they don't have any tool to dig up what's buried. They end up using their hands. Shovels are easy to find. Fold-up shovels are good to have. They are cheap, and easy to carry. When the detector goes off, take out a shovel, unfold it and dig up what's buried.

Brush

This can be a small paint brush. Sometimes the treasure is a delicate item and you need to remove it slowly from its resting place. Also some items are too big to remove without cleaning up around them. A clue to the treasure might be a carving on a large boulder or rock and you'll need to clean up around the carving to get a better look at it. A brush is a good item to use. I like to use a small paint brush. They are not expensive and they do the trick.

When a two-member team is out, one member of the team can lead the way, while the other works the

200

metal detector. If another member is available, they can also look for clues as well as monitor the radio. Each team should stay on their paths or dirt roads. When it comes to rivers, walk along the shoreline and look for anything that might have washed up—but you need to watch out for quicksand. It's not easy to see. Work the shallow waters with an underwater detector and find things that have been pushed closer to shore by storms. When in the woods be careful of what is around. In the eastern part of the country, which is very hilly, there are a lot of cliffs.

I have stated the following in each legend trip where you go into the woods. I do not apologize for repeating myself on this subject. There are dangerous animals you need to be aware of which should be considered when venturing into the woods. The most dangerous animals are bears, large wild cats, wild pigs, alligators, snakes, and certain insects. You should avoid these dangers at all costs. In Chapter 4, I go into detail on each of these animals. I am not an expert on animals, but I do know there are dangerous animals out there. There are popular stories about attacks on humans by animals and there is some truth to those stories. Do not underestimate any kind of wildlife, even small foxes and armadillos.

After a couple of hours, if nobody has found anything, call them in and reassign AORs so teams don't get bored looking at the same thing all day. Call them in when the sun goes down and it gets dark.

If a team finds some kind of clue, they should immediately call it in and then check it out. If warranted, have the rest of the teams come to that location.

When all teams are back, inventory gear. If on a team getting back to base camp late, as a safety measure, call on the radio and let the base know you have stopped and are checking for something. Give them the location as well. It only takes a couple of seconds to do this. If a team does not show up at the prescribed time, don't panic. First, call them on the radio and see where they are. On the way back, a team may notice something and stop to investigate. If they don't answer (radio/cell phone) and it has been a while, then send only one team with a member who knows the area.

Remember there is still treasure out there and so are the maps. A lot of people, especially groups like outlaws, pirates and the Spanish left the clues to their treasures carved in rocks and on rock bluffs. It's something that happens quite often, but if not looked at it in the proper way one might not realize when a clue is directly in front of them. When most people see a map or a clue carved into a rock or bluff they assume it is some type of graffiti because they aren't looking at it the way it was intended to be seen. Finding these types of clues and even an entire map is almost as exciting as working the map to a discovery. Good luck with this legend trip and I hope you find something.

Here is the equipment list I use when I go out legend tripping for treasure:

Treasure Legend Trip

- Camera—one that has IR capabilities
- Camera stands and pods
- GPS
- Cold weather clothes
- Backpack (with items mentioned in backpack list)
- Metal detector
- Shovel (folding)
- Binoculars
- Poncho

202

Chapter 13
Mysterious Places

There are more than a few mysterious places on this planet. There are too many to count in the United States and Canada. If you don't believe me, just look it up on the Internet. Now when it comes to legend tripping I always like the free or inexpensive mysterious places. In this chapter, I picked out some of my favorite mysterious places. Most of them you have heard of, some of them maybe not.

Ringing Rocks Park.

I first read of Ringing Rocks Park in Ivan T. Sanderson's 1967 book *Things*. In this unique place, located deep in the woods of Upper Black Eddy, Pennsylvania, is a large field of mysterious boulders which, when struck, sound like bells as if hollow and made of metal. Each summer, hundreds of visitors flock there, hammers in hand, to perform their own "rock concerts." While scientists have determined the stones are made from a volcanic substance called diabase, there's no explanation for their unusual ringing properties, nor for

the eight-acre field itself, which is situated high on a hillside, not at the bottom, which may rule out it having been formed by a glacier or avalanche. This is not the only place on Earth where this phenomenon

The Ringing Rocks of Upper Black Eddy, PA.

203

happens; there is a similar location outside Whitehall, Montana. I've visited this incredible place during my visits to Pennsylvania. It is free to visit, but you need to bring your own hammer. There is also a waterfall near the rocks, making the trek a scenic adventure.

Coral Castle

This strange-looking site is on the top of most lists of mysterious places in the United States. The enigmatic structures here are made from 1,100 tons of megalithic-style limestone boulders—some heavier than the Pyramids' and bigger than those at Stonehenge. This unusual structure is located in the town of Homestead, Florida, just 25 miles south of Miami. Built from 1923 to 1951 by a single man, a diminutive Latvian immigrant named Edward Leedskalnin, this collection of stones was supposedly an homage to the love of his life who left him on the eve of their wedding. But how did he do it? Leedskalnin claimed he knew the secret to the Great Pyramid's construction, and was once witnessed levitating stones. Other construction details—no mortar, precision seams, and impossible balancing acts—have also stumped scientists for decades. This mysterious place has been featured on numerous television shows like *In Search Of, Unsolved Mysteries,* and *That's Incredible*, to name a few. The price for admission is $15.00 for adults and $7.00 for children. There are holiday special deals so I recommend you check before visiting.

204

Part of Coral Castle in Homestead, FL.

Mount Shasta

This beautiful and stunning snow-capped peak located right outside of Redding, California has long been shrouded in mystery. It is part of the Cascade Mountain range and is located 60 miles south of the Oregon border. To UFO and paranormal enthusiasts this area has long been considered one of the planet's great "cosmic power spots," luring everyone from Native Americans to Buddhist monks and hippies. Its sacred slopes are home to a potpourri of mysteries: spontaneous altered states; UFO sightings; crystal caves; encounters with Ascended Masters; underground military bases; even the rumored home to two alien races. The Lemurians, surviving members of a sensitive super-race some believe existed 12,000 years ago during the time of Atlantis and the lost continent of Mu (in the Pacific) are said to abide thre. The idea of aliens using Mount Shasta may have been the inspiration for author Alexander H. Keys' book *Escape to Witch Mountain* which features two alien children trying to piece together their past, making their way with a secret map to Witch Mountain. There have also been numerous Bigfoot sightings on the

Mount Shasta in northern California.

205

Legend Tripping

mountain, making it a hotbed for crytpozoologists. There are also numerous trails along the mountain making it a popular place for avid hikers. The mountain was featured on the popular television show *Ancient Aliens*.

In the Oregon Vortex House of Mystery.

Oregon Vortex

This curious and enigmatic site in southern Oregon has long attracted visitors and has been a tourist stop since the 1930s. Here, balls roll uphill, brooms stand on end, and people appear to grow and shrink inside its centerpiece, a former gold mining outpost called the House of Mystery. Measuring 165 feet in diameter the area is known for producing intense feelings of vertigo. Native Americans referred to it as Forbidden Ground. The vortex's strange phenomenon is well documented, and animals still refuse to enter its sphere. Skeptics state the whole thing is an optical illusion with other mystery houses around the United States using the same gimmicks as the Oregon Vortex. This is not true. Not all the strange things happening there are seen in other mystery houses, nor can they be logically explained, which is why every year thousands of visitors come to the Oregon Vortex. The attraction has been featured on television shows like *Incredible, Fact or Faked: Paranormal Files* and *Ancient Aliens*.

Roanoke Island

This island in Dare County on the Outer Banks of North Carolina is known for the abandoned

206

settlement or "The Lost Colony of Roanoke." The island was named after the historical Roanoke Carolina Algonquian people who inhabited the area in the 16th century at the time of English exploration. In 1587, the English again tried to settle Roanoke Island. John White,

Roanoke Island.

father of the colonist Eleanor Dare, and grandfather to Virginia Dare, the first English child born in the New World, left the colony to return to England for supplies. He expected to return to Roanoke Island within three months. Instead, with England at war with Spain, all ships were confiscated for use of the war office. White's return to Roanoke Island was delayed until 1590, by which time all the colonists had disappeared and the settlement was abandoned. The only clue White found was the word "CROATOAN" carved into a tree. Before leaving the colony three years earlier, White had left instructions that if the colonists left the settlement, they were to carve the name of their destination, with a Maltese cross if they left due to danger. "Croatoan" was the name of an island to the south (modern-day Hatteras Island), where a native tribe friendly to the English was known to live. Colonists might have tried to reach the island. However, foul weather kept White from venturing south to search on Croatoan for the colonists, and he returned to England. White never returned to the New World. Unable to determine exactly what happened, the fate of the people has become a source of legend.

Bridgewater Triangle

In the southeastern part of Massachusetts is an area of about 200 square miles where alleged unexplained

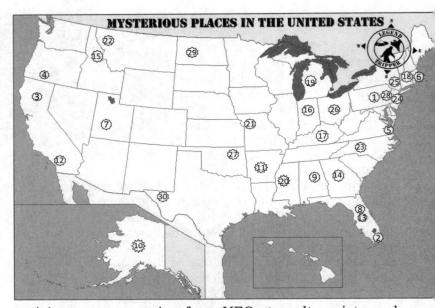

activity occurs, ranging from UFOs to poltergeists and orbs, balls of fire and other spectral phenomena, various Bigfoot sightings, giant snakes and thunderbirds, as well as the mutilation of cattle and other livestock. Cryptozoologist and paranormal investigator Loren Coleman conducted an investigation of the area in 1970 and dubbed it the Bridgewater Triangle. Paranormal-Encyclopedia.com calls the triangle one of the world's most concentrated areas of diverse paranormal reports. The towns of Raynham, Taunton, Brockton, Mansfield, Norton and Easton are all located in the triangle with Bridgewater nearly in the dead center. The Hockomock Swamp is the hub of many paranormal reports within the triangle, and remains shrouded in superstition to this day. The Wampanoag Tribe feared the swamp, calling it "the place where evil spirits dwell." Since 1908 there have been a multitude of UFOs sighted within the triangle. Reports of a large hairy bipedal creature prowling the area have come in since the 1970s. Also

208

1. Ringing Rocks, PA
2. Coral Castle, FL
3. Mount Shasta, CA
4. Oregon Vortex, OR
5. Roanoke Island, VA
6. Bridgewater Triangle, MA
7. Skinwalker Ranch, UT
8. Astor, FL
   Gravity Hills:
9. Oak Grove, AL
10. Anchorage, AK
11. Alma, AR
12. Altadena, CA
13. Lake Wales, FL
14. Cummings, GA
15. Grangeville, ID
16. Mooresville, IN
17. Covington, KY
18. Greenfield, MA
19. Blaine Township, MI
20. Burnsville, MS
21. Freeman, MO
22. Columbus Falls, MT
23. Richfield, NC
24. Franklin Lakes, NJ
25. Middlesex, NY
26. Kirkland Hills, OH
27. Bartlesville, OK
28. New Paris, PA
29. Rapid City, SD
30. El Paso, TX

giant birds have been seen in Hockomock Swamp. There is a DVD released in 2015 on Bridgewater Triangle phenomena.

The Skinwalker Ranch

The east coast has the Bridgewater Triangle and the west coast has Utah's Skinwalker Ranch. Originally called Sherman Ranch, it is located in west Uintah County, southeast of Ballard, Utah bordering the Ute Indian Reservation; it is approximately 480 acres. According to UFO enthusiasts, it is a hotbed of extraterrestrial and paranormal activity. Since 1974 there have been hundreds of reports of unexplained incidents including vanishing and mutilated cattle, sightings of UFOs, large glowing orbs, large animals with piercing red eyes, and invisible objects emitting destructive magnetic fields. The last family who lived on the ranch were plagued with poltergeists, shape shifters, and other forms of paranormal harassment, and moved out after twenty months. They sold the property to the National Institute for Discovery Science (NIDS) director/owner Robert T. Bigelow in 1996. The new ranch owner conducted a thorough, round-the-clock investigation of the property. The ranch is considered private property and is set up like a fortress, nearly impossible to access. You can however, drive the roads bordering the ranch. Some investigators have done this with some successful results. There are numerous books on the Skinwalker Ranch.

Astor, Florida

This small town located in north central Florida is considered by many investigators to be ground zero for the paranormal, the extraterrestrial and the unexplained. I mentioned this town here because it has every legend out there. I could write a book on this creepy hamlet alone.

Astor is located almost due north of Orlando and due west of Daytona Beach, with the St. Johns River running along the west side. The land around Astor was originally inhabited by the Timucua Indians. If you travel on State Road 40, you will go right through Astor.

This little town has had reports of Skunk Apes prowling the surrounding forest; a dinosaur-like river monster known as "Pinky" sighted by numerous witnesses in the Saint Johns River (Chapter 5, Aquatic Cryptids); numerous UFO sightings nearby; various disappearances in the nearby swamps from pirates to surveyors and soldiers. Reports of hauntings include a haunted lighthouse and the ghostly specter of a monk tied to a tree by Indians and left to die in the swamps.

Astor, along with Lake and Marion counties, has a long history of Skunk Ape sightings. Many of the sightings have occurred just south of Astor near Alexander Springs, an area popular for Florida Bigfoot hunting groups.

Gravity Hills

Another oddity with a possible paranormal origin is the mystery of the gravity hills. These are places where unseen forces will move objects uphill. Though most are believed to be optical illusions, they are fun to visit. Stephen Wagner writes about them on the website About.com:

There are dozens of mystery spots to be found around the U.S., and many more gravity hills—places where gravity itself seems to be warped. Our perceptions of up, down, straight

210

and crooked are confused by what some say are powerful gravitational anomalies and dizzying magnetic vortexes. Is this the case, or are our senses being fooled by clever man-made and natural optical illusions?

Two interesting places defying all laws of gravity are both called Spook Hill. You have one in the small town of Middlesex, New York, on Newell Road. Right before you reach a driveway and Spike Road on your left, place your car in neutral and you will find your car is moving backwards …uphill! This strange phenomenon also works with people on bikes, general round objects and even water. Legend has it near Canandaigua Lake lies a Native American burial ground, causing the strange things to happen in this area. To get there you follow Route 364 through Potter and Middlesex. Turn left onto South Vine Valley Road and then turn left onto Newell Road.

The other Spook Hill is located in Lake Wales, Florida, close to the downtown area and across the street from the Lake Wales High School. This quaint citrus and cattle town surrounds Lake Wailes for which the town was named, yet misspelled. One of Florida's oldest tourist attractions, it is still free to see. Legend behind the gravity hill tells of an Indian village on the shores of Lake Wailes that was plagued by the raids of a huge gator. The chief, a great warrior, killed the gator in a

A sign for Spook Hill, Lake Wales, FL.

211

battle that created a small lake, and where the chief was later buried on the north side. Pioneer mail riders first discovered their horses laboring downhill, thus naming it "Spook Hill." When the road was paved, cars coasted uphill. I remember visiting this when I was young. Unfortunately, with the refurbishing of the road and the housing area next to it, the gravity effect is not as prominent as it used to be when I was a kid. The adjacent elementary school in Lake Wales is named Spook Hill Elementary and features Casper the Friendly Ghost as its mascot. This is the only time Harvey Comics has allowed Casper to be used. A sign marking the start point of Spook Hill is on the east side of N. Wales Drive/5th St. about a quarter mile south of Hwy 17/Burns Ave. Spook Hill Elementary is right next to it and the high school is across the street.

There is a gravity hill in Richfield, North Carolina. Legend says a young woman was trying to push her stalled car up the hill, her baby in the back seat, when a truck struck and killed both instantly. Today, if you go to the hill and put your car in neutral, your car will go up the hill on its own. Also, if you apply baby powder to the back of your car, you will see the mother's handprints.

I was going to list more gravity hills, but that information would fill an entire book. There is a gravity hill in almost every state in the US. Look on the Internet to find the one nearest you. They are all free to visit and experience.

Chapter 14
Day Legend Trips

These people have seen something. What it is, I do not know and I am not curious to know.
—Albert Einstein, physicist, on UFO sightings

When it comes to legend tripping, it's not just about Bigfoot or ghost hunting. It's about everything from the beginning, middle to the end. What I mean by this is plan stuff en route to the legend trip. There is nothing saying you can't stop along the way and look at other sites. Sometimes the journey is just as important as the destination.

There are what I call day legend trips. These are places you can go visit during the day or nighttime but you can't camp out or stay there. An example would be Coral Castle. You can pay and visit it, but you can't stay and conduct an investigation. Your first thought may be this isn't very exciting. My answer is day legend trips can and are just as exciting as other legend trips. You'll find you will feel the same excitement doing this as you would if you were looking for Bigfoot or ghosts. What is more exciting than standing on a mountain and watching mysterious lights dance around? Are they the lights from UFOs or from Indian spirits wandering the mountains, looking for their lost loves? What about standing where a flying saucer crashed and its occupants died, only to have the military spirit it away to some hidden warehouse? There are all kinds of different day legend trips to do.

Halloween is a great time to go legend tripping. A lot of haunted places have special ghost hunts and tours.

Legend Tripping

I'm not talking about haunted houses that have been fixed up with people in costumes or electronic devices. I mean real—or supposed real—haunted places.

Also some people can only do day trips as their schedules allow. Me, I like to incorporate day legend trips into my other ones. In other words, if I'm heading up to New York for an aquatic cryptid legend trip, I'll check and see what's on the way up and do day legend trips.

Museums

I like to visit museums on the way to or returning from legend trips. I am a huge Ripley's Believe It or Not fan. There are over twenty-two Ripley's Odditorium sin the United States and Canada. Every one of them has a section on the unexplained. Whenever I plan a legend trip to a different state I look to see if there is a Ripley's Odditorium on the way or close by. Especially when I take my family on trips, I'll check to see if there is an Odditorium in the area. The entrance price is not bad and there is a lot to see. My family and I have been to a total of twelve of Ripley's attractions, including the now-closed World of the Unexplained. The great thing about Ripley's attractions is they are located all over the United States and they're all different. My favorite Ripley's is the one located in St. Augustine, Florida. It is the first and oldest permanent collection of Ripley's, and it is located in a castle that is reported to be haunted. I have also had the privilege of visiting the Ripley's warehouse in Orlando. Ripley's Believe It or Not in St. Augustine also has a ghost train to take tourists to locations in the city that are supposed dwellings of the paranormal.

If a legend trip is going to take more than a day while traveling to a different state, this is where these museums come in. Plan a pit stop to look at things on the way. It doesn't have to be Ripley's museums; stop and check out other museums and aquariums. Some of them even have a section on local legends and mysteries. The roadside stops can be fun.

There is one museum I would like to mention. It was probably the neatest one I ever went to and the memories of the place have always stuck with me. It also inspired me to go legend tripping.

Back in the mid-1970s, Ripley's had three museums, one being located in Chicago and the others at Fisherman's Wharf, California, and Gatlinburg, Tennessee. The Gatlinburg museum was called World of the Unexplained. I had the privilege of visiting the latter one in 1976. I remember finding the museum's pamphlet at the Tennessee visitor's center and I begged my parents into letting my brother and me go into the museum, since we were passing through Gatlinburg. Since my mom wanted to stop for lunch, my dad relented and allowed us to go. As luck would have it, the museum was easy to find on the main street. There on the television hanging over the entrance was Leonard Nimoy talking about the unexplained and encouraging viewers to go in and see

The original brochure for World of the Unexplained.

the incredible exhibits. I didn't need much encouraging. My brother and I entered and were in awe at what we saw. The first thing we saw was a life-size statue of Bigfoot. They even had whole sections on UFOs and the Bermuda Triangle. There was a séance display with the table actually moving. There was also a fortuneteller with a crystal ball. Inside the crystal ball was a talking head of a woman. There was also a really neat werewolf exhibit. The museum had exhibits about voodoo, witchcraft, and ghosts. They even had a section on ancient astronauts.

For me, a kid who loved mysteries and the unexplained, this museum was awesome. On the humorous side, there was an exhibit in the witchcraft section of a young witch who was totally nude standing by a fireplace. Now remember, I was only twelve years old. My brother and I just stood there transfixed by this lovely young witch. Unfortunately, what I didn't know was my parents also went into the museum and caught up to us at the end. My mother was a little ticked off about the witch. My dad, on the other hand, also thought she was attractive. The whole experience further educated me on the unexplained and whet my appetite for more. The only thing that disappointed me was the museum didn't have a gift shop. It had a magic shop, which did not sell anything related to the museum except a souvenir booklet, postcards, and a lucky token coin. I still have the coin, booklet, and postcards. Unfortunately, all three

216

museums shut down in 1980s due to low ticket sales. All the attractions were either sent back to the Ripley's warehouse or relocated to other Ripley's establishments.

The International UFO Museum.

In Roswell, New Mexico there is an excellent museum. It is called the International UFO Museum. It first opened its doors in 1990 and is a 501(c)(3) non-profit educational organization with the mission of educating the general public on all aspects of the UFO phenomenon. People from around the world come to see some awesome exhibits of not only the Roswell Incident, but also crop circles, UFO sightings, Area 51, ancient astronauts and alien abductions. The museum is located at 114 North Main Street, Roswell, New Mexico and is open daily from 9:00 am to 5:00 pm. There is also an excellent gift shop in the museum.

Roswell also has an annual UFO festival around the end of June. It is a three-day event featuring guest speakers, authors, live entertainment, an alien and Men in Black costume contest, a pet costume contest, a parade, family-friendly activities and more. The festival starts off with a parade to celebrate one of the most debated incidents in history. Thousands of people attend this growing event each year. It is a must for any UFO enthusiast.

In Point Pleasant, West Virginia there is the Mothman Museum. This museum has the largest collection of memorabilia in the town where the Mothman sightings and encounters actually occurred, and props from the movie *The Mothman Prophecies*. There are also rare historical documents from Mothman eyewitnesses

217

Legend Tripping

Linda and Steve Scarberry, Steve and Mary Mallete and Mary Hyre, documenting what they experienced that fateful night of November 15, 1966. There are rare historical press clippings and photographs of the Silver Bridge disaster, and of author and historical figurehead John Keel of the Mothman legacy.

There is also a Mothman Festival in Point Pleasant during the third weekend in September. This festival commemorates the visit of the mysterious entity known as the Mothman. The festival features a wide variety of vendors, live local music, delicious food, a Miss Mothman pageant, a five-kilometer Mothman run and a tour of the areas where the Mothman was seen. Patrons from all over the world come to experience the unique atmosphere and learn more about the mysterious cryptid the Mothman.

Another museum that has a legend-tripping theme is the Museum of the Weird in Austin, Texas. This awesome museum has not only weird and mysterious attractions but also famous monsters of the movies, including King Kong. It reminds me of the old carnivals and their sideshows. During the Halloween season, the museum features a live midnight spook show reminiscent of the scary shows featured at movie theaters in the 1940s. The price is excellent, and there is something for everybody to enjoy. It also has one the best gift shops I have ever seen.

In 2013 the museum acquired the famous "Minnesota Iceman" exhibit. This famous roadside attraction from the 70s was thought to have been

218

lost, but was then discovered in a closed-down carnival. This attraction featured a large hairy bipedal creature frozen in ice. The figure fit the exact description of what witnesses claim Bigfoot looks like. If you were lucky enough to be growing up along the upper east coast of the United States, then chances are the exhibit was at a nearby mall or carnival.

Frank Hanson, the owner, claimed it was real and he had purchased it after it was found floating in the South China Sea. He later made claims he had, in fact, shot the animal on a hunting trip in Minnesota. After the FBI got involved over the display of a real cadaver, the attraction was revealed to be a fake. Mr. Hanson later stated he substituted the real one for a fake one he had had constructed in Hollywood to avoid problems with the authorities. There has always been speculation about whether the creature was real or a hoax. But now this rare oddity of the cryptozoology world can be seen at its permanent home at the Museum of the Weird. The Museum of the Weird is located on Sixth Street in downtown Austin, Texas. It is open daily from 10 am to midnight, seven days a week.

There are three Bigfoot museums, two in California and one in Georgia.

The first one in California is called the Capri Taurus Bigfoot Discovery Museum and is located at 5497 Hwy 9, Felton, CA. This museum mixes educational displays and serious evidence with a couple of generations of

219

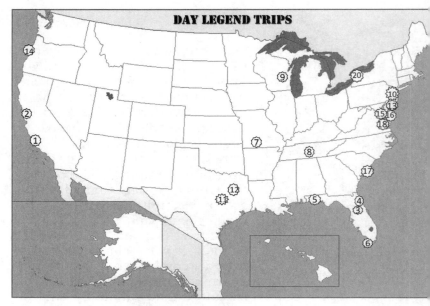

pop culture exploitation artifacts. It features Bigfoot in movies and fiction. A line of woodcarvings of creatures stands outside the museum. The Bigfoot Discovery Museum is open six days a week, closed on Tuesdays, 11 am to 6 pm.

The second one is called the Willow Creek China Flat museum and it features a Bigfoot collection housed in its own wing. The museum is located on the west edge of the town of Willow Creek, on the north side of Hwy 299/Trinity Hwy just west of its intersection with Hwy 96. It's impossible to miss this museum, as it features a large Bigfoot statue right outside. The museum opened its Bigfoot collection in May of 2000. Many notable Bigfoot hunters, like author John Green, were there for the opening of the collection. The wing has on display one of the largest collections of Bigfoot footprint casts, and Bigfoot related pop culture toys, doodads, and collectibles. It should be noted the first Bigfoot sighting in the 1950s was at

220

Ripley's Believe It or Not Odditorium
1. Hollywood, CA
2. San Francisco, CA
3. Orlando, FL
4. St Augustine, FL
5. Panama City, FL
6. Key West, FL
7. Branson, MO
8. Gatlinburg, TN
9. Wisconsin Dells. WI
10. Atlantic City, NJ
11. Grand Prairie, TX
12. San Antonio, TX
13. New York City, NY
14. Newport, OR
15. Ocean City, MD
16. Baltimore, MD
17. Myrtle Beach, SC
18. Williamsburg, VA
19. Cavendish, CAN
20. Niagara Falls, CAN
Museums
21. International UFO museum, NV
22. Mothman Museum, WV
23. Museum of the Weird, TX
24. Capri Taurus Bigfoot Discovery, CA
25. Willow Creek/China Flat museum, CA
26. Expedition Bigfoot, GA
27. International Cryptozoology museum
28. Paranormal Museum, NJ
29. Warrens Occult Museum, CT
30. Zaffis Museum of the Paranormal, CT

Day Legend Trips

Willow Creek, when a logger named Jerry Crew wandered into town with a plaster cast of a giant footprint he found around the equipment being used for logging. Willow Creek is known as the Bigfoot Capital of Northern California.

Willow Creek also has an annual Bigfoot Celebration. Each Labor Day weekend the small town celebrates the life and times of the large hairy giant. The whole thing kicks off with a Bigfoot parade and then there are vendors and presentations by famous Bigfoot hunters. One of the popular items to purchase is a map showing all Bigfoot sightings. Willow Creek claims to have had the most sightings of Bigfoot anywhere in the world. The celebration was featured on Discovery Channel's *Bigfoot Country* special.

The new museum in Georgia is called Expedition Bigfoot. It opened in February 2015. It is the first museum in the eastern United States totally dedicated the large cryptid beast. The museum not only features Bigfoot, but also the Yeti and large cryptids from other countries. There are life-size displays of Bigfoot and a large collection of Bigfoot castings. There are displays of the famous 1924 Ape Canyon incident, where miners were attacked by a group of angry Bigfoot. There is an excellent gift shop with an awesome T-shirt design. The museum is located north of Atlanta

Legend Tripping

at 1934 Highway 515-S in Cherry Log, Georgia. It is open six days a week (closed on Tuesday) 10 am to 5 pm.

The next museum I want to talk about is the International Cryptozoology Museum. It is the only museum of its kind in the world. Author and cryptozoologist Loren Coleman first opened the museum in the first floor of his home about 10 years ago, but as the collection got bigger, moved to a more central location in downtown Portland, Maine. The museum has been featured on numerous television shows, the most recent being the Travel Channel's *Mysteries of the Museum*. The museum contains roughly 10,000 items displayed in cases within two main rooms. Over 50 years of collecting by Loren Coleman are displayed in this museum, with some pieces donated by cryptozoologists around the world. Over 10,000 visitors flock each year to examine evidence of Bigfoot and other cryptids. The International Cryptozoology Museum is open from 11 am to 3:30 pm, six days a week, including Monday holidays. It is closed on Tuesdays.

The names Ed and Loren Warren are synonymous with ghost hunting. In fact, they wrote the book on conducting paranormal investigations. Their investigations have become a thing of legend in the paranormal investigation world. The 2013 movie *The Conjuring* is about one of their investigations. The Warrens collected hundreds of items from their investigations that they put in a room in their house. One of the popular items in the collection is a Raggedy Ann doll named Annabelle that sits in a glass cabinet with a sign saying, "Do Not Open." This doll gained fame from the 2015 movie by the same name. Legend has it that in 1970 this demonic doll terrorized a family for months until the Warrens were called in and an exorcism was performed. Although Annabelle has been exorcised several times, the Warrens believe that some energy is still attached to this doll. Annabelle is believed to be responsible for the death of a young man who came in and taunted it. The collection is now a must-see for paranormal investigators or legend trippers. This world-renowned museum has attracted hundreds of thousands of visitors from across the world. The museum is located at Monroe, Connecticut. It is not open to the general public. Go to the museum's website for information on tours and events. http://www.warrens.net/Occult-Museum-Tours.html

If you are ever in Ashbury, New Jersey there is a little paranormal bookstore that is also a paranormal museum. It is a small, storefront museum, which has a collection of historical and educational exhibits that explore the unexplained myths, legends and folklore; it has a whole section on New Jersey's famous cryptid the Jersey Devil. The museum was created for the purpose of exploring those mysteries that remain in our modern world of science and reason. It is a showcase of all that exists in the borderland betwixt imagination and reality. The exhibits featured in the museum bring to life the myths, legends, folklore and superstitions through genuine artifacts and artful interpretations. Visitors to the museum are invited to explore the real-life history and diverse culture woven into the fabric of each unsolved paranormal mystery. In the end, it is up to each of us to decide what is a fantasy and what could be truly possible. The Paranormal Museum is located in downtown Ashbury Park at 627 Cookman Ave. It is open Monday, Thursday, Friday, Sunday 12 pm to 6 pm. Saturday it stays open to 9 pm. Tuesday and Wednesday closed.

Conferences/Conventions
Another great thing to do with legend trips is the conferences. There are different kinds of conferences from cryptozoology and the paranormal to UFOs. To find when and where the next conference is check the Internet; all these conferences have websites.

One of the most popular in the cryptozoology field is the annual International Cryptozoology Conference. The first one was held January 2016 in St. Augustine, Florida and featured many notable experts in the cryptozoology field like Loren Coleman, Lyle Blackburn, Cliff Barackman, Kathy Strain, and Paul LeBland.

There are numerous Bigfoot conferences around the United States. I'm going to go over them according to the month the conference takes place. There is always a new conference each year, so I apologize for not mentioning all of them.

Probably one of the most popular Bigfoot conferences is the Ohio Bigfoot Conference. It is held during the month of May. The conference has grown into the premier Bigfoot conference, drawing thousands of people each year. The event features top-rated speakers from across the Bigfoot community who share their experiences and knowledge on the subject of Sasquatch. From television personalities, academics, local and national investigators and other prominent figures, the conference has something for everyone. The conference is held at Salt Fork State

224

Park Lodge in Cambridge, Ohio

In August there is a Virginia Bigfoot Conference held at the Hemlock Haven Conference Center in Hungry Mother Park. The park itself has a bizarre legend of a mother who died with her child in her arms. The child and the mother perished.

There is the International Bigfoot Conference held in Kennewick, Washington during the month of September. It too features many notable experts in the Bigfoot field.

Texas has a Bigfoot conference during the month of October. It is held in the city of Jefferson. This conference started in 2001 and has been getting bigger every year.

There are also numerous paranormal conferences held around the country. Here is some information about a few.

The Haunted America Conference in Alton, Illinois is considered one of the premier paranormal conferences. Started in 1997 by author/legend tripper Troy Taylor it is called America's Original Ghost Conference and is one of the longest running. It features lectures and workshops on ghost hunting. It also features tours/ghost hunts of local haunted locations. The conference is held in June at the Atrium Hotel in downtown Alton. There are vendors selling some of the new ghost hunting equipment.

Another popular paranormal conference is the Las Vegas Paracon held in Goldfield, Nevada. It features a lot of the paranormal investigators seen on popular ghost hunting shows. It is held in August and features a parade as well as ghost hunts in popular locations around Goldfield.

In October there is the Utah Paranormal Festival. It is held at Crone's Hollow in downtown Salt Lake City. Like all conferences there are guest speakers quite prominent in the paranormal field, and lectures and workshops.

Here is a list of some of the popular UFO conferences around the country.

The UFO/Paranormal Summit is a showcase of presentations featuring research and evidence of unidentified flying objects, alien life, portals and the paranormal, presented by the world's highest authorities on such topics. It is one of the only conferences for both ghost hunters and UFO investigators. It is held in March at Quinault Beach Resort in Ocean Shores, Washington.

MUFON (Mutual UFO Network) has an annual conference, which is presented at a different location each year. It is considered one of the premier UFO conferences in the country. Guest speakers talk about some of the latest news in the extraterrestrial world.

The MUFON Symposium, like the conference, is held in different locations each year. This is for MUFON field investigators and features lectures, but also up-to-date training in the world of UFOs and extraterrestrials.

Obviously, it is not hard to find conferences to gain and develop knowledge of cryptids, ghosts, and UFOs.

I want talk about some of the day legend trips I've done over the years. I'm relating thesw adventures to show how easy and exciting day tripping can be.

In 2010 my wife Tracy and I were in Bucks County in Pennsylvania on vacation. Tracy grew up there and knows the area like the back of her hand. As I said earlier, we stayed at a haunted bed and breakfast. We also visited some areas described in the book *Weird Pennsylvania* by Matt Lake. We went to Ghost Mountain, where legend has it a bunch of albino cannibals in Upper Black Eddy attack motorists whose cars have broken down. The legend also says

226

the albinos live in a glass house easily seen from the road. We didn't see any albinos but we did see the glass house, which turned out to be a pool house owned by a doctor.

We also went and saw the Bucks County pyramids. They belong to a secret society and are on private property. Visible from the road, it is not accessible by foot. We also went to Ringing Rocks Park and got to bang on the rocks that sound just like bells. It's amazing and it's free. All the previously-mentioned locales are free. Granted, the pyramids are not open to the public, but pictures can be taken of them from the road.

My stepson Jesse found an old cave and he took us there to see it. It was one of the neatest things I've seen. We found out that it was an old smuggler's

The author with his stepson at the Bucks County pyramids.

227

cave that was also used by the Underground Railroad. Again, it is not visible from the main road and a walk through the woods is required to find it. We didn't find any beer cans there or graffiti on the walls, so obviously not a lot of people know about this cave.

In 2012 I took my family on a legend trip down to Homestead, Florida, to visit Coral Castle. It was just as I remembered it being when I last visited when I was five years old. After staying in the area overnight, we proceeded to the Everglades and visited Dave Shealy's Skunk Ape Research Headquarters at Ochopee, Florida. Dave has a small petting zoo, and we had a great time holding snakes and alligators. I have known Dave a long time and consider him a close friend. He opened his zoo to my family and they got more hands-on with the alligators and snakes than at any expensive animal park. We then visited Solomon's Castle in the small little town of Ona. Howard Solomon has a great art museum and excellent restaurant that is not too expensive All these places on one legend trip. The weather was great, and we stayed at hotels were not expensive.

On a day legend trip we took to Jupiter, Florida we did have a strange experience while visiting the lighthouse. We (Tracy, our six kids, my father-in-law, and I) went to the top of the lighthouse as part of a tour. My mother-in-law could not come up because of knee problems, so remained at the bottom, near the lighthouse entrance. While we were looking around at the view, we all heard what sounded like somebody coming up the metal stairs. I instantly thought my mother-in-law had changed her mind and was coming up. I immediately looked inside but saw nobody. I went back out and looked down and saw her sitting on a park bench. I yelled down to her and asked if anybody was coming up. She replied there was nobody down there with her. I thought this strange. The tour guide, who was watching me, came over and related the lighthouse was supposed to be haunted. We all went back inside and looked down the lighthouse shaft and listened. We didn't hear anything more.

Recently I found something really cool in central Florida. There is a Boy Scout camp called Bigfoot Wilderness Camp, which happens to be located in the middle of the Green Swamp. One time, I took our cadets (Venturing Crew) on a weekend outing to Bigfoot Wilderness Camp. During the day, we taught the cadets outdoor survival skills such as using a compass, making a shelter, and making a fire with wood. In the early evening, I broke the cadets into three groups and, along with an adult they did a Bigfoot hunt down some of the hiking trails. One of the groups ended up hearing some noises they couldn't identify. When they all returned, I got them around the campfire and started telling scary Bigfoot stories. When I knew they were all getting scared and looking over their shoulders into the woods, I had my son jump out in a gorilla suit. After a lot of screaming and running, they all enjoyed a big laugh at their own expense, and they all got their picture taken with Bigfoot.

On a side note: if hotels are the preferred form of lodging on a legend trip, then make sure to scout around for the best deals. Remember, unless the hotel is the object of the investigation, it is only there as a place to crash in the evening. If bringing kids, then the hotel will have to have a swimming pool. If traveling with an active duty military or retired, check and see if there is a military post close by and stay at the guesthouse. The navy base in Key West has some awesome guesthouses to stay in at a really great price. Don't waste trip money on hotels. The great

229

thing about the Internet is every tourist attraction and lodging has a website to check the prices. Sometimes you can find seasonal deals and discounts. A word of caution: a lot of the really cheap motels are located in the bad part of town, so be careful.

Here is what to carry in the backpacks for day legend trips:

- Camera with night vision
- Survival kit
- First-aid kit—include poison ivy cream, moleskin for blisters
- Foot powder (cold weather)
- Petroleum jelly (hot weather and swamps)
- Extra socks
- Canteen with cup
- Flashlight (two)—always carry a headlamp and an extra flashlight
- GPS (with extra batteries)/Map of area
- Compass—in case the GPS stops working
- Poncho (for use in bad weather or as a shelter)
- Rain gear
- Back-up knife
- Water purifier pump
- Plaster casting kit
- Binoculars
- Trail camera
- 550 parachute cord
- Marking kit
- Bear mace
- Machete
- Food (beef jerky, trail mix, peanut butter crackers, and an MRE)
- Solar wrap used to recharge a cell phone or GPS
- Toilet paper/baby wipes (you will need them)
- Sunscreen/bug spray

230

Chapter 15
Critical Thinking

Science is defined in the dictionaries as
the pursuit of the unknown; yet science
today is coming more and more to insist
that it not be bothered with this, and it
has reached a point where anything that
is not already known is frowned upon.
—*Ivan T. Sanderson*

One day, I stopped at a gas station to fuel up my
vehicle. On the back on the spare tire, I have my legend
tripper logo on the tire cover. Some young men pulled
up to the gas pump behind me. I heard them laughing
and talking about my logo. Then one of the boys stated,
"You know there is no Bigfoot out there." I looked over
at them and smiled and said, "Well that's a matter
of opinion." Again the boys laughed and whispered
comments to each other. Then out of the blue, one of
the boys stated, "My dad saw this large and hairy thing
in the woods a while back, and he said it wasn't a bear."
The boys all stopped laughing and looked at the boy.
The boy looked at his friends and said, "You know my
dad, and you know he wouldn't make that up." I asked
the boy where his dad saw it, and he told me the area.
One of the other boys then said to me, "Are you going to
look for it?" To which I nodded my head. I then finished
fueling up the vehicle and I waved back at the boys and
left.

When I started legend tripping, the first thing I
ran into was people who didn't believe in legends and
some would say that I was wasting my time. With
legend tripping, why is dealing with people that do not

believe in legends or the unexplained necessary?

Critical thinking is defined as disciplined thinking that is clear, rational, open-minded, and informed by evidence.

Unfortunately, there are people out there who think there are no such things as monsters, ghosts, or UFOs, and that legend tripping is a waste of time. I've noticed a lot of "city folk" are quick to dismiss the existence of cryptids or unknown creatures or ghosts. I guess they sleep better at night believing there is nothing in the woods or in old abandoned houses to scare them. One gentleman didn't want me talking about Bigfoot around his kids for fear they would have nightmares. After seeing the movie *The Legend of Boggy Creek*, the whole "being scared" thing didn't sit well with me. I didn't like being scared, and I had to find out more about this large hairy monster. I started reading about cryptozoology and I have been interested in this stuff ever since. Not everybody believes in Bigfoot, flying saucers, or ghosts. As a legend tripper, running into skeptics is always a hazard. Be ready for that kind of negativity regarding certain legends. I'm not saying these people are right, but they are entitled to their opinion. When it comes to family, remember the saying, "You can lead a horse to water, but you can't make it drink." In other words, you can take your children on a Bigfoot hunt, but that isn't necessarily going to make them a believer. Actually, don't push your beliefs on them. I do ask my family to keep an open mind when we go on a legend trip. I encourage them to really listen to what people are telling them and remember that not everybody tells the

232

truth.

A legend is still a legend until it is confirmed, and then it becomes a fact. As the definition of critical thinking says: "open-minded." I always tell people I am open-minded to any theory out there. As our children become young adults, their ideas, values, and morals develop. We need to encourage them to take all the information they are given and create their own hypothesis for what they believe exists and how they want to handle a legend, a problem in their life, peer pressure, or life itself.

Today's schoolteachers use critical thinking as part of their teaching strategy because it encourages students to think beyond what they are reading. Most students will read what they are told to read. But because they have no interest in the text, they are just looking at words. They do not comprehend what they are reading. With critical thinking, people are encouraged to analyze and question what they are reading. Doing this helps them retain what's in the text. With critical thinking, challenge what is read or heard. With legend tripping, challenge belief in the unexplained.

There is nothing wrong with this kind of thinking and I encourage everybody to do this. My good friend and fellow teacher Ann McCarty related to me that, "The scientific method lets scientists study the unknown and then compile that data to see what is real and what is not, what is worth studying, and what is not. They can then create experiments that will allow thinking outside the existing 'facts' or 'world as we know it.' That is what scientists have been doing for hundreds of years. So, through the creative process it is possible to expand the way young people view the world or problem-solve, or even a vital part of their lives... just think about it, and the possibility that other things could exist."

My students love when I tell them stories of legend

tripping exploits. I don't order or tell them to believe my stories. I give them a little background on where I heard the legend. I don't want them believing in everything. If something sounds unbelievable, then they have every right to challenge it. I have found this out not only during my years as a legend tripper but as a military policeman. People don't always tell the truth, and they do make up stories of seeing Bigfoot, ghosts, or flying saucers. I have found they do this for a number of reasons. One is that they want to get on television. The second is that they do it for kicks and want to see if they can fool the experts. The third reason is that they do it out of boredom just to see what happens. Whatever the reason, it happens a lot. I treat all my sighting reports with skepticism. I'm very polite to the witness, but I do question if they did in fact see something. This is critical thinking, and there is nothing wrong with it. If we believed everything that was reported, then we would be the laughingstock of the scientific world.

Encourage critical thinking in your legend trips. If a friend or family member shares that they don't believe in Bigfoot or ghosts, then respect their belief. You can expose someone to these legends, but you can't make them believe. Have them give you good reasonable data why they think a legend doesn't exist! Tell them that they have to back their opinions up with facts or tests they have done or could do; this teaches them to take a stand, maybe different from everyone else, and have information to back their opinion. Unless you can produce a live Bigfoot for them to see or touch, then people are entitled to be unbelievers.

This doesn't mean you don't take people who don't believe on legend trips. It just means they are going to see things differently than you, and you all are going to have some pretty good conversations. There is nothing like debating a legend. It is a great way to communicate and makes for some interesting conversations. It shows them you are listening to them and that their opinions matter. My friend Ann McCarty is not a believer in Bigfoot, and she and I have had some great debates on the subject. I like hearing the "why" when scientists say an animal doesn't exist. This motivates me to go and find concrete facts to back up my beliefs.

Legend tripping is about exploring legends. Unfortunately, sometimes finding the legend reveals exactly that—it is just a legend and nothing more. That happened to an author friend while completing research for a book. It can be disappointing, but sometimes finding provocative information or inspirational locations can ease the pain of disappointment. Truth can sometimes be just as exciting as the legend. Young people will be more willing to go outside the box, in life, if they know what to expect from others, and if they learn to stand up for their ideas and debate them with others

The author at a Swamp Ape exhibit.

who do not think just as they do. This teaches them to work with others in their community because they become good listeners; and when they say something, it has true meaning to them because they have thought it over first.

Now, you may have family members who are too scared to go on a legend trip, especially if they're young. There have been many movies on the subject of Bigfoot and ghosts, and most show them in a scary, violent manner. Movie companies today do not want to make movies like *Harry and the Hendersons* or *Ghostbusters*, which show Bigfoot and ghosts in a friendlier way. The commercials for Jack Link's beef jerky have popularized Bigfoot and portrayed him in a manner to show he does exist. Young kids watch all of these and start to form their own opinion on the legends.

Ann suggested a way for parents to help their children develop critical thinking and learn to conduct simple experiments:

> With developing students, the teacher begins with small amounts of information and then scaffolds from that point and adds a little more each year—or as the students conquer one area, or step, at a time. Begin a science experiment by looking at and explaining the background information that already exists. This should be done to make known what is already out there to work with; do not reinvent the wheel. Then, begin with a simple hypothesis.
>
> For example: "If large animals walk on four legs, then the prints they leave behind will be smaller or shallower than the prints of animals that walk on only two." Then, run an experiment in the house or the backyard with a small pile of dirt and things you have at home. Children

can compare the household pet's paw prints to their own footprints; they can make prints of themselves walking on all fours and see how that compares with just standing, etc. They can compare by looking at them and talking about how they look different. As the children get older, they can compare them by measuring the depth of the prints from the surface of the dirt. This simple experiment can create long-lasting art, things to send to friends and family and to put on the Christmas tree: "My prints when I was five years old."

My father and mother do not believe in UFOs, ghosts, or monsters. Oddly enough, it was my mother who told me about the Loch Ness Monster. She grew up in Scotland and knew all about the famous cryptid. My parents even took me to see *The Legend of Boggy Creek*, but they don't believe in the unexplained. This does not bother me. It probably would bother me if they pretended to believe in it for my sake. My father is probably one of the most levelheaded men I have ever known, and he will tell it like it is. I always tell people, don't ask my dad if you don't want to hear the truth. He is what I call brutally honest, and I have always respected him for it. If he doesn't want to talk about a certain subject, he'll tell you point blank that he doesn't want to hear about it. He never put down my belief in the unexplained, but I don't suppose he cared for it. His thinking would be, "How can you make a living hunting ghosts or monsters?"

The point I'm making (and what I said at the beginning) is that not everybody is going to believe in monster hunting, and that shouldn't bother you. I show my friends and family members legend tripping, but I do not make them go. I do ask them to keep an open mind.

When my father would take me out fishing, we would talk for hours about things, and he would listen to what I was interested in. He would listen to my stories about Bigfoot and the Fouke Monster, but I think he just wanted see what degree of expertise I had on the subject. Again, he never put me down for my interest in legend tripping. My parents instilled one thing in both me and my brother: finish what you start. Never quit.

So I have promised myself that I will not stop looking for legends until I find them all. We know that is not going to happen, but at least I have a goal. Of course, I enjoy going out and looking for legends, and seeing things I would not see if we did not go out there. I am not afraid to let those who think differently question me or ask me why or how I believe this way. I know that I have changed my life and my family members' lives for the positive by teaching them this way to attack a problem or idea. Research always brings rewards, though it may not bring confirmation of your stated hypothesis; it could reveal a need for a new and better hypothesis for the next experiment.

There are many people putting videos on the Internet of supposed Bigfoot or other cryptids. Legend trippers definitely need to be critical about what appears on the Internet. Some people enjoy making bogus cryptid videos and putting them on the 'net and thinking they are fooling the monster hunters. Most cryptid hunters today are very critical of all videos that appear on the 'net.

I think that if a person believed he or she had actually filmed a real animal, the last place he or she would put it would be on the Internet, where everybody could download the video for free. Contrary to popular belief, not everything on the Internet is legit. Some reference sites have come under fire because they allow anybody

238

to go on them and change information. I tested this by going on a reference site and changing the birthplace of actor Leonard Nimoy to "Vulcan, Illinois." The sad part was that it remained on the site for a couple of months before the site owners discovered it and changed it back.

Recently I had the privilege of meeting Ed and Marsha Edmunds of Distortions Unlimited at the Spooky Empire horror convention in Orlando, Florida, where they had a booth. They make Halloween-type masks and props for haunted houses and other attractions, and are featured on the hit television show *Making Monsters*. Tracy and I are big fans of the show. One episode featured Ed and Marsha making a Sasquatch costume for Phillip Morris, who is the costume maker who claims to have made the original costume on the 1967 Roger Patterson film. I know of Mr. Morris from the book *How to Operate a Financially Successful Haunted House,* which he co-wrote with Dennis Phillips. Though I do like Mr. Morris's work, I'm not quite sure I believe he is the one who made the costume. I need to see more proof. When I met Ed and Marsha, I brought up the Bigfoot episode, and Ed told me—as he stated on the show—that he didn't believe in Bigfoot. We talked for about thirty minutes on the subject, and in the end Ed said that if I bring him a real Bigfoot he will believe in it. So now all I have to do is find me a real one. Easier said than done. But I did enjoy talking to him and his wife. They are extremely nice people, and I don't take offense that he doesn't believe in Bigfoot. I respect that he is honest about it. For the record, he makes an awesome Bigfoot costume.

Now I always believe it is important to keep an open mind when out legend tripping, but don't open it so wide brains fall out. In other words don't believe everything everybody says. Unfortunately, people, for whatever reason, do lie. There has been a recent increase in Bigfoot hoax videos on the Internet.

The most important idea to carry away from this is not everyone will share the same level of enthusiasm for legend tripping. This should not be a deterrent to going out and looking. Embrace it and use it to motivate the search for truth behind the legend. If family proves to be skeptical, then instead of getting upset, encourage them to join the next legend trip and show them how exciting it can be.

The author in his hammock doing some critical thinking.

Chapter 16
Outdoor Survival

Being prepared means no surprises.
"First Words," by Barri Segal,
American Survival Guide Magazine, Issue 6, Fall 2013

With the popularity of shows on Bigfoot and other cryptid animals, more and more people are taking to the woods and forests to find elusive animals. Most think it will be a simple day trip where they only have to bring out a camera, and many don't even have the thought cross their minds they could get lost. Some people don't even bring out a flashlight, fearing it might scare Bigfoot away. While most Bigfoot investigations take place at night, some investigators do look for footprints and evidence during the daylight hours. Novices make the mistake of journeying into the woods alone.

I have had the opportunity to go on Bigfoot hunts with many people. Some have been doing it for years and some are new to the field. Some of these fellow Bigfoot enthusiasts have never even gone camping and know nothing of the woods. Numerous times I have found myself showing people how to make fires and navigate in the woods, or telling them what to bring, instead of looking for Bigfoot. I've had to go look for people who have gotten lost when they set out to search for the cryptid animal, and I've had to help some set up their camp. I have no problem helping people in need. However, ignorance of the forest shouldn't be an issue when the general knowledge is that the wilderness can be dangerous. People who are new to Bigfoot hunting need to prepare themselves for this adventure.

I always think of the worst case scenario whenever

Legend Tripping

I go on outings. No matter how long I plan on being out there, I always plan for the worst. A legend trip should never be a spur of the moment thing. You need to always plan out your trip and plan for what might go wrong, like getting lost in the woods.

I know I have said this, but I can't stress enough: if you are new to legend tripping, specifically monster hunting, DO NOT GO OUT ALONE! Always have somebody with you; in fact it's better to have two extra people. I have learned that if one of you gets hurt, it's easier for the other two to aid the injured person and carry them back to the starting point. I find it better to go out with a fellow Bigfoot hunter and someone who's familiar with the area. Never go to an area at night without checking it out in the daytime and always let somebody know where you are going in case something should happen.

Every successful trip or expedition is a result of the people and the equipment. A well-planned-out legend trip is a successful and exciting one. I make no apologies about going into depth about putting together an equipment list. All the items I will go over with you are ones I have used and have worked for me. With equipment, I look for dependability and not a name brand. You may have different items than what I use. What you prefer to take is up to you. You need to bring equipment you are comfortable with and know how to use. You can add to or take away from these lists, depending where you are going and how long you are staying at the location. I am offering the basics. I always make a list to ensure I don't forget anything. Some people like to take a lot of electronic equipment with them. Don't go buy something because it looks neat. I, personally, like to keep it simple and not take extra weight.

Outdoor survival should be considered a priority

242

and incorporated into every legend trip plan. Every year, hundreds of hikers and campers get lost, and some die, out in the woods. The reports show they didn't properly think through what they would need or what could go wrong. I think it is great that people are starting to get back to nature and some are actually going on monster hunts. But I can't stress enough the importance of preparation and outdoor survival when it comes to legend tripping. If you are going to be out in the swamps or woods, your safety and that of your family and teammates should be a top concern, and this is where outdoor survival and self-reliance come into play.

Let me say for the record, I am not a survival expert, nor do I pretend to be. I have not attended any formal civilian or US Army Special Forces survival training. I have received basic survival training in the US Army. I have read a number of books on the subject and practiced some of the survival techniques, such as starting a fire. I have been deployed numerous times in the military and have spent a lot of time living in the woods. To date, I have not been in a survival situation, and I attribute that to good planning. I always try to prepare for the unexpected, especially if we are going into the woods. I always keep safety and survival in mind when preparing for a trip into the swamps or woodlands. For the sake of my team and my family, I don't want to be unprepared if something goes wrong.

One time while I was on a monster hunt, I observed some people who had never been in the woods before trying to start a fire. They took some big logs and tried to light them with a small plastic lighter. They didn't have a clue what they were doing and justified their actions by stating they had seen somebody do it on a television show. After observing their fruitless attempts, I showed them how to do it. Later I found out they also were not

243

prepared to go navigating at night. Again, I had to show them how to do it, and I ended up going with them to make sure they didn't get lost.

Another time, I went on a Bigfoot expedition and two of the members didn't bring a sleeping bag or tent. I asked them why not and they replied it doesn't get cold enough at night in Florida. Boy, were they ever wrong. One of them was military, and he said he knew what he was doing. I guess he knew he was going to be sitting by the campfire all night trying to keep warm. Don't ever plan to rough it in the wild. That is how people die. I always take a sleeping bag and tent with me whenever I go camping. You have to always plan for the unexpected.

If you are new to camping, then you should do a camp out at a local campground with facilities (i.e., showers and bathrooms). Sleeping outside for the first time is quite an experience. Also, you may want to attend an outdoor survival course, if one is available in your area. I highly recommend it. They can be expensive, but if you can't afford to go on a course, there are plenty of books on the subject. If you go this route, you need to practice outdoor survival skills before you go into the woods. Once you are out in the wild, there is no turning back.

One of the first best sellers was the *SAS Survival Handbook* by John "Lofty" Wiseman. It is a fully illustrated and practical guide to outdoor survival. Lofty has made two instructional videos on outdoor survival and recently introduced a survival app for your cell phone which is actually his book put into app form.

There are also plenty of survival shows on television. I like watching survival shows, and I am friends with a couple of the shows' hosts. They provide good information, and you can learn a great deal from watching them. One thing I have learned is to make sure you know every plant out there—especially poison ivy and oak.

I feel it important to talk about certain pieces of equipment you must have, and I want to go into detail on why and how to use these items. The items I believe are a must for an outdoor legend trip are knives, survival kits, first-aid kits, water, and safety necklaces. The last thing I want to mention is being in the proper shape, and as you will see, this does fall into outdoor survival.

Knives

The first thing I want to talk about is knives. A knife is one of the most important items to have whenever you go into the woods or swamps. Remember, a knife should be considered a tool and not a weapon. Small children should not have knives until they know and understand the importance of knife safety. Knives were not originally designed as weapons. A knife is only as good as the person who owns it and takes care of it. Every camping and survival book I have read says, "You've got to have a good knife." All I can add is it's true. Every time I have gone out to the swamps or woods, I've had to use a knife for some task.

There are all different kinds of knives and all with various uses. The purpose of this discussion is not to get you to buy a certain kind of knife, but I have learned a couple of lessons in my military career about the kinds of knives not to buy. When the *Rambo* movies came out, everyone had to go buy one of the survival knives. I bought one and it looked so cool and it had everything I would need to survive in the wild—or so I thought. The knife broke the first time I used it. The embarrassing part was, I was showing it off to some friends. Now I don't own or carry a big fancy survival knife or a "Rambo"-style knife. I don't choose a knife for its fancy looks, but get one that has everything for a survival situation. I will no longer buy a knife because some famous person has his name on it or endorses it.

At the end of World War II, returning American soldiers introduced the Swiss Army knife to the American public, and they have been popular ever since. My dad gave me my first Swiss Army knife, and I carried one for most of my childhood into my teens. Then I was introduced to the multi-tool. To this day, I carry a multi-tool with me. When my sons were deployed overseas, I made sure they had a multi-tool to take with them. I knew they would need it. There are one hundred different versions of multi-tools by different companies.

As you can imagine, there is quite a selection to choose from when it comes to knives. You need to choose the type of knife you are going to be comfortable using. I know people who spend a lot of money on a certain kind of knife and then don't know how to use it properly. I continue to test knives new to the market, but only if I think they are worthy of a try. If you have a knife you have been using for years and it works for you, then by all means continue to use it and carry it with you. Again, I'm not trying to push any kind of knife on you.

Here is a quick lesson on knives. There are two kinds of knives. The fixed blade is a knife with a blade and handle which are connected or are one piece, an example of which would be the army bayonet and the Ka-Bar. The other style is the folding blade knife which has a blade that will either be open or retracted into the handle, and the best known examples are the Swiss Army type and pocket knives. Outdoors, I prefer the fixed blade. When I was young, I owned a Swiss Army knife and it was pretty handy. But with the introduction of multi-tools, the Swiss Army knives are not as popular anymore.

Recently the small Swedish knife called a Mora knife has gained in popularity. The funny part is it looks like a steak knife with a dark green handle. At first I was hesitant to use it because it doesn't look like an outdoor knife. This little knife has held up to everything I have put it through so far. I'm not easy on knives, and I need a dependable one to withstand constant use. It's not a fancy-looking knife, but it hasn't broken on me, and it keeps its edge after continuous outdoor use. The only thing you can't do with it is chop down small trees, and if you are not careful you can in fact bend it. I'm not endorsing this knife; I'm just saying, don't be put off by a knife because of its appearance. It's a great knife, but there are some other great knives out there as well. You need to find a knife to meet your individual needs, when outdoors.

Some knives are made overseas in the Orient and the quality is poor and they break the first time you use them. Not all knives made in the Orient are poor quality, however. I own a handmade parang from Malaysia, and I think it is a great knife. My Mora-style knife was made in Sweden, and my multi-tool was made in the US; I have used them numerous times, and neither have ever let me down. When picking out a knife, make sure it has the metal tang, which is an extension of the blade that runs through the entire handle. Some of them don't, and they break the first time you use them. They are called rat tail knives and claim to be full tang knives. Stainless steel is a good metal, and it will not rust as easily. You'll know you've got a cheap one when it rusts the first time you take it outdoors.

I actually carry three knives with me. I have the knife I got when I was in the military, and I carry it on my belt. I carry my Mora knife inside my rucksack and a third backup knife on my rucksack strap. I always have backup knives in case I lose my main knife. I also have a multi-tool, which I also carry in my rucksack; it comes in handy when I need to fix equipment or make vehicle repairs. It is not an expensive one, and I carry it in my vehicle at all times.

Water

Water is the second thing I want to talk about, and I think it's pretty obvious why. Let's be real: you can't survive without it. A lot of weekend hikers and legend trippers do not take enough water with them. They think they are just going to be in the woods or forest for a couple of hours, and why carry around a heavy canteen? This is a disaster waiting to happen. I have been dehydrated, and I can tell you is not something I want to have happen again.

There is a survival saying: "humans can live three minutes without air, three days without water, and three weeks without food." Because of this, water needs to be a top priority on your packing list. If you are out in the woods and run out of water, then you're going to have to end your legend trip and go back. It happened to me with a friend, and now I don't go legend tripping with him anymore. I don't buy cases of water; instead I buy big collapsible water containers. It is a lot cheaper, and it gives you more room in your vehicle. Plus, you won't have all those empty plastic containers to deal with.

I always take a canteen with me, and I make sure it is filled up with water before I go out hiking. I prefer the two-quart military-style canteen. It is easier to carry than some of the new styles of containers. I also take water purification tablets and iodine in case I run out of water and have to get it from a stream or creek. I always put the water containers in a cooler with ice. There is nothing better than coming back to some cold

248

water after a hike. I'm not a big fan of energy drinks. They only work for a short period of time, plus, you have to deal with those empty plastic containers. I just stick to water.

In Cody Lundin's book *98.6 Degrees: The Art of Keeping Your Ass Alive!*, he puts 550 cord in a loop secured with duct tape on his canteen. This is a great idea and it doesn't take up any extra room. If you have to lower your canteen into a creek or stream, the loop makes it easier. In the southeastern part of the country you have to be careful of alligators and you might not want to get too close to the banks, so this really helps out. I highly recommend this book if you are looking for no-nonsense ideas for going out into the wild and surviving. I recently purchased a water purifier pump I carry with me. It was not expensive, and I now have another way to get clean water if ever I need it. Make sure you also carry iodine, either liquid or tablets, to purify water if you have to. Some of the purifying tablets on the market do not kill all the bacteria, like Giardia, and once bacteria get into your system, you can't find a bathroom quick enough. You can also purchase Iodine Tincture Solution which is two percent iodine and about forty-seven percent alcohol. Bottles of this solution should be available at your local drugstore, and a two-ounce bottle is usually three dollars or less. Just to let you know, iodine tastes awful but it does make the suspect water safe to drink. Keep the iodine in a dropper bottle for easy use. You can keep the iodine with the first-aid kit; just make sure you know exactly where it is when you need it.

If you do run out of water and you find a pond, lake, river, or stream, please remember this: clear water is better than cloudy water, and flowing water is better than still water, but even if the water looks extremely pure and clean, it should always be purified before drinking. Looks can be deceiving! If you can't boil the water (which the best way to purify water) then add five to ten drops of iodine tincture per thirty-two fluid ounces (about one liter) of water. The exact number of drops is a personal choice. Personally, I'm a fan of eight drops. If you are filling up a bottle or container that is not thirty-two fluid ounces or one liter, change your measurements accordingly. A two-liter bottle will require twice the number of drops. How much you use should depend on the water source (if your source is a lake or some other still body of water, you will want to add closer to ten drops; if the source is flowing, you can add fewer) and the clarity of the water (you should add closer to ten drops if the water is cloudy). Then you need to wait at least five minutes before you start drinking it. Be ready; it is still going to mess with your system. Have the toilet paper ready!

Survival Kit

The third thing that is a must is a survival kit, and I do stress the importance of having one with you. Though it is considered pretty standard, it should have everything you need in a survival situation. There are plenty of really good survival kits available on the market today. Most are priced at about thirty dollars and come in small, compact containers. There are even zombie survival kits and end-of-the-world survival kits. Whatever kit you purchase, just make sure you can carry it with you. I'm not going to endorse any particular one. Most of them essentially have the same stuff. Remember, a survival kit is only as good as the person who owns it. In other words, you can have all this fancy stuff to help you in a survival situation, but if you don't know how to use it, the kit is worthless to you.

You can even make your own survival kit. I made

250

up my survival kit based on what I think I will need in a survival situation. I keep my kit with me at all times when I go into the woods, even if it is just a day trip. You never know when something will happen. It is a good idea to make sure your family members or teammates have one as well.

Before you go into the woods, make sure you know how to make a fire with the stuff in the kit. It's better to learn how to use it before you are in a real survival situation. Learning to make a fire is not an easy task, and it takes practice. I added a sewing kit to my survival kit, because of my habit of ripping my clothes or losing a button. You don't want to turn your trip into a survival situation, but it can happen. You can read stories about people who went on a day trip and found themselves in a survival situation. If you prepare accordingly and make sure you bring everything you need, you can minimize any emergency. I recently downloaded a survival app to my cell phone. It looks pretty good and has a lot of information, but I have not tried it yet. I hope I won't have to, but it's there if I need it.

When it comes to survival situations involving young kids, the only things useful to them in a survival kit are the emergency blanket and a signaling mirror. The most important thing to relate to them is when they find themselves disoriented, they should stay where they are. The safety necklace (described below) is a must for young members of the team or first-time outdoor legend trippers.

First Aid kit

The fourth must-have item is a first-aid kit. If you are bringing the whole family, you have two options. You can bring a large one for everybody or you can have the team members each bring a small individual kit.

251

Most first-aid kits are pretty standard, with alcohol and band-aids, but you will have to personalize them depending on the kind of trip you are taking. Some survival kits have small first-aid kits in them. If you are taking medicine of any sort, you need to make sure you bring it and notify everybody on your team that you are taking it. For example, if you are allergic to bee stings then you need to bring your EpiPen (epinephrine injection). I have hay fever, so I always bring my antihistamine medicine with me just in case. I don't have it as bad as when I was a kid, but you never know, and the worst time to forget it is when you are deep in the woods and your eyes start to itch.

Most standard first-aid kits do not have it, but make sure you bring some poison ivy cream. It would be a good idea to add moleskin to your kit, in case you or your team get blisters walking around. Petroleum jelly is good to have in tropical weather. You can also waterproof gear with it. I add cough drops to my first-aid

252

Legend Tripping day gear

1. Backpack
2. Extra T-shirt and socks in waterproof bag
3. Sleeping bag
4. Emergency sleeping bag
5. Bug spray, Sunblock and other medicine
6. 2-quart canteen
7. Casting powder in water proof bag
8. LifeStraw go water bottle
9. Bear mace
10. Snake boots
11. Rain coat
12. Collapsible solar lantern
13. Binoculars
14. Bluetooth speaker for call blasting
15. Survival Kit/First Aid kit
16. Camera with night vision
17. Map in waterproof container
18. Head light
19. BioLite Nano light with attachments
20. Solar recharger
21. Night vision scope
22. Thermal imager for cellphone
23. Knife and sheath
24. Spare knife and sheath

Not pictured: compass and spare batteries

kit. They are great in the morning when you get a weird cough and sore throat, called camper's cough. Most people do not take enough band-aids with them. They figure if they cut themselves, they will only need one band-aid the whole time they are out there. Wrong; you need to change the band-aid once a day, and if you are in a survival situation you don't know how long you are going to be out there. Make sure you take extra band-aids with you. Put a drop of iodine on the cloth part of the band-aid and it will speed up the healing. One word of caution: some people are allergic to iodine because it contains shellfish, so make sure you know what every member of your party is allergic to.

Flashlight

The fifth item is a flashlight, which is essential in a survival situation at night. Humans are not nocturnal. I always make sure I bring a couple of them with me. One is a small pocket light I carry in the pocket flap of my jacket. I like to wear a head light at night. It makes monster hunting easier, and it leaves your hands free to operate your camera. And it makes going to the bathroom outside a lot easier. I always make sure I carry a couple of light sticks I can break open and use in case my flashlights stop working.

When you go legend tripping at night, you really need to be proactive on this. If your light source goes out and you are in the middle of the woods, you are screwed, and you're going to end up lost for hours. If

Legend Tripping

you are Bigfoot hunting, it is good to have a red or blue lens flashlight. It doesn't give off a strong light and it helps your eyes adjust more quickly to the darkness—a technique I learned in the military. I even installed a blue light in my Jeep for the same reason.

Safety Necklace

The last thing I want to talk about is ensuring every team member has a safety necklace. When we all go into the woods, I always make sure each person has a safety necklace around his or her neck. The items on it are a whistle, a pen light, and a couple of optional items I will talk about later. Though some hikers and outdoorsmen like to secure these items to a shoulder pad of their backpack, I found this isn't always a good idea. When you are out rucking and you come to a stop, the first thing you do is take off your ruck. Most people, myself included, will take off the ruck to go to the bathroom. Now your safety items are away from you and on the ruck, and this can be bad at night. It is easier to have them on a necklace, which is readily accessible to you at all times.

I remember one night in the military when we were out at night doing a mission. One of my soldiers took off his rucksack to go to the bathroom. He heard a loud noise and took off running back to us. We had to stop everything to go find his rucksack. It took us all night and we finally found it when the sun came up. I have all first-time legend trippers sleep with their safety necklaces on when we are camping. You never know when you are going to have to urinate, and it's usually at night. I go over each item on the safety necklace and explain its importance to the trip participants.

Whistle

Do not just buy any old whistle. A lot of them can't be heard over long distances. I highly recommend

254

storm whistles. My friend and survival expert, Kevin Jackson, introduced me to storm whistles and how effective they are. Storm whistles are a little more expensive than average whistles, but when it comes to you and your teammates' safety the extra cost is well worth it. It was developed after recreational divers who used a standard whistle when they were in distress found they could not be heard at relatively short distances. Later, the US Coast Guard introduced whistles designed to be heard over the high winds of a hurricane or other storm. They were appropriately named "storm whistles" and are now considered standard on all diving gear.

Making a palm teepee shelter.

Pen Light

I try to get a variety of colored lights and assign a different one to each team member, so I know who it is at night. They come in pretty handy when you have to go to the bathroom outside. They can also be used in conjunction with the whistle at night, so you can find someone who is lost. It is even easier to see them when you use a night vision scope.

The next items are optional on the safety necklace. A compass is great to have when you know how to use it. They are easy to find and are very inexpensive. There are some cheap ones that don't work right, though, so be careful. Small kids really won't use one. They understand the arrow points north, but don't understand the importance of a compass. Of course, a legend trip might be a great time to teach them.

255

Small Folding Blade Knife

A small folding knife is a good item to have on your safety necklace. I don't really like folding knives, but this is a good place to keep one as a backup knife because they are light and compact. Do not purchase cheap ones at a dollar store. You never know what you are going to have to cut yourself loose from, and cheap knives do not hold up. If you have small children, you might want to reconsider putting this on their safety necklace. Small kids love to play with stuff, and knives are not a good idea. I have a little fixed-blade knife on my necklace, because I didn't know where else to put it. The smaller, the lighter, the better. All these items are secured on an orange 550 paracord.

Being in Good Physical Shape and Health

The last thing I want to emphasize about outdoor survival is being in the right shape when you go into the woods for your legend trip. If you want to go hiking or even climbing up hills, you and your team members need to be in the right shape. One way to accomplish this is to go out and start walking around. Most state parks have walking trails, so take the team and walk one of the trails. Not only are they getting in shape, but they are also getting used to the outdoors. Some of you are going to use a legend trip as a way to get your team out and exercising. If they are not used to it, then I recommend you start off with just a day-long legend trip. This will get them used to being outside. Be patient, and don't push too hard if your team members are not used to it. If you feel that either you or they are not in the right shape, then don't

The author with his gear.

256

wear a backpack, but you do need to have water with you. Your first outing may not involve a lot of walking, and that's OK. Be prepared to have plenty of stops to help them get used to being outdoors. Make sure they have the right foot gear (see Chapter 17, Equipment and Tools). Bring plenty of bug spray; you are going to need it.

You also have to be aware of what time of day you are going hiking. During the summer months it is not wise to go hiking in the middle of the day, due to the heat. Do not plan long walks during the hottest part of the day. I recommend you hike in the morning, before it has gotten hot. I like to go hiking in the morning, or in the early evening when it starts to cool down.

Also, don't bring any unnecessary gear. I have seen many people bring a lot of survival gear and knives. They bring heavy packs with them and end up getting tired quickly and can't finish the expedition. If you are going up any mountains or hills, you need to prepare yourself to do this. A heavy pack is not a good thing to have when you are rucking up hills. You are going to lose your team and friends if you have to end the expedition because they have taken too much.

I like to go rucking on weekends through the woods with at least fifty pounds in my backpack. When it comes to hiking and climbing in the outdoors, you can't just hope you're in the right shape. You have to be in the right shape. Again, never go rucking alone.

My team is my priority out there, and I always make sure they are prepared and won't panic if anything goes wrong. We all carry the right equipment, which I will go into in detail in the next chapter.

But you've got to expect the unexpected even if it is only a day trip. People have gotten lost and died on day trips. Make sure you make survival a priority in your legend tripping plan.

Legend Tripping

You need to remember: "go prepared." You can journey out on your legend trip and discover something you wish you had brought, but as long as you have the basics, as I mentioned above, your trip will be exciting and enjoyable. Never treat any trip into the woods as a simple day trip. Always prepare for the worst. That way it will give you peace of mind and you can concentrate on finding Bigfoot and other legends.

Chapter 17
Equipment & Tools

Every successful trip or expedition is a result of not only the people but also the equipment. A well-planned-out legend trip is a successful and exciting one. I make no apologies about going into depth about putting together an equipment list. This book does not endorse any specific product. All the items that I will go over are those that I have used and that have worked for me. With equipment, I look for dependability and not a name brand. You may prefer to take different items than what I use. That is up to you. You need to bring equipment that you are comfortable with and know how to use.

With every legend trip, add and remove items from the equipment list according to purpose and weather. I have a friend who always brings his ninja sword; I don't know why, but he likes to bring it. I like to bring items that I used in the Army; they worked for me then. When I was on active duty, I would watch some younger soldiers go out and buy what I call "G.I. Joe stuff" to take into the field. They ended up not using it; they wasted their money on gadgets. Bottom line: out in the woods or jungle, that is added, unneeded weight. When it comes to preparing for legend tripping or any kind of trip, if there is any new equipment or apparatus to try out, make sure it is actually needed before investing the money. It's like a person who tries out golfing. He goes and buys an expensive set of golf clubs and then finds out he can't stand it. Now he's stuck with expensive golf clubs.

Legend Tripping

Legend tripping should not be an expensive experience, but spending some money is a requirement of any adventure or hobby. I refuse to lie about the expense. An example is gas; fuel for the vehicle is a requirement to get to any location. What I am saying is that when planning ahead, look around for the right equipment. It doesn't have to be expensive, but remember, "You get what you pay for." To go on a good legend trip and have a great experience, the right equipment is needed. It doesn't have to be expensive, but don't go out and buy cheap stuff, especially clothing.

Like I said, it is important to make an equipment list. If being outdoors is already important to you, going out and buying a lot of stuff won't be necessary. If camping is already your pastime, then everything required for a Bigfoot hunt will be easily at hand. A lot of the ghost hunting equipment my wife has was purchased at the hardware store. She paid a fraction of the price that some online ghost hunting stores are charging for the same items. Also, go to some of the online bidding websites and check out some of the equipment they have there. Just because an item is new and expensive does not necessarily mean that it is better than the same item that is used and cheaper. I have gotten some name brand items, because I have tried cheaper versions that did not hold up. When deep in the woods, reliable equipment is needed.

I am going to go over some things that I think are important to have on any legend trip. I already mentioned survival kits and knives in the previous chapter on outdoor survival. Just make sure to have both whenever out in the jungle or woods. In the following discussion, pay particular attention to my side notes.

260

Equipment for Legend Tripping

Camera: This is one of the most important pieces of equipment on a legend trip. There needs to be some device to record the experience. There might be a Bigfoot or ghost and a camera is necessary to get a picture or video of it. To me, the best part of legend tripping is recording the experience. When it comes to cameras, don't buy cheap. I'm talking about the disposable ones that have to be turned in to get the pictures back. Most cameras are digital now, and it is really easy to download the pictures right onto the computer. I recently purchased a small digital camera that has IR capability from a ghost hunting store. "IR" means infrared, and it takes pictures with night vision. This is a must when looking for Bigfoot, ghosts, or other nocturnal legends. Looking at some of the online retail sites makes finding a decent camera at a good price much easier. I find most of my equipment online using these non-specialty websites.

Side note: When on a legend trip, take a whole bunch of pictures. The background of the picture could reveal more than the original target. Also video each other and talk about the legend trip and the stories behind the legends. I know it sounds weird, but imagine being on one of those reality shows. This actually makes it easier to do, and can encourage the entire team to "buy in" to the experience. Make sure to bring extra batteries and car chargers so the cameras are ready.

Money: Some wonder why I listed this. The reason is that some families fail to check their bank accounts and find out later they don't have the money. Part of planning is to make sure there is adequate money and put some aside for the trip. Carry some checks in case a debit or credit card gets lost. Always keep a stash of cash to put gas in the car. Check the car before the trip. Like I said earlier, all the money should not go to the lodging.

Side note: Always put the money/debit cards in a safe place. Keep them in a waterproof container or pouch.

Equipment for Camping

For a legend trip that requires camping, the following gear is important:

Clothing: When it comes to "what to wear" on a legend trip, it is not about fashion. Make sure the clothing is comfortable, not heavy, quick-drying, and—most important—durable! Like I said earlier, "You get what you pay for." I once bought some cheap clothing items and they fell apart the first time I washed them. Never again will I buy cheap clothing.

I am very careful about the clothing I buy because I am pretty hard on clothes and I've been known to tear them up. Regardless of the brand names, I purchase outdoor clothing that I know is going to stand up to trips into the woods or swamps. That being said, I don't dress up as if I were going to be on television. I do wear some camouflage or hunting items. I didn't buy them because they were camouflage; I bought them because they were durable and comfortable. I don't have anything against camouflage clothing; I wore it for more than twenty-one years in the Army. I just don't see the necessity in wearing it. I like light-colored (usually tan) clothing that will dry quickly and keep me cool when it gets hot.

Plenty of companies produce outdoor clothes that are reasonably priced. Some of it can be kind of expensive, though, and I recommend looking for seasonal sales. My wife found good deals on the clearance rack. I see

262

people going out and buying expensive clothing and gear for their first legend trip. Make sure legend tripping is a priority before you invest too much money.

Clothing should be the last thing to worry about when deep in the woods on a monster hunt. Again, make sure the clothing is durable and light if it is summertime. During the wintertime, make sure the clothing is made to keep the cold out and keep the wearer warm and dry. If going on a monster hunt, wash the clothes in anti-scent detergent found in the sports and hunting sections of outdoors equipment stores, as well as the anti-scent dryer sheets, because even the no-scent dryer sheets have a scent.

Side note: Make sure to take the "snivel" rain gear whenever hiking or in the woods.

Gore-Tex can be expensive but it does work, and it will also keep wearers warm during cold nights. I still have my original Gore-Tex rain jacket from the Army and I still use it. Yes, it is camouflage, but I don't use it for that reason and I didn't have to pay an outrageous price. I recommend buying them at a military surplus store where they are used, but cheap.

Side note: If purchasing any Gore-Tex gear, make sure to take care of it and be careful when cleaning and storing it. Prolonged exposure to the sun can cause it to dry out.

During colder months, warmer clothes are a requirement. Don't go with some television survivalist attitude and think roughing it is an option. Without the right gear in cold weather, you can and will die. I highly recommend fleece shirts and caps, a warm coat and gloves. A lot of people don't think about how cold it can get at night. While I was in Afghanistan, it was blazing hot during the day and below zero at night. If rucking in cold weather, have the coat handy to put on during stops to stay warm. When actually rucking (hiking), the

263

Legend Tripping overnight gear

body heat will keep a body warm.

Side note: During hunting season, wear items that have orange in them so you don't get mistaken for a deer and get shot in the butt.

Believe it or not, most of my outdoor gear has some orange color in it. You'd think it would be a straight camouflage pattern. I'm not saying I don't own camouflage clothing or that I am dressed head-to-toe in orange. What I'm saying is that a lot of my gear has orange parts to it. My cell phone has an orange case, and I have an orange zip drive on my key ring. My Crocs sandals have an orange band on them. I put orange tape on my knife sheath, and I use an orange 550 paracord. Unless it is glow-in-the-dark gear, the orange is just as invisible at night as a hunter with all his camouflage gear on. None of my orange gear glows in the dark. The

264

1. Tent
2. Backpack
3. Extra clothes and socks
4. Sleeping bag
5. Emergency sleeping bag
6. Water bottle with built in filter
7. Bear mace
8. Snake boots
9. Kettle pot
10. Stove
11. Grill
12. Trench shovel
13. Tent light
14. Medicine
15. Survival kit/First Aid kit
16. 2-quart canteen
17. Casting powder
18. Rain coat
19. Portable fishing pole
20. Collapsible solar lamp
21. Binoculars
22. Night vision scope
23. Bluetooth speaker
24. Video camera with night vision
25. BioLite Nano light and attachment
26. Solar charger
27. Thermal imager for cellphone
28. Knife and sheath (2)
29. Map in water proof case
30. Head light

reason for the orange is that I don't want to lose any of my gear when I'm out in the woods. If it was camouflage and I dropped it (especially at night), I would never find it again. On one of our outings, a friend of mine could not find his sleeping bag, which, of course, was camouflage in color. It turned out it was right next to him the whole time. A lot of hunters wear gear that is orange. Deer are supposedly color blind, and it helps in that other hunters do not mistake each other for deer or other animals. In Florida, the main areas where the Swamp Ape is seen are also designated hunting areas, so I highly encourage possessing items with orange on them.

Side note: A lot of new survival gear is bright in color, so it can be used as a signaling device and it makes it easier to be seen for rescue. If properly planned, rescue won't be needed.

Headgear: To start off, I am not a big fan of hats. I'm not saying I don't wear them; I'm just saying I don't like to wear them. I understand the importance of wearing them in extreme hot weather climates and they offer protection from the harmful UV rays of the sun.

When I was on active duty and deployed to Afghanistan, we were all required to wear boonie hats. These hats offered protection not only to the face but also to the back of the neck in the extreme desert heat. When I first started monster hunting in Florida, I didn't wear a hat, and one time when we were walking a trail during July, I got sunburned on the top of my head. It was a painful lesson. Skin cancer caused by the harmful UV rays of the sun is difficult to cure.

Now, when on legend trips, I take along a hat if I know we'll be walking around in the sun. But when I'm in the deep swamps, I don't wear a hat. I find it gets in the way when I'm pushing through the thick bushes and plants. When I have to, I wear a simple tan baseball cap. It is light and comfortable. I do recommend some form of headgear when doing any kind of trip in the sun. Some people like to wear head wraps, and they are effective in keeping sweat out of the face, but they do not keep the sun out of the face, or the harmful UV rays that can cause skin cancer. Ensure that every member of the team has some kind of headgear. In cold weather I bring what the military calls a "watch cap." It is like a large sock for the head. It is extremely useful for wearing in a sleeping bag during a cold night. It also helps keep the body heat in when hiking in the winter.

Side note: Pick out headgear that you will wear; do not buy it because it looks good.

Gloves: These may not be needed all the time, but prove handy when chopping wood with an axe or machete. They are good to have when roughing it through the high bush or grass. There are thorn bushes out there, and wearing gloves makes it easier to get through. Inexpensive work gloves are sufficient, so please ignore expensive combat gloves.

Sunglasses: Always bring them as they are needed for daytime use. Get a strap to put on the back so you won't lose them. Make sure everybody in the team has sunglasses. Some people pay a fortune for them, but you can just buy some cheap ones. I don't like expensive ones, for fear of losing or breaking them. The great thing about mine is that they are also bifocal, and I use them for reading. In my travels, I have gone through many pairs of sunglasses. I buy ones that are durable and not expensive.

Footwear: The hiking boots I wear on my legend trips are broken in and comfortable, and I can walk for miles in them. Proper footgear can make or break the legend trip. If buying new boots, don't start wearing them on the expedition. If you do, have some moleskin for blisters. I have seen this happen many times. Break in new boots before the expedition, especially if hiking a long distance; foot powder is also a suggested addition to the packing list. If getting feet wet is a possibility, bring petroleum jelly to stop the development of foot fungus frequently found in tropical environments.

On a recent outing in the Florida swamps, I joined some Bigfoot hunters. We walked a couple of miles in water up to our knees. Everyone developed "trench foot" except me. I took the liberty of covering my feet with petroleum jelly before departing on the trail. I always pack extra moleskin and petroleum jelly for my team, just in case. A good rule for hiking is: use foot powder for cold weather and petroleum jelly for tropical weather.

I also own some snake boots, but I only wear them when I'm walking through the deep swamps. I prefer to wear my hiking boots whenever I can. Snake boots are great for what they are designed for, and there are some areas where wearing them is recommended, but they are not designed for long-term walking. In Florida we have rattlesnakes and cottonmouths. Both are extremely poisonous and aggressive. A bite from one of these reptiles will quickly end the legend trip. On a safety note, stay away from areas that might have snakes. Snake boots are expensive and will cost about one hundred bucks on average. They are cheaper during the off-season. I only use them when I have to or when my wife makes me.

Another type of footwear I always bring is my Crocs sandals. I like to wear them when I am not hiking or out in the woods. They are great to put on in the morning when first waking up. They are also great to change into after a long hike or ruck march. They help my feet relax. They are better than normal sandals because they cover up the toes and are extremely comfortable. The straps on my Crocs sandals are orange and easy to find when I need them.

Socks: This item is as equally important as footwear. Make sure the socks fit properly and do not rub when they get wet. Most standard white socks are terrible when wet, and fungus develops quickly because of the cotton. I wear nylon socks that dry quickly and are made for hiking. They aren't too expensive, and help prevent foot fungus and blisters. Properly-sized hiking socks will help prevent blisters.

Tent: Make sure to buy a tent that is the right size. If legend tripping with the family and the only tent taken is made for two people, family togetherness becomes very uncomfortable. Don't buy an expensive tent, just make sure it is big enough for all who are sleeping in it.

Side note: Make sure to bring some ant spray to put around the tent, otherwise you are going to have a fire ant problem.

Sleeping Bags: There are different kinds of sleeping bags for different temperatures. If camping out and it gets really cold but the bag is designed for summertime, campers end up wearing all the packed clothes to keep warm. I know I said I don't spend a lot of money on certain things, but when it comes to a good night's sleep, invest in a good sleeping bag. The military has great sleeping bags and they sell them at Army surplus stores. I recently purchased one that could handle the different climates. It consisted of two actual sleeping bags, a small one for mild temperatures and a larger one for cold temperatures. For extreme cold, take the small one and put it into the larger one, creating an

268

extreme cold weather sleeping bag. The best two things about the sleeping bag are that it folds to a tiny size for my rucksack and it only costs sixty dollars. When purchasing a sleeping bag, look at the tag and make sure it is designed for the temperature in which the planned trip will take place.

Air Mattresses: The family and I like to bring them when we use tents. It makes sleeping outside a lot more bearable. My wife refuses to go camping without them. They can be found in the camping section of any store, and the great thing is that they are not expensive. I also have a self-inflating mattress that I bring. Let's be real, a good night's sleep is incredibly important, otherwise the whole legend trip turns into a bad experience and puts everybody in a bad mood. Get the body off the cold ground at night; it's not healthy to sleep on the ground. For me, there is nothing better than a nice comfortable bed after a nighttime ruck march.

Side note: Make sure to bring a repair kit, in case a team member gets a leak in their mattress. I don't know why, but it always seems to happen.

Lanterns: I highly recommend the battery-operated ones over the kerosene ones. They come in a wide range of sizes, and they are not expensive. Always remember to bring extra batteries and replacement light bulbs.

Side note: I always bring two lanterns, in case one breaks.

Bug Spray: When it comes to bug spray, all I can say is purchase a lot of it. Make sure everybody on the trip has his or her own bug spray. It has been my experience that unless the bug spray contains DEET, it will not work, or it won't work for long. The new mosquito devices with a cartridge insert that clip to the belt work, when there are only a few of the darn bugs around or in the tent. One time I wore it in the woods and I still got covered in those bloodsucking insects, so I ended

269

up putting bug spray on. They work well in tents, but make sure the tent has an open mess at the top. In a closed tent, it may not be safe to breathe that stuff in.

Side note: There is a new device to clip on the belt to keep mosquitoes away. It does work, but only for a limited time, plus it is kind of noisy. I prefer bug spray.

Mosquito Net: This is a great thing to bring if going into the swamps or woods. Mosquitoes will drive anyone crazy when they're trying to sleep at night. A net doesn't cost a lot, and will pack into a small ball to carry in either a pocket or backpack. It can provide added protection if secured over the tent. When out in the swamps, throw it on for additional bug defense.

Cleansing/Baby Wipes: One item that I swear by and always bring is baby wipes. When going to the bathroom outside, either in the woods or in a portable toilet, paper is not enough. Wipes are great to clean the hands before eating, and cleaning all parts of the body when a bath or shower isn't available. In today's military, all soldiers bring baby wipes with them. Don't get the scented ones without expecting funny looks from the teammates. Now, stores sell wipes for camping.

Side note: Make sure to not litter when out in the woods. Used wipes attract flies and other critters. Pack out what is brought in.

Food: When I am not taking the camper out, I usually take military meals called MREs (Meals Ready to Eat). It's easier than carrying around huge coolers of food. But that is me, and MREs get old quick. A cooking stove can be purchased for a good price, and it is fun to cook over the campfire. Because of the recent droughts, some campgrounds prohibit campfires. A camping stove will come in handy. Waking up on the first morning will be a wonderful experience for those camping for the first time. I say that facetiously. For me, a good hot cup of coffee is the way to start the morning, so I always make sure I bring coffee with me.

Side note: I bring sugar substitute because sugar brings in ants. If you do bring sugar, just make sure it is in a strong Ziploc bag.

Snacks: Trail mix, energy bars, and beef jerky are great to take along for hikes and rucking. As any parent knows, when kids get hungry, they also get irritable. They then have one thing on their mind and that's food.

Side note: When packing in snacks, make sure to bring plenty of water.

Machetes: These large knives are good to have in the jungle or swamps. But when only going out to the jungle once a month, don't invest in an expensive one. A while back, I ordered a Parang machete online because I thought it was just what I needed in the jungle and swamps. When it arrived I found it to be too heavy, and it gave me blisters every time I used it. I ended up dropping it off a cliff in Ecuador, when I almost fell off the cliff. It was going to be either me or the Parang, and I chose my own life. Our Ecuadorian guides had cheap machetes, which they sharpened the heck out of. They had no problems cutting through the jungle with them. Now I don't buy fancy machetes. I own a cheap one that I rarely use, which I got for a reasonable price at a hardware store. If I go back to Ecuador, I won't be taking an expensive Parang with me. Remember, just because it looks neat, doesn't mean that it is practical.

Side note: Machetes and little kids do not mix. An accident always happens when a kid gets a machete.

Bear Mace: If worried about the local wild animals, then I suggest bear mace rather than a gun as most public park areas prohibit guns. When on an outing with the family, it might make everybody uncomfortable, knowing a member of the team is armed. Also, if exploring on private or government property with a gun, the person carrying the firearm can be charged

271

Legend Tripping

with poaching. Poaching comes with a heavy fine, and the gun will be confiscated. If caught trespassing with only bear mace, the fine can only be for trespassing. It happened to me, and I was able to talk my way out of it, with only a butt-chewing from the Fish and Wildlife people. Actually, I think the Fish and Wildlife officers were amused when I told them I was Bigfoot hunting. Bear mace is not that expensive and it will do the trick if a bear, panther, or wild pig sneaks up. Snakes hate the stuff as well.

Side note: I suggest adults, and not children, carry the bear mace. I made the mistake of allowing my son to carry it, and he ended up using it on me. For the record, he stated he thought I was a Bigfoot. I think he just wanted to see how the stuff worked. Boy, I was irate. That mace burned for two days. I will never make that mistake again.

Fishing Gear: Bring it just in case there is a chance to fish. It will be something to do during the day when waiting for the evening. There is nothing worse than being bored, and a bored family is less likely to return for another legend trip. If catching fish for dinner, it will save money down the road. The fish or fish guts can also be used as bait for the trail camera. Just make sure to stay in compliance with state law when fishing. Most fishing permits may be purchased online. Fishing poles are a great thing to add to the packing list. Fishing itself is enjoyable, and I have found that for some reason, when father and son are alone out there, there is better communication. I don't know why, but there is something about a father and son fishing trip; sons seem to understand the bonding factor with fishing, and start to open up and communicate. If skeptical, give it a try. It works. My sons and I have some awesome conversations when we're out fishing.

Fishing Poles: I always bring my "Pocket Fisherman"

pole with me. It is a small compact fishing device that can be taken anywhere (I sound like a commercial), and it is inexpensive. I bought mine on an online auction site for five dollars, including postage, and it is made in the USA. It works great, and I've caught quite a lot of large fish with it.

Side note: If going fishing, make sure to adhere to local and state laws and have a fishing license.

Rope: This should always be part of the gear when camping. Rope must have a thousand uses. I use it to cross rivers or streams and to secure gear. I like to bring 550 paracord with me. It is actually parachute cord, but it is extremely strong and can hold 550 pounds, hence the name 550 paracord. I like to use it for my safety necklaces, and I also replaced my bootlaces with it. I use it when I put up my hammock and to help secure my trail cameras to trees. It seems to always be used on survival shows to set up animal traps. Again, I like to use orange-colored 550 paracord so that it's easy to see in the woods. It comes in all different colors.

Side note: Bring bungee cords. Like 550 cord, bungee cords have a hundred different uses. They make setting up a shelter a lot easier.

Duct Tape: This extremely strong and durable tape also has a hundred different uses. I bring dark green tape, and orange, of course. It can be used to fix tears in tents and tarps. I had to use it on my Gore-Tex rain jacket one time, and it worked like a charm. I use the orange tape to mark certain items of equipment.

Flares: Flares are a good thing to have if you are a die-hard legend tripper and go miles into the wilderness. If a weekend warrior, like most family guys are, then keep flares in the car. If I bring the family then I stay close to the main paths, so I don't get into a survival situation. If canoeing downriver to another site, flares might not be a bad idea.

Side note: Keep flares away from small kids. They can be dangerous.

Emergency Locators: These are a must for die-hard legend trippers that go deep into the wilderness, miles from any human population. If you are lost or run into a survival situation, then simply push the button and emergency personnel are contacted with the location. The only problem is that they are expensive. Most cell phones have an emergency locator on them. Some parents have added it to their cell phone service in order to keep a heads up on their kids' location. Once the child is eighteen, the service is not allowed. Only emergency services and police authorities are allowed to use them to locate individuals.

Side note: If the batteries run out, then the cell phone only records the last position when the cell phone was working. Stay put when this happens if that is at all possible

Cool Wrap Towel: This is a new item that is gaining in popularity. The towels are made of absorbent material and are so cool when wet. They are great when sweating the butt off; they take the sweat off and feel nice and cool against the skin.

Side note: They have to be kept wet in order to work properly.

Global Positioning System (GPS): I recently purchased a GPS, and now I make sure I always bring it with me. They are great and easy to use. A lot of cell phones now have GPS on them. My wife loves using hers, and she can always tell me where we are. They are good to use at night when location is difficult to determine. Make sure there are good batteries in them. I remember one time when I was Bigfoot hunting up near the Suwannee River, when my friend Eric and I were checking a trail camera. After we put it up, I couldn't see where we were or how far we had gone from the dirt road we were using. In fact, I couldn't tell what direction the road was in. Eric pulled out his GPS and switched it on. It turned out the dirt road was just to our left and about ten feet away. It was so dark in the woods and every tree looked the same. I should have gotten a compass reading before we went into the woods that night, but I didn't think it was going to be hard to find the road again. Boy, was I wrong. Now, no matter what, I always take a compass reading when I go Bigfoot hunting.

Side Note: GPS depends on the use of satellites, and if it is extremely cloudy the reading may not be accurate. Always bring a compass and map as backup.

Solar Battery Rechargers: Another new item I just bought is a solar battery recharger. Whoever invented this little item is a genius. They make them small enough to carry in a cargo pocket or rucksack. Just make sure to have rechargeable batteries. I use it for my cell phone and flashlight.

Binoculars: These are another great item to bring along. If a serious legend tripper is developing, then get a good pair. Make sure to look online before buying, as binoculars can be expensive. I found a great pair at a garage sale. If there are younger kids, then purchase a relatively cheap pair for them. It gets them into the mood and ready for adventure. It also gives them something to do when they are riding in the car, and they feel part of the experience.

Backpacks: Last but not least, have a backpack or rucksack to carry the gear. There is a new term, "bug out bag," which refers to a portable emergency bag, usually a backpack, that's thoughtfully filled with critical gear and supplies needed in order to survive a multi-day journey to a safe location in the event of a crisis.

I don't keep my bag ready for a crisis. I like to have a bag with all the stuff I use on a legend trip. It does

275

have critical survival gear and some supplies, but only because I want to be prepared for anything while I'm out in the woods. I carry my trail camera and evidence-collecting equipment in case I find something, as well as casting powder in case I find a large footprint.

I have my family members each put together a bag of stuff for a legend trip, and they have designed their bags according to what they feel they need. My sons always make sure they have their music listening devices. There are plenty of good backpacks on the market. I have two packs. The ruck that I carry for day trips is one I had in the military. It is the one I'm used to, and I find it comfortable. The second one is a large backpack for when I go rucking back into the woods and I expect to camp over time. I bought it used on the Internet. If one is needed, I suggest first looking on the auction websites before buying anything new. Some backpacks can be expensive.

Recreational Vehicles (RVs) or Campers: These are great to use, and there is the added comfort. If you are like my wife, and sleeping in a tent on the ground is a deal breaker for adventure, then maybe an RV is the right way to go. They are great, but expensive to rent. I don't like them because I can't take them back to the areas where I Bigfoot hunt. They can be set up at the nearest campground and trippers may bicycle over to the area where the investigation will be conducted.

In some states, the RV is required to be parked at a campground, and that will cost money. RVs are great for long distance legend trips if tent camping is out, although if an RV is used instead of hotels, it may cost the same or more. RVs take a lot of fuel, and setting one up at camp can prove to be a challenge. They should make solar-powered RVs.

I recently purchased a pop-up camper, and we now have a reason to go legend tripping. It wasn't expensive and it meets all our needs. Now when we go out, we don't have to worry about getting a hotel room. We all think it's fun to take the camper out and set up in the woods for the weekend.

They also make little campers called "teardrop campers," which can go into areas where a standard-size camper won't fit. The problem is that they are expensive and only (sort of) fit two people. My wife doesn't like them. Handy types can buy a set of plans to build one of their own, but it requires a trailer frame to build it on. When I have to set up in an area where a camper can't go, I just take my tent. It's a lot easier and less expensive.

Vehicles: When on a legend trip, one of the most important items is the one most families don't think about. When it is not working, the legend trip is over. I'm talking about the vehicle. I own a Jeep Wrangler. I have always owned a Jeep. It has always been dependable and I never get stuck. Well, I did get stuck once.

The point I am trying to make is take the right kind of vehicle for a legend trip. Some vehicles can't handle off-roading, and that is a disaster ready to happen. I'm not recommending you go out and buy an off-road vehicle. I am saying make sure to take the vehicle only where it can safely go. I have had to pull numerous vehicles out of the mud because the driver took the vehicle where it wasn't equipped to go.

It's really simple: if the vehicle (for example, a minivan) can't go off road, then stay on the hardtop. Either that or park it and walk. Check out the vehicle before departing for a trip, especially the tires. Make sure the spare tire is good to go. I always carry a vehicle emergency kit in the back. They cost about thirty dollars and they will come in handy.

If bringing an ATV, that can add to the legend trip. Not only are they fun to ride but they can increase the search zone. Be careful on them. They do not have a good track record, and people have been killed on them. I know a person who got his ATV stuck out in the swamp and it is still out there. It's located in a spot where a recovery vehicle can't get to it.

Inflatable Boat or Canoe: This is nice to bring, if there is room. Be careful when taking it out. Make sure there are no alligators in the water if using an inflatable raft. Some lakes and streams have sticks poking up that can puncture it. I am the proud owner of a hovercraft. I bring it on occasion just to have something fun to do if the trip turns out to be a bust. Always have a backup plan for entertainment and fun when bringing children. It is fun to go canoeing, and the family gets some exercise and sees things. Always locate nearby places that rent boats and canoes. This might be something to think about, especially if the area where you are legend tripping has a lake, river, or creek.

Side note: For safety, make sure all members have life vests, and safety necklaces.

Equipment for Monster (Bigfoot) Hunting

The next listed items are for a monster (Bigfoot) hunt.

Night Vision Goggles: These are nice to have, but they can be expensive. I bought a set online for fifty dollars. They work, but only for about fifty feet in front of you. Even though the device is a toy, eye reflections from animals are easily seen from more than one hundred feet away. My camera also has night vision capabilities, and with it I can see a lot further than fifty feet. It's a small camera that I can carry in my breast pocket, which makes it easier to grab when I need it. I'm not a big fan of using night vision devices to maneuver through the woods. They have no depth perception, resulting in you tripping over plants or branches. I like

278

to get my eyes adjusted to the dark and go from there.

Side note: If it gets too dark I pull out my flashlight and use that. As I stated before, I don't like tramping around the woods because I end up making too much noise.

Trail Camera: If going on a monster or ghost legend trip, please get one. Called a "trail cam" for short, it is a camera that has an automatic device which triggers when something walks by. It is good for Bigfoot and ghost hunting. Trail cams used to be really expensive, but are now available from any outdoor store for a reasonable price. I like to find a game trail (a path made by some animal through the brush) and put the trail camera on a tree with a good field of view. I then spray it with a chemical that takes away the human smell. I leave it out there for about two weeks or a month, long enough for the human scent to go away. I go back and retrieve it and check the pictures. If I get nothing, then I move it to another location.

Side note: Always put a lock on a trail cam, to make sure nobody will steal it.

Camouflage Netting: I like to conduct most of my monster investigations in the early morning or early evening. From my research I have observed that a lot of Bigfoot sightings take place during these time frames. Because the animals are believed to be nocturnal, this is the best time to see a Bigfoot, in my opinion. I have acquired some netting that I like to bring. Believe it or not, I bought it at a toy store. Sometimes I will sit in a tree stand (used for hunting) and put the camouflage over me and wait. The camouflage helps break up my human pattern or silhouette. I also wrap my trail cameras in it when I set them up in trees. It disguises them better. It doesn't matter what clothing you're wearing unless hunting for deer or other animals. Being visible is a safety guideline when in the habitat of certain animals such as panthers and hogs—and people; if you can be seen, animals and hunters will leave the area and no one gets shot accidentally. I can't stress enough how important it is to be visible to hunters. Every year somebody gets mistaken for a deer and shot. One of our former vice presidents shot somebody during a hunting trip, thinking the person was a deer. Luckily the person lived.

Footprint Casting Kit: I bring one of these when I go out monster hunting, just in case I find the footprint of an unidentified animal. Refer to Chapter 4: Bigfoot Legend Trip, on how to properly make castings. The kit should consist of the following items:

• Plaster casting powder: can be purchased from any hardware store. Double what is recommended. I purchase two of the eight-pound tubs. I carry a Ziploc bag of plaster powder when I go deep into the woods. I always say that if I don't bring it, I'm going to end up finding a print.

• Rubber gloves, because the process can be messy

• Water—using too much, the plaster takes forever to dry and the material is not as strong. If too little water is used, the plaster becomes a thick paste that can damage the footprint

• Soft brush

• Large plastic or bendable copper strip (2" x 24" or two pieces of 2" x 13")

• Hairspray (in an aerosol can)

• Measuring tape

Evidence Kit: Bring one if the legend trip involves collecting evidence. This is going to sound funny, but a good evidence kit can be purchased at any toy store. With the popularity of crime scene investigation TV shows, evidence kits are now readily available and not expensive. They have everything needed for hair samples or scat (animal poop). Just a friendly warning, it is extremely expensive to have DNA samples sent off and professionally examined. I leave that for the monster hunting TV shows, which have the money.

The evidence kit should consist of the following items:

- Plastic tackle box—to keep the kit together
- Plastic bags of assorted sizes—for collecting hair or scat samples
- Rubber gloves
- Tweezers
- Small shovel
- Plastic medicine containers
- Measuring tape

Side note: Make sure the evidence kit includes gloves to protect the evidence and the hands. Also, do not leave any trash after collecting the evidence.

Trail Markers: These are brightly colored strips of cloth or plastic that hunters use to mark their area in the woods or swamps. They are great for marking the trail for guidance at night. They can also be used to find the way back to a main road or trail. I use them during my scouting trips during the daytime. They are inexpensive and easy to see at night. Some of them are reflective and can easily be spotted at night with a flashlight. Especially use them in thick, wooded areas, but make sure to retrieve them during the daytime so they can be reused.

Parabolic Listening Device: It looks like a toy gun with a satellite dish on the front of it, and it comes with a set of earphones. It is also referred to as a Bionic Ear. It is great for listening to noises, especially at night. I can plug it into my wife's voice recorder and tape what I am listening to. The only problem is that it is bulky and hard to pack away in my backpack. This is not much of problem if I am set up on a static post with the vehicle,

Legend Tripping

but when rucking, it is not easy lugging around a lot of gear in the woods or jungle.

Portable (Walkie Talkie) Radios: These are great items to bring and they help keep track of everybody and can be purchased from most department stores. They are great to have when the group is divided up into smaller teams. I make sure the base camp has a radio and is always in communication with all the teams.

Equipment for Ghost Hunting

When it comes to ghost hunting, there is a lot of fancy equipment out there to buy. If you don't quite believe me, just type in "ghost hunting equipment" on the Internet and look. My wife bought all of hers, with the exception of the camera, at a hardware store. We have friends who own a lot of equipment for ghost hunting. Tracy thinks it is too time-consuming to lug all that equipment around and set it up. It never fails that at least one piece does not work right or is missing a power cord.

We did an investigation in an old shut-down school, and it turned out there was no power source to plug all the equipment into. We ended up just using just our cameras and recording devices, and we still got great results. My wife caught a voice on her recording device. With a lot of the equipment ghost hunters use, it is still just theory if it works or not. Ghost hunting has not turned into a money-making endeavor. Here are some items needed to conduct an effective paranormal investigation.

EMF Reader and Temperature Reader: These can be found in any hardware store (I say that a lot). An EMF (electromagnetic field) reader picks up on the electronic signature given off by any electrical fixture. Ghost hunters swear by them. Many online ghost hunting stores sell them for much more than the

282

hardware store. Why pay more? It is the same thing. Where do you think these ghost hunters originally got them from? They did not invent them. The temperature reader looks like some space-age laser gun. Point at any object with the red light dot and it will relate the temperature given off by the object. They are great to use when monster hunting at night to see if anything is out there.

Sound Recorder: My wife always brings one with her when she conducts a paranormal investigation, so she is always ready in case we run into a haunted location. During a ghost hunt, Tracy will find a spot, hit record, and leave it there. She will go retrieve the device later and listen to the recording and see if she can hear anything. She claimed success when we did an investigation on an old school.

Standard 35mm Camera: Believe it or not, these old-fashioned film cameras pick up everything that some digital cameras won't. The great part is that they are very inexpensive. The only thing is the film has to be developed, which costs money.

Night Vision Game Camera: They work great on both monster and paranormal hunts. There are different versions out today. Some are expensive and some are affordable. Personally I do not invest in the expensive ones due to the fact that they can get stolen once placed out in the woods or forests. I have even put a lock system on one and it was still stolen. Also, if buying the inexpensive ones, purchase more than one and saturate an area with trail cameras. Some Bigfoot hunters believe that the Bigfoot can see the IR and stays away from the cameras, so that is something to think about

Here is a list of other tools and devices that paranormal investigators use on investigations. I'm going over this just to share what they are and how they are used, so if ghost hunting with experts, the equipment will be familiar. Do not purchase these items unless you are serious and planning to continue doing paranormal investigations.

Thermal Imager: This is an excellent tool to have on a monster hunt or paranormal investigation, but unfortunately they are extremely expensive. They are for serious monster/paranormal hunters who have the money to buy them. I have used them in the military, but didn't own one until recently. I found out that most television shows rent them because of the cost; they do break, and they are expensive to have repaired. The good news is that the prices are dropping, and there is one that is durable enough for outdoor use. I recently purchased one which attaches to my cell phone.

Full IR Camera/DVR Set Up: DVR (Digital Video Recorder) systems with night vision can be a powerful way to capture great paranormal evidence. Using multiple cameras, you will record and cover large areas for long periods of time with one easy set-up.

Dowsing Rod: These L-shaped rods have been used for centuries by different cultures. The word "dowsing" means to use a rod or pendulum to find something. These have been used to find water and minerals. In our modern day, large oil companies, police forces, mining operations, and farmers employ skilled dowsers. After World War I and during the Vietnam War, soldiers equipped with rods were able to locate booby traps and underground tunnels. Dowsing rods have been found useful by paranormal investigators as a device to communicate with spirits. The investigator will hold the rod and ask the spirit questions. These questions can be answered either with a "yes" or "no" or by the spirit directing the rods at an object or person. The rods are inexpensive and easy to find on the Internet.

Laser Grid Pen: This high-powered laser emits a grid

of green dots useful for detecting shadows or general visual disturbances during an investigation. Set it in front of a running camera to catch potential evidence when something goes through the dots.

EM Pump: An electromagnetic (EM) pump creates a low level magnetic field to help provide energy. The theory is that spirits use it to manifest or communicate. Since the frequency and duration changes, it is thought of as a beacon or trigger device.

Motion Sensor: This device will detect any movement and alert you with a blinking light (for visual alerts and video documentation) or the choice of a pleasant chime or piercing alarm when you are not near the unit. Just place it in any room where it is claimed that movement can be detected, and it gives an alert when it happens.

REM Pod: This new item for ghost hunting uses a mini telescopic antenna to radiate its own independent electromagnetic field around the instrument. The EM field can be easily influenced by materials and objects that conduct electricity. Based on source proximity, strength, and EM field distortion, four colorful LED lights can be activated in any order or combination. This device is expensive, and is only intended for the serious paranormal investigator.

Ghost Box: This device utilizes various environmental cues through software to give the spirits a voice while the spirit box emits raw radio frequencies. These are popular in paranormal television shows. Like the REM Pod, this item is expensive, and it is only intended for serious paranormal investigations.

Chapter 18
Your Legend Trip Begins Now!

Your time is limited—so don't waste it living someone
else's life. Don't be trapped by dogma—which is living
with the results of other people's thinking. Don't let
the noise of others' opinions drown out your own
inner voice. And most important, have the courage to
follow your heart and intuition.
—*Steve Jobs*

"It is all about the experience." I don't know who
said it first, but he or she is definitely right. Legend
tripping is all about an awesome experience. Now that
you've nearly finished reading this book, you are all
psyched up to go out and look for Bigfoot or maybe do
a ghost hunt. I have related my knowledge of legends
and mysteries and I've given you all the tools needed to
have a successful and safe adventure.

Now that the next legend trip is planned and all
the gear is loaded in the vehicle, the family or team
are off on the adventure. I need to bring up one point
about leadership. Being retired military, I have always
found that somebody needs to be in charge at all times.
Somebody has to be there to make the command
decisions and stick with those decisions. I'm saying
while actually walking into the woods or swamps, this
is not a good time to change plans. Being flexible is
always a factor and plans change due to unforeseen
events. An example of this would be arriving at a chosen
campground to find it is closed or full. Always have a
backup plan or an alternate place to go.

One time, we got to a campground and found it full,
so we had to drive around and find another place to

camp. It ended up taking us all day, and we lost one day of walking around. But as the leader, you need to be ready for it. If something goes wrong, and it will, fix it and drive on. In other words, don't stand around mad and complaining about it. Go to Plan B and continue on.

The next step is to find a legend to go check out, find out everything you can about it, then make a plan that includes location. Gather up the family or call some friends to join in, pack the gear and then head out. I wish you all the luck and I hope you find the truth behind the legends you look for.

Once you are traveling with the legend tripping team or family down the highway on the way to adventure, what else can else can be done to create the right mood for this legend trip? The quick answer is to bring reading material related to the subject of the legend trip. If a DVD player is brought on the trip, look for shows about it on DVD. As I mentioned, back in the mid-seventies there was an awesome show called *In Search Of...* which was hosted by *Star Trek* great Leonard Nimoy, and the show dealt with the unexplained. The show featured episodes about Bigfoot, UFOs, lake monsters, ESP, witchcraft, the Oak Island Money Pit, the Bermuda Triangle, and Coral Castle. The show is now on DVD and previous episodes are easily located on YouTube where it is easier and cheaper to watch. The shows are well done and really help set the mood. We watched the episode on Coral Castle on our way to Homestead to see the castle.

Another good thing to bring along is books on the unexplained which help educate the family. There are books on almost every legend and mystery, such as *Weird US* and the rest of the series by Mark Sceurman and Mark Moran. I love these books and I use them all the time when I go on a legend trip. If planning a visit to a different state, check and see if there is a *Weird* book about it. Recently, this series has been released

288

in paperback and are quite affordable. They have many pictures, and younger adults will enjoy them.

If the chosen location offers a tour, take it. The tour guides know their job and location better than most historians and can share personal experiences and anecdotes not found in a guidebook or website.

There is no reason not to go legend tripping. I hate it when I hear someone tell me that he/she doesn't do anything because they're too busy. Planning at least one legend trip a month can create an adventurous mood at home. Look for a group that goes legend tripping; just make sure to check and understand their rules. If a legend trip organization isn't found locally then form a group or take the family. As I said, not a lot of money is needed to trip locally. Just make time and a plan to go out and experience stuff.

I learned being in the military that life is short, and without adventure or challenge, there isn't much to live for. Sometimes, when I hear of a Bigfoot sighting or of a recent haunting, I contact some friends or a family member, and head to the location as soon as I can. I always keep my LT bag in my vehicle just in case I get a call.

I also want to talk about safety. Children watch what adults do and say. As any parent knows, be careful, because what children see, they imitate. When on a legend trip, never take unnecessary risks. Do not try and show off in front of the family. There are numerous horror stories where the father was doing just that and an incident happened, and sadly, in some cases, a family member died. As a parent, put safety first. Set the example of safe practices and behaviors. If a sign says it's private property, then set an example for the kids: stay behind the fence. If the leader acts safely, then the rest of the family will follow suit. If not, most of the trip will be spent worrying about something happening or somebody getting hurt. Explain to the family or team that safety is the top priority.

With that being said, today's youth are not easily stimulated by outdoor vacations. The reaction of most teenagers when told they are going camping is "whatever." Tell them it's a monster hunt, and they will get excited and look forward to the expedition and doing something out of the ordinary. I believe the youth of today are craving adventure. They like video games because in the game they are participating in an adventure. Legend tripping is a way for them to have a real adventure

If looking for something exciting to do with the family or scout group, then maybe going on a legend trip might be the thing. With legend tripping, I know I am doing two good things. First, I'm getting out there and getting exercise and being outdoors instead of being a couch potato. The second is I'm doing what I enjoy doing and looking for legends. I hope you find as much excitement on your legend trips as I do on mine. Don't be deterred and discouraged if nothing is found the first time out. Patience pays off on this field. Albert Einstein said it best: "The important thing is to not stop questioning. Curiosity has its own reason for existence. One cannot help but be in awe when he contemplates the mysteries of eternity, of life, of the marvelous structure of reality. It is enough if one tries merely to comprehend a little of this mystery each day."

GET OUT THERE AND LOOK OUTSIDE THE BOX
GO LEGEND TRIPPING!

Chapter 19
Who's Who in Legend Tripping

The term "legend tripping" is relatively new, but the idea has been around for a really long time. Since explorers first started looking for legendary places such as the Lost City of El Dorado and the Fountain of Youth, legend tripping has been going on. As long as there are still legends and mysteries, legend tripping will continue.

There are many famous legend trippers in history. These people had the courage to stand up and say not everything in this world is explainable and there are strange things out there. They weren't afraid to openly talk and lecture about Bigfoot, UFOs, and haunted places, and put them on the map. Here are a few of these remarkable people, those I feel embody the true spirit of legend tripping. The lives of these adventurers could fill volumes, and numerous biographies have been written about them; consult the bibliography for specific book titles. I will say this: without these people and their brave exploits, there would be no legend tripping. I listed them alphabetically because they are all equally ranked in the legend tripping field. Some, sadly, have passed on.

Cliff Barackman
Cliff was born and raised in Long Beach, California. Throughout his youth, his interests were drawn toward both the physical and biological sciences, as well as to music. Cliff has been a dedicated Sasquatch field researcher for the past two decades. Over the years, he has managed to gather data supporting the hypothesis Sasquatch are an undiscovered species of bipedal great

ape living in North America. Cliff's growing interest in the Bigfoot phenomenon drove him to travel to other parts of the country to investigate the mystery. After extensively travelling the West Coast, he found himself unsatisfied with living in southern California and wanting to live closer to Bigfoot habitat. After living in various parts of California and Washington State, he eventually settled in Portland, OR where he lives today. In 2007, Cliff was contacted to be on the History Channel's *Monster Quest*. The episode, entitled "Legend of the Hairy Beast," featured Cliff and fellow Bigfoot researcher James "Bobo" Fay investigating Bigfoot sighting reports on the Klamath River in northern California. In the spring of 2010, Cliff was asked to accompany Bob Saget on a Bigfoot expedition in northern Washington State. Bob was filming an episode of his A&E series, *Strange Days with Bob Saget*, where he would partake in an eccentric subculture's way of life for a weekend. Cliff is currently one of the investigators on Animal Planet's popular series *Finding Bigfoot*. It premiered on May 30, 2011, and on January 3, 2016 started its ninth season. Teaming up with colleagues James "Bobo" Fay, Matt Moneymaker, and Ranae Holland, Cliff travels around the world investigating Bigfoot evidence.

Jeff Belanger
Jeff was the first to write on the subject of legend tripping. He has written more than a dozen books on the paranormal and legends. His book *Picture Yourself Legend Tripping* is excellent. He is the writer and researcher for the paranormal show *Ghost Adventures* on the Travel Channel and he has appeared on hundreds of radio and television programs worldwide. He is a sought-after lecturer. To find more information on Jeff and where he is speaking, go to his official website at www.jeffbelanger.com. Jeff also maintains an excellent

legend tripping website at www.legendtripping.com.

Charles Berlitz

Berlitz was a best-selling author on paranormal phenomena. His book on the Bermuda Triangle was his biggest best seller. He wrote a number of books dealing with Atlantis, the Roswell Incident, the Philadelphia Experiment and other unexplained mysteries. Berlitz was also an ancient astronaut proponent who believed extraterrestrials visited Earth. He has passed on.

Lyle Blackburn

Lyle wrote *The Beast of Boggy Creek*, which is the definitive guide to the Fouke Monster and one of my favorite books. He conducted the most thorough research of the Fouke Monster ever done, and his book has the most complete up-to-date information on the movie and the legend. Lyle accomplished the same thing with his new book, *Lizard Man*. His books are now considered classics in the cryptozoology field. Lyle has also been featured on television shows such as *Monsters and Mysteries in America*, *Finding Bigfoot*, and *Weird Homes*. Lyle's official website is at http://www.lyleblackburn.com.

Charles Carlson

Charles was an American author, actor, and film producer, as well as a Vietnam veteran. Known as "Florida's Man in Black," or "Master of the Weird," he specialized in the paranormal, and I call him Florida's first legend tripper. He is the author of *Strange Florida*, as well as many historical books and a novel, *Ashley's Shadow*. He retired as a Command Sergeant Major after twenty-five years in the US Army. Charlie, whom I consider a second father, encouraged me to write this book about legend tripping. Sadly Charlie passed

293

away in 2015, but I will always remember him and his guidance.

David Hatcher Childress
David is an adventurer, world traveler, and author whose fans consider him to be the real-life Indiana Jones. David is a legend tripper in every sense of the word. His interests are mainly history, archeology, and cryptozoology, and he has appeared on many TV and radio shows. He is one of the main personalities featured in the nine seasons (so far) of the History Channel's *Ancient Aliens* series. I have had a subscription to his magazine, *World Explorer*, for years. David maintains an excellent website at http://davidhatcherchildress. com.
The World Explorers Club website is at http://wexclub. com.

Loren Coleman
Loren Coleman is one of the world's leading cryptozoologists; some say he is "the" leading living cryptozoologist. Certainly, he is acknowledged as the current living American researcher and writer who has most popularized cryptozoology in the late 20th and early 21st centuries. He started his fieldwork and investigations in 1960, traveling and trekking extensively in pursuit of cryptozoological mysteries. In 1969, Coleman began writing to share his experiences. An honorary member of Ivan T. Sanderson's Society for the Investigation of the Unexplained in the 1970s, Coleman has been bestowed with similar honorary memberships in other groups: the North Idaho College Cryptozoology Club in 1983, the British Columbia Scientific Cryptozoology Club, CryptoSafari International, and other international organizations. He was also a Life Member and Benefactor of the

International Society of Cryptozoology (now-defunct). Loren Coleman's daily blog, as a member of the Cryptomundo Team, served as an ongoing avenue of communication for the ever-growing body of cryptozoo news from 2005 through 2013. He returned as an infrequent contributor beginning Halloween week of 2015. In 2003, he founded the International Cryptozoology Museum in Portland, Maine, where he is the current director. It was his *Mysterious America* which inspired me to go out and look for legends. I first meet Loren at Ripley's Believe It or Not! Odditorium in St. Augustine and we have remained good friends ever since. He maintains a great website called "The Cryptozoologist" at http://lorencoleman.com.

Marc A. Dewerth
Marc DeWerth of Columbia Station, Ohio has been a longtime Ohio Bigfoot investigator since 1990, actively pursuing Bigfoot creatures throughout the country. Marc has interviewed over 200 witnesses who have claimed seeing a large, hair-covered creature roaming the Ohio woodlands and has participated in many public and private expeditions over the years. After many years in the field throughout Ohio and beyond, he's quite confident in the existence of Bigfoot. He's been a longtime investigator with the BFRO (Bigfoot Field Researchers Organization), and is the President of the Ohio Bigfoot Organization. Currently, Marc and his group are the hosts of the Ohio Bigfoot Conference every year, a nationally recognized event taking place every spring at Salt Fork State Park. To learn more, go to www.ohiobigfootconference.org.

Col. Percy Fawcett
Col. Fawcett was an English explorer and legend tripper. He is considered a groundbreaker in the field of exploits

into the unknown. Percy wrote about creatures called the Maricoxi which he described as large bipedal apelike creatures. This Bigfoot was a household word. He saw a huge hundred-foot-long anaconda, he claimed. Fawcett disappeared during an expedition to find the legendary lost city of Z in the jungles of South America. A more complete bio and story of his expeditions can be found at Virtual Exploration Society at www. unmuseum. org/fawcett.htm. He disappeared in 1925.

Charles Fort
Charles researched the mysterious and the unexplained, and he wrote about these subjects in several books, including *The Book of the Damned*. There isn't a legend tripper out there who doesn't know or read Charles Fort's work. He is credited with inventing the word "teleportation." The great thing is the books are still in publication today. The International Fortean Organization publishes a magazine, *INFO Journal*, and hosts an annual convention to commemorate the work and spirit of Charles Fort. He passed on in 1932. Read more about him at www. forteans.com/ and www.forteana.org.

Vincent Gaddis
Vincent was an American author who coined the phrase "Bermuda Triangle" in a February 1964 *Argosy* cover piece. He popularized tales of anomalous phenomena in a style similar to Charles Fort. His two books *Invisible Horizons* (1965) and *Mysterious Lights and Fires* (1967) are classics and are popular among legend trippers. He has passed on.

Josh Gates
Josh is the star and producer of the hit television show *Destination Unknown* on the History Channel, and *Destination Truth* on the SyFy channel, one of my favorite

296

shows. He has traveled to more countries and looked for the existence of more unknown creatures than any other television host in history. Josh and his crew found the most indisputable proof of the Yeti's existence when they found large bipedal tracks in Nepal. I highly recommend his book *Destination Truth: Diary of a Monster Hunter*. I got to meet and talk with Josh at the 2013 Texas Bigfoot Conference in Fort Worth, Texas. His official website is at http://joshuagates.com.

Ken Gerhard

Ken, an author and explorer, is one of the top cryptozoologists and field researchers in the field today. Ken has traveled the world searching for evidence of mysterious beasts including Bigfoot, the Loch Ness Monster, the chupacabras, flying creatures and even werewolves. He has authored three best-selling books on the subject and his research has been featured on many television shows including *MonsterQuest* and *Ancient Aliens*, as well as on several networks including National Geographic, Science Channel, Animal Planet, SyFy Channel and the Travel Channel. He has been featured on numerous television shows about cryptozoology and is an active member of the Centre for Fortean Zoology and the Gulf Coast Bigfoot Research Organization. He serves as a consultant for various paranormal groups. He has investigated reports of cryptids and mysterious animals around the world. He currently lectures and exhibits at events across the United States. As of 2016 he was co-host of the History Channel series *Missing in Alaska*.

Linda Moulton Howe

Linda is an American investigative journalist and documentarian. She is best known as a UFOlogist and advocate of a variety of conspiracy theories. She is well known for her investigations of cattle mutilations, and her conclusion that they are of extraterrestrial origin. She is also noted for her speculations that the US government is involved with aliens.

Steve Kulls
Steve has had a lifelong fascination with the Bigfoot phenomenon since an early age. In 1998, after reading *Monsters of the Northwoods*, Steve learned there were numerous sighting reports close to his residence in upstate New York. Steve has had three sightings in the last ten years and a handful of what he describes as "most likely, close encounters" with the creatures, after initially entering the field quite skeptical. Steve has appeared on numerous local news programs around the country and national venues such as *Fox and Friends*, and been interviewed in print in over 100 newspapers over the last ten years. Steve has appeared on the History Channel and the National Geographic Channel, featured on several programs. Steve is a former Licensed Private Investigator in New York of 28 years.

Edward Meyers
Ed is Vice President of Ripley's Believe It or Not!, Inc., based out of Orlando, Florida. Ed is also Ripley's curator and archivist and has taken up where Robert Ripley left off, scouring the world searching for weird items for the Ripley's Odditoriums. Ed can tell more exciting stories of far-off travels than anybody I know. He definitely has my dream job: to travel all over the world and look for legends. Ed is a true legend tripper.

Christopher O'Brien
Since 1992, Christopher O'Brien has investigated over one thousand paranormal events reported in the San Luis Valley located in south central Colorado/north

298

central New Mexico. Working with law enforcement officials, ex-military, ranchers and an extensive network of sky watchers, he documented what may have been the most intense wave of unexplained activity ever seen in a single region of North America. His ten-year investigation resulted in the three books of his "mysterious valley" trilogy, *The Mysterious Valley*, *Enter the Valley*, and *Secrets of the Mysterious Valley*. His meticulous field investigation of UFO reports, unexplained livestock deaths, Native American legends, cryptozoology, secret military activity and the folklore found in the world's largest alpine valley, has produced one of the largest databases of unusual occurrences gathered on a single geographic region. His latest book, *Stalking the Herd*, has been released by Adventures Unlimited Press and explores the cattle mutilation mystery. His website is at http://www.ourstrangeplanet.com

Nick Redfern

Nick is a British best-selling author, UFOlogist, and cryptozoologist now living in Dallas, Texas. Nick is a legend tripper in the truest sense. Nick has traveled the world investigating the unexplained, and written numerous books on the subject. He is also a regular on television. His official website is www.nickredfern.com.

Robert L. Ripley

Legend tripping cannot be mentioned without bringing up Robert Ripley. He traveled all over the world looking for the weird, the bizarre, and the unexplained. He first became famous for his *Ripley's Believe It or Not!* comic strips. He went on to publish books and have a radio program and a TV show. He opened his first Odditorium Museum in Chicago in 1933, and today there are dozens of Ripley's Believe It or Not! Museums

299

in the USA and beyond. Ripley passed on in 1949. For the record, I am a huge Ripley's Believe It or Not! fan. I remember as a kid thinking, "What a great job to have, traveling all over the world looking for the strange and unexplained." To read more about Mr. Ripley, go to the official Ripley's website at www.ripleys.com.

Ivan T. Sanderson
Mr. Sanderson was a biologist and writer born in Edinburgh, Scotland, who became a naturalized citizen of the United States. Sanderson is remembered for his interest in cryptozoology and paranormal subjects and is credited with coining the term "cryptozoology." A pioneer in the field of cryptozoology, he founded the Society for the Investigation of the Unexplained (SITU). As a kid I read all his books, and they inspired me to go legend tripping. I was a member of the SITU organization, and I idolized him and his adventures. I remember wanting to be just like him when I grew up. Sanderson passed on in 1973. A lot of great information about this man, who cryptozoology owes so much to, can be found on Richard Grigonis's website, www.richardgrigonis.com.

Tom Slick
Tom was a Texas oilman who was also an inventor and an adventurer. He was responsible for a number of successful expeditions to look for the Yeti and Bigfoot. Loren Coleman has written several books about him, including *Tom Slick: True Life Encounters in Cryptozoology*. In 1962 while flying in a small plane over Montana, his plane disintegrated. He was killed.

Pat Spain
Pat Spain is a young wildlife scientist. For the past eight years, he has worked at one of the world's leading

300

biotechnology companies, helping to develop and apply the most advanced technologies in the life sciences. His wildlife expertise spans from caring for exotic reptiles at a major reptile distribution center to teaching students about marine life at the New England Aquarium. In 2005, Spain created a nature web show titled "Nature Calls" and chronicled his "ridiculous adventures to find, film and interact with wild animals all over the planet." His exploits for the program ranged from examining scorpions and black widows in the Arizona desert to wolves in New England. Spain has a Bachelor of Science in biology from Suffolk University. His great-uncle, Charles Fort, was a paranormal pioneer in the early 20th century who investigated strange reports from around the world. Pat was the star and host of the popular NatGeo cryptozoology show *Beast Hunter*.

Troy Taylor

Troy Taylor is a researcher of history, crime, and the supernatural, and the author of 116 books on ghosts, hauntings, history, crime and the unexplained in America. Taylor shares a birthday with one of his favorite authors, F. Scott Fitzgerald, but instead of living in New York, Hollywood and Paris like Fitzgerald, Taylor grew up in Illinois. Raised on the prairies of the state, he developed an interest in "things that go bump in the night" at an early age and as a young man, developed ghost tours and wrote about haunts in Chicago and central Illinois. He began his first book in 1989, which delved into the history and hauntings of Decatur, Illinois. Troy has appeared in documentary productions for TLC, The History Channel, A&E, Discovery Channel, PBS, CMT, Travel Channel, Investigation Discovery and in various network programs and syndicated news shows. These programs have included *America's Ghost Hunters*, *Ghost Waters*, *Night Visitors*, *Beyond Human*

301

Legend Tripping

Senses, Scariest Places on Earth, Children of the Grave, The Possessed, America's Most Terrifying Places, Unexplained Files, and *Evil Kin.* Troy is the founder and owner of American Hauntings Tours and Events.

David Weatherly
David has been exploring the world of the strange for more than thirty-five years. He has written and lectured on a diverse range of topics including cryptozoology, UFOlogy, and hauntings. David has also studied shamanic and magical traditions with elders from numerous cultures. Dave is a true legend tripper who is not only knowledgeable but also extremely funny and a first rate storyteller. I consider it a real privilege to have Dave as a friend. You can follow Dave on his website at http://twocrowsparanormal.blogspot.com/ and Twitter: https://twitter.com/#!/TwoCrowsPara.

Craig Woolheater
Craig is another great friend and legend tripper. Craig runs the popular website *Cryptomundo,* which features the most up-to-date information on cryptozoology on the web. Craig is the former director of the Texas Bigfoot Research Conservatory. When Tracy and I visit Texas, we always stop in to see Craig and talk about what is going on in the monster hunting community. Craig's website is at www. cryptomundo.com.

No doubt I have out left many important researchers and authors... sorry about that! I am limited in space!

302

Chapter 20
Legend Tripping in
Popular Fiction

Believe it or not, legend tripping has always been a mainstay of popular fiction in both books and movies. It was just never referred to as legend tripping, but as mystery hunting. Many grew up watching these shows and reading the books without realizing they were about legend tripping. There are legend trippers in novels, on television, and on the silver screen. Here are some of them:

The Adventures of Tom Sawyer by Mark Twain presents one of the earliest concepts of legend tripping, with tales of adolescents visiting haunted houses and caves. The book has inspired many people to go out and look for adventure.

The Adventures of Tintin series by Hergé is about the globetrotting adventures of the intrepid young reporter Tintin who goes looking for legends with his dog Snowy. I highly recommend these books for children if they have never read them, as they encourage and build a sense of wonder and intrigue.

The Hardy Boys series by Frankin W. Dixon. These stories feature the Hardy Boys, teenage brothers and amateur detectives who have adventures while investigating haunted places and lost treasures.

The Three Investigators series by Robert Arthur. Three children set up a secret detective agency and solve mysteries. This series has a special place in my heart. I would never have become a book reader without it.

The Trixie Belden series by Julie Campbell. Trixie

and her friends solve mysteries. She has a run-in with Bigfoot in *The Sasquatch Mystery*. These books are great for young girls.

Indiana Jones may not be the first, but he is without a doubt the most famous of fictional legend trippers. *Raiders of the Lost Ark* and the other Indiana Jones movies inspired many, including me, to go out on a legend trip. There is also a book series on the further exploits of the great adventurer by authors Rob MacGregor, Martin Caidin and Max McCoy.

Lara Croft is a legend tripper from the hit video games and *Tomb Raider* movies. Considered a modern, female Indiana Jones, her adventures start when she is sent on missions that usually involve legends. The games also feature crytpids such as the Yeti and a giant octopus.

The Goonies is an action-adventure movie about a group of youths who go on a legend trip. The movie has everything a legend tripper seeking adventure would want: buried treasure, a cave maze with booby traps, and (in the recent Blu-ray edition) a giant octopus.

Scooby-Doo, Where Are You? was the original cartoon series, in which four teenagers and their talking Great Dane dog go legend tripping and solve mysteries. When I was a kid, everybody wanted to go mystery hunting with Scooby Doo. If you have younger kids, I highly recommend the series; they will understand why you like legend tripping.

Jonny Quest is a cartoon series about a boy adventurer who goes on adventures with his father and his friend Hadji. Many of the adventures involved legends like the Yeti, but they also featured gadgets that would make James Bond jealous. I think these shows are one of the reasons I own a hovercraft and go legend tripping.

The X-Files is a science fiction, horror, drama

television series that featured everything related to legend tripping. The award-winning series focused on FBI Special Agents Fox Mulder and Dana Scully as they investigated X-Files, unsolved cases involving paranormal phenomena. I became a huge fan of this show and never missed an episode. The series spawned two movies, *The X-Files* and *The X-Files: I Want to Believe.*

Author and Illustrator's Bio

Robert C. Robinson was born at Hamilton Air Force Base, California. He grew up an Army brat and had the privilege of visiting numerous countries. After graduating high school in 1982, in Lansing, Kansas, Robert enlisted in the United States Army. He received his Basic and Advanced Individual Training as a Military Policeman at Fort McClellan, Alabama. He completed the Basic Airborne School, Air Assault School, Jumpmaster School, and Military Police Special Reaction Team Course. Rob has a Bachelor's Degree in Criminal Justice from Everest University and is a certified PADI wreck diver.

During his twenty-one years of service, Rob served in South Korea, Texas, Italy, North Carolina, Johnston Island, Germany, Cuba, Panama, and participated in Operation Enduring Freedom in Afghanistan. Rob retired as Sergeant First Class from the Army in 2003 and started teaching JROTC in Okeechobee, Florida. Rob then relocated to the beautiful city of Winter Haven, Florida, and continued teaching JROTC at Summerlin Academy in Bartow.

Rob is married to the former Tracy L. Bonfransico and they have four sons (Sean, Christopher, Joshua, and Jesse) and two daughters (Brittany and Kera).

Robert first became interested in cryptozoology after watching the movie *The Legend of Boggy Creek* when he was young. His mother, who is from Scotland, would tell him about the Loch Ness Monster. Also, his uncle would relate scary stories of the Fouke Monster and other monster legends. Because the whole subject of real monsters scared him, Rob started researching monsters by reading every book on the unexplained that he could find. The fear turned into intrigue and

Rob has continued to follow this passion.

After Rob retired from the Army, he started going on Swamp Ape expeditions as well as other monster hunts, including a hunt for a reported serpent in Frostproof, Florida. Tracy introduced Rob to the paranormal, such as hauntings and ghosts, and Rob has accompanied Tracy on numerous ghost hunts.

Rob and his family appeared on ABC's *Wife Swap* on July 30, 2010, as the monster and ghost hunting family. The Robinsons try to go on at least one monster or ghost hunt each month, when their schedules allow. Rob is an active member of Sasquatch Hunters, the Independent Sasquatch Research Team, the North American Wood Ape Conservancy, Mutual UFO Network, and the Alliance for Unveiling and Researching Anomalies.

Rob appeared in the second installment of PBS's *Weird Florida* series, titled "Weird Florida: On the Road Again," which began airing January 9, 2013. He will also appear in segments on the Skunk Ape in *Monsters and Mysteries in America* and *Bigfoot in America* on the Destination America channel. Rob currently gives lectures on legend tripping at various events.

J. Kent Holloway is the international bestselling author of six paranormal thrillers. He also co-writes Jeremy Robinson's 'Jack Sigler Continuum' series. Kent has finally completed his very first forensic crime thriller, *Clean Exit*, the first book in the 'Ajax Clean Thriller' series. With more than twenty years of experience as a forensic death investigator for two different medical examiner offices within the state of Florida, as well as several years of work as both a private investigator and a newspaper reporter following the crime beat, he brings a unique and authentic perspective to the genre. He also grew up in a haunted house in southeastern Kentucky, leading him to develop a healthy respect and affinity for the paranormal, folklore, and all things legend. Find Kent at his website: www.kenthollowayonline.com or by following him on Facebook.

www.AdventuresUnlimitedPress.com

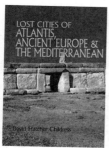

LOST CITIES OF ATLANTIS, ANCIENT EUROPE & THE MEDITERRANEAN
by David Hatcher Childress

Atlantis! The legendary lost continent comes under the close scrutiny of maverick archaeologist David Hatcher Childress in this sixth book in the internationally popular *Lost Cities* series. Childress takes the reader in search of sunken cities in the Mediterranean; across the Atlas Mountains in search of Atlantean ruins; to remote islands in search of megalithic ruins; to meet living legends and secret societies. From Ireland to Turkey, Morocco to Eastern Europe, and around the remote islands of the Mediterranean and Atlantic, Childress takes the reader on an astonishing quest for mankind's past. Ancient technology, cataclysms, megalithic construction, lost civilizations and devastating wars of the past are all explored in this book. Childress challenges the skeptics and proves that great civilizations not only existed in the past, but the modern world and its problems are reflections of the ancient world of Atlantis.

524 PAGES. 6x9 PAPERBACK. ILLUSTRATED. BIBLIOGRAPHY & INDEX. $16.95. CODE: MED

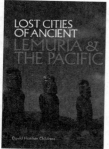

LOST CITIES OF ANCIENT LEMURIA & THE PACIFIC
by David Hatcher Childress

Was there once a continent in the Pacific? Called Lemuria or Pacifica by geologists, Mu or Pan by the mystics, there is now ample mythological, geological and archaeological evidence to "prove" that an advanced and ancient civilization once lived in the central Pacific. Maverick archaeologist and explorer David Hatcher Childress combs the Indian Ocean, Australia and the Pacific in search of the surprising truth about mankind's past. Contains photos of the underwater city on Pohnpei; explanations on how the statues were levitated around Easter Island in a clockwise vortex movement; tales of disappearing islands; Egyptians in Australia; and more.

379 PAGES. 6x9 PAPERBACK. $14.95. ILLUSTRATED. CODE: LEM

LOST CITIES & ANCIENT MYSTERIES OF SOUTH AMERICA
by David Hatcher Childress

Rogue adventurer and maverick archaeologist David Hatcher Childress takes the reader on unforgettable journeys deep into deadly jungles, high up on windswept mountains and across scorching deserts in search of lost civilizations and ancient mysteries. Travel with David and explore stone cities high in mountain forests and hear fantastic tales of Inca treasure, living dinosaurs, and a mysterious tunnel system. Whether he is hopping freight trains, searching for secret cities, or just dealing with the daily problems of food, money, and romance, the author keeps the reader spellbound. Includes both early and current maps, photos, and illustrations, and plenty of advice for the explorer planning his or her own journey of discovery.

381 PAGES. 6x9 PAPERBACK. ILLUSTRATED. FOOTNOTES. BIBLIOGRAPHY. INDEX. $16.95. CODE: SAM

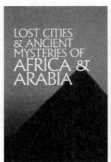

LOST CITIES & ANCIENT MYSTERIES OF AFRICA & ARABIA
by David Hatcher Childress

Across ancient deserts, dusty plains and steaming jungles, maverick archaeologist David Childress continues his world-wide quest for lost cities and ancient mysteries. Join him as he discovers forbidden cities in the Empty Quarter of Arabia; "Atlantean" ruins in Egypt and the Kalahari desert; a mysterious, ancient empire in the Sahara; and more. This is the tale of an extraordinary life on the road: across war-torn countries, Childress searches for King Solomon's Mines, living dinosaurs, the Ark of the Covenant and the solutions to some of the fantastic mysteries of the past.

423 PAGES. 6x9 PAPERBACK. ILLUSTRATED. FOOTNOTES & BIBLIOGRAPHY. $14.95. CODE: AFA

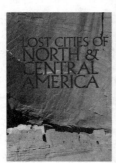

LOST CITIES OF NORTH & CENTRAL AMERICA
by David Hatcher Childress

Down the back roads from coast to coast, maverick archaeologist and adventurer David Hatcher Childress goes deep into unknown America. With this incredible book, you will search for lost Mayan cities and books of gold, discover an ancient canal system in Arizona, climb gigantic pyramids in the Midwest, explore megalithic monuments in New England, and join the astonishing quest for lost cities throughout North America. From the war-torn jungles of Guatemala, Nicaragua and Honduras to the deserts, mountains and fields of Mexico, Canada, and the U.S.A., Childress takes the reader in search of sunken ruins, Viking forts, strange tunnel systems, living dinosaurs, early Chinese explorers, and fantastic lost treasure. Packed with both early and current maps, photos and illustrations.

590 PAGES. 6x9 PAPERBACK. ILLUSTRATED. FOOTNOTES. BIBLIOGRAPHY. INDEX. $16.95. CODE: NCA

LOST CITIES OF CHINA, CENTRAL ASIA & INDIA
by David Hatcher Childress

Like a real life "Indiana Jones," maverick archaeologist David Childress takes the reader on an incredible adventure across some of the world's oldest and most remote countries in search of lost cities and ancient mysteries. Discover ancient cities in the Gobi Desert; hear fantastic tales of lost continents, vanished civilizations and secret societies bent on ruling the world; visit forgotten monasteries in forbidding snow-capped mountains with strange tunnels to mysterious subterranean cities! A unique combination of far-out exploration and practical travel advice, it will astound and delight the experienced traveler or the armchair voyager.

429 PAGES. 6x9 PAPERBACK. ILLUSTRATED. FOOTNOTES & BIBLIOGRAPHY. $14.95. CODE: CHI

TECHNOLOGY OF THE GODS
The Incredible Sciences of the Ancients
by David Hatcher Childress

Popular *Lost Cities* author David Hatcher Childress takes us into the amazing world of ancient technology, from computers in antiquity to the "flying machines of the gods." Childress looks at the technology that was allegedly used in Atlantis and the theory that the Great Pyramid of Egypt was originally a gigantic power station. He examines tales of ancient flight and the technology that it involved; how the ancients used electricity; megalithic building techniques; the use of crystal lenses and the fire from the gods; evidence of various high tech weapons in the past, including atomic weapons; ancient metallurgy and heavy machinery; the role of modern inventors such as Nikola Tesla in bringing ancient technology back into modern use; impossible artifacts; and more.

356 PAGES. 6x9 PAPERBACK. ILLUSTRATED. BIBLIOGRAPHY. $16.95. CODE: TGOD

ARK OF GOD
The Incredible Power of the Ark of the Covenant
By David Hatcher Childress

Childress takes us on an incredible journey in search of the truth about (and science behind) the fantastic biblical artifact known as the Ark of the Covenant. This object made by Moses at Mount Sinai—part wooden-metal box and part golden statue—had the power to create "lightning" to kill people, and also to fly and lead people through the wilderness. The Ark of the Covenant suddenly disappears from the Bible record and what happened to it is not mentioned. Was it hidden in the underground passages of King Solomon's temple and later discovered by the Knights Templar? Was it taken through Egypt to Ethiopia as many Coptic Christians believe? Childress looks into hidden history, astonishing ancient technology, and a 3,000-year-old mystery that continues to fascinate millions of people today. Color section.

420 Pages. 6x9 Paperback. Illustrated. $22.00 Code: AOG

LOST CONTINENTS & THE HOLLOW EARTH
I Remember Lemuria and the Shaver Mystery
by David Hatcher Childress & Richard Shaver

A thorough examination of the early hollow earth stories of Richard Shaver and the fascination that fringe fantasy subjects such as lost continents and the hollow earth have had for the American public. Shaver's rare 1948 book *I Remember Lemuria* is reprinted in its entirety, and the book is packed with illustrations from Ray Palmer's *Amazing Stories* magazine of the 1940s. Palmer and Shaver told of tunnels running through the earth—tunnels inhabited by the Deros and Teros, humanoids from an ancient spacefaring race that had inhabited the earth, eventually going underground, hundreds of thousands of years ago. Childress discusses the famous hollow earth books and delves deep into whatever reality may be behind the stories of tunnels in the earth. Operation High Jump to Antarctica in 1947 and Admiral Byrd's bizarre statements, tunnel systems in South America and Tibet, the underground world of Agartha, the belief of UFOs coming from the South Pole, more.

344 PAGES. 6x9 PAPERBACK. $16.95. CODE: LCHE

YETIS, SASQUATCH & HAIRY GIANTS
By David Hatcher Childress

Childress takes the reader on a fantastic journey across the Himalayas to Europe and North America in his quest for Yeti, Sasquatch and Hairy Giants. Childress begins with a discussion of giants and then tells of his own decades-long quest for the Yeti in Nepal, Sikkim, Bhutan and other areas of the Himalayas, and then proceeds to his research into Bigfoot, Sasquatch and Skunk Apes in North America. Chapters include: The Giants of Yore; Giants Among Us; Wildmen and Hairy Giants; The Call of the Yeti; Kanchenjunga Demons; The Yeti of Tibet, Mongolia & Russia; Bigfoot & the Grassman; Sasquatch Rules the Forest; Modern Sasquatch Accounts; more. Includes a 16-page color photo insert of astonishing photos!
360 pages. 5x9 Paperback. Illustrated. Bibliography. Index. $18.95. Code: YSHG

SECRETS OF THE HOLY LANCE
The Spear of Destiny in History & Legend
by Jerry E. Smith

Secrets of the Holy Lance traces the Spear from its possession by Constantine, Rome's first Christian Caesar, to Charlemagne's claim that with it he ruled the Holy Roman Empire by Divine Right, and on through two thousand years of kings and emperors, until it came within Hitler's grasp—and beyond! Did it rest for a while in Antarctic ice? Is it now hidden in Europe, awaiting the next person to claim its awesome power? Neither debunking nor worshiping, *Secrets of the Holy Lance* seeks to pierce the veil of myth and mystery around the Spear.
312 PAGES. 6x9 PAPERBACK. ILLUSTRATED. $16.95. CODE: SOHL

THE CRYSTAL SKULLS
Astonishing Portals to Man's Past
by David Hatcher Childress and Stephen S. Mehler

Childress introduces the technology and lore of crystals, and then plunges into the turbulent times of the Mexican Revolution form the backdrop for the rollicking adventures of Ambrose Bierce, the renowned journalist who went missing in the jungles in 1913, and F.A. Mitchell-Hedges, the notorious adventurer who emerged from the jungles with the most famous of the crystal skulls. Mehler shares his extensive knowledge of and experience with crystal skulls. Having been involved in the field since the 1980s, he has personally examined many of the most influential skulls, and has worked with the leaders in crystal skull research. Color section.
294 pages. 6x9 Paperback. Illustrated. $18.95. Code: CRSK

THE LAND OF OSIRIS
An Introduction to Khemitology
by Stephen S. Mehler

Was there an advanced prehistoric civilization in ancient Egypt? Were they the people who built the great pyramids and carved the Great Sphinx? Did the pyramids serve as energy devices and not as tombs for kings? Chapters include: Egyptology and Its Paradigms; Khemitology—New Paradigms; Asgat Nefer—The Harmony of Water; Khemit and the Myth of Atlantis; The Extraterrestrial Question; more.
272 PAGES. 6x9 PAPERBACK. ILLUSTRATED. COLOR SECTION. BIBLIOGRAPHY. $18.95. CODE: LOOS

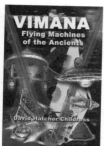

VIMANA:
Flying Machines of the Ancients
by David Hatcher Childress

According to early Sanskrit texts the ancients had several types of airships called vimanas. Like aircraft of today, vimanas were used to fly through the air from city to city; to conduct aerial surveys of uncharted lands; and as delivery vehicles for awesome weapons. David Hatcher Childress, popular *Lost Cities* author and star of the History Channel's long-running show Ancient Aliens, takes us on an astounding investigation into tales of ancient flying machines. In his new book, packed with photos and diagrams, he consults ancient texts and modern stories and presents astonishing evidence that aircraft, similar to the ones we use today, were used thousands of years ago in India, Sumeria, China and other countries. Includes a 24-page color section.

408 Pages. 6x9 Paperback. Illustrated. $22.95. Code: VMA

MIND CONTROL AND UFOS:
Casebook on Alternative 3
By Jim Keith

Keith's classic investigation of the Alternative 3 scenario as it first appeared on British television over 20 years ago. Keith delves into the bizarre story of Alternative 3, including mind control programs, underground bases not only on the Earth but also on the Moon and Mars, the real origin of the UFO problem, the mysterious deaths of Marconi Electronics employees in Britain during the 1980s, the Russian-American superpower arms race of the 50s, 60s and 70s as a massive hoax, more.

248 Pages. 6x9 Paperback. Illustrated. $14.95. Code: MCUF

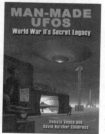

MAN-MADE UFOS
WWII's Secret Legacy
By Renato Vesco & David Hatcher Childress

The classic book on suppressed technology: the early "flying saucer" technology of Nazi Germany and the genesis of man-made UFOs. Examined in detail are secret underground airfields and factories; German secret weapons; "suction" aircraft; the origin of NASA; gyroscopic stabilizers and engines; the secret Marconi aircraft factory in South America; and more. Chapters include: June 24, 1947: A Day to Remember; The True Story of Project Blue Book; Mysterious Night Lights Over the Rhineland; Revolutionary German Anti-Aircraft Weaponry; How To Do the Impossible; Marconi's Secret Saucer Base; more.

524 Pages. 6x9 Paperback. Illustrated. $22.95. Code: MMU

ROSWELL AND THE REICH
By Joseph P. Farrell

Farrell comes to a radically different scenario of what happened in Roswell in July 1947, and why the US military has continued to cover it up to this day. Farrell presents a fascinating case that what crashed may have been representative of an independent postwar Nazi power—an extraterritorial Reich monitoring its old enemy, America, and the continuing development of the very technologies confiscated from Germany at the end of the War.

540 pages. 6x9 Paperback. $19.95. Code: RWR

IN SECRET MONGOLIA
by Henning Haslund

Haslund takes us into the barely known world of Mongolia of 1921, a land of god-kings, bandits, vast mountain wilderness and a Russian army running amok. Starting in Peking, Haslund journeys to Mongolia as part of a mission to establish a Danish butter farm in a remote corner of northern Mongolia. With Haslund we meet the "Mad Baron" Ungern-Sternberg and his renegade Russian army, the many characters of Urga's fledgling foreign community, and the last god-king of Mongolia, Seng Chen Gegen, the fifth reincarnation of the Tiger god and the "ruler of all Torguts." Aside from the esoteric and mystical material, there is plenty of just plain adventure: Haslund encounters a Mongolian werewolf; is ambushed along the trail; escapes from prison and fights terrifying blizzards; more.

374 PAGES. 6x9 PAPERBACK. ILLUSTRATED. BIBLIOGRAPHY & INDEX. $16.95. CODE: ISM

MEN & GODS IN MONGOLIA
by Henning Haslund

Haslund takes us to the lost city of Karakota in the Gobi desert. We meet the Bodgo Gegen, a god-king in Mongolia similar to the Dalai Lama of Tibet. We meet Dambin Jansang, the dreaded warlord of the "Black Gobi." Haslund and companions journey across the Gobi desert by camel caravan; are kidnapped and held for ransom; witness initiation into Shamanic societies; meet reincarnated warlords; and experience the violent birth of "modern" Mongolia.

358 PAGES. 6x9 PAPERBACK. ILLUSTRATED. INDEX. $18.95. CODE: MGM

This rare 1935 book is back in print!
Mystic Traveller Series

MYSTERIES OF ANCIENT SOUTH AMERICA
by Harold T. Wilkins

Wilkins digs into old manuscripts and books to bring us some truly amazing stories of South America: a bizarre subterranean tunnel system; lost cities in the remote border jungles of Brazil; cataclysmic changes that shaped South America; and other strange stories from one of the world's great researchers. Chapters include: Dead Cities of Ancient Brazil, The Jungle Light that Shines by Itself, The Missionary Men in Black: Forerunners of the Great Catastrophe, The Sign of the Sun: The World's Oldest Alphabet, The Atlanean "Subterraneans" of the Incas, Tiahuanacu and the Giants, more.

236 PAGES. 6x9 PAPERBACK. ILLUSTRATED. INDEX. $14.95. CODE: MASA

SECRET CITIES OF OLD SOUTH AMERICA
by Harold T. Wilkins

The reprint of Wilkins' classic book, first published in 1952, claiming that South America was Atlantis. Chapters include Mysteries of a Lost World; Atlantis Unveiled; Red Riddles on the Rocks; South America's Amazons Existed!; The Mystery of El Dorado and Gran Payatiti—the Final Refuge of the Incas; Monstrous Beasts of the Unexplored Swamps & Wilds; Weird Denizens of Antediluvian Forests; New Light on Atlantis from the World's Oldest Book; The Mystery of Old Man Noah and the Arks; and more.

438 PAGES. 6x9 PAPERBACK. ILLUSTRATED. BIBLIOGRAPHY & INDEX. $16.95. CODE: SCOS

ATLANTIS REPRINT SERIES

www.AdventuresUnlimitedPress.com

LOST CITIES & ANCIENT MYSTERIES OF THE SOUTHWEST
By David Hatcher Childress
Join David as he starts in northern Mexico and then to west Texas amd into New Mexico where he stumbles upon a hollow mountain with a billion dollars of gold bars hidden deep inside it! In Arizona he investigates tales of Egyptian catacombs in the Grand Canyon, cruises along the Devil's Highway, and tackles the century-old mystery of the Lost Dutchman mine. In California Childress checks out the rumors of mummified giants and weird tunnels in Death Valley—It's a full-tilt blast down the back roads of the Southwest in search of the weird and wondrous mysteries of the past!
486 Pages. 6x9 Paperback. Illustrated. $19.95. Code: LCSW

AXIS OF THE WORLD
The Search for the Oldest American Civilization
by Igor Witkowski
Witkowski's research reveals remnants of a high civilization that was able to exert its influence on almost the entire planet, and did so with full consciousness. Sites around South America show that this was a place where they built their crowning achievements. Easter Island, in the southeastern Pacific, constitutes one of them. The Rongo-Rongo language that developed there points westward to the Indus Valley. Taken together, the facts presented provide new proof that an antediluvian civilization flourished several millennia ago.
220 pages. 6x9 Paperback. Illustrated. $18.95. Code: AXOW

SECRETS OF THE MYSTERIOUS VALLEY
by Christopher O'Brien
No other region in North America features the variety and intensity of unusual phenomena found in the world's largest alpine valley, the San Luis Valley of Colorado and New Mexico. Since 1989, O'Brien has documented thousands of high-strange accounts that report UFOs, ghosts, crypto-creatures, cattle mutilations, and more, along with portal areas, secret underground bases and covert military activity. Hundreds of animals have been found strangely slain during waves of anomalous aerial craft sightings. Is the government directly involved? Are there underground bases here?
460 PAGES. 6x9 PAPERBACK. ILLUSTRATED. BIBLIOGRAPHY. $19.95. CODE: SOMV

PIRATES & THE LOST TEMPLAR FLEET
by David Hatcher Childress
The lost Templar fleet was originally based at La Rochelle in southern France, but fled to the deep fiords of Scotland upon the dissolution of the Order by King Phillip. This banned fleet of ships was later commanded by the St. Clair family of Rosslyn Chapel. St. Clair and his Templars made a voyage to Canada in the year 1398 AD, nearly 100 years before Columbus! Chapters include: 10,000 Years of Seafaring; The Templars and the Assassins; The Lost Templar Fleet and the Jolly Roger; Maps of the Ancient Sea Kings; Pirates, Templars and the New World; Christopher Columbus—Secret Templar Pirate?; Later Day Pirates and the War with the Vatican; Pirate Utopias and the New Jerusalem; more.
320 PAGES. 6x9 PAPERBACK. ILLUSTRATED. BIBLIOGRAPHY. $16.95. CODE: PLTF

EYE OF THE PHOENIX
Mysterious Visions and
Secrets of the American Southwest
by Gary David

GaryDavid explores enigmas and anomalies in the vast American Southwest. Contents includes: The Great Pyramids of Arizona; Meteor Crater—Arizona's First Bonanza?; Chaco Canyon—Ancient City of the Dog Star; Phoenix—Masonic Metropolis in the Valley of the Sun; Along the 33rd Parallel—A Global Mystery Circle; The Flying Shields of the Hopi Katsinam; Is the Starchild a Hopi God?; The Ant People of Orion—Ancient Star Beings of the Hopi; Serpent Knights of the Round Temple; The Nagas—Origin of the Hopi Snake Clan?; The Tau (or T-shaped) Cross—Hopi/Maya/Egyptian Connections; The Hopi Stone Tablets of Techqua Ikachi; The Four Arms of Destiny—Swastikas in the Hopi World of the End Times; and more.
348 pages. 6x9 Paperback. Illustrated. $16.95. Code: EOPX

THE ORION ZONE
Ancient Star Cities of the American Southwest
by Gary A. David

This book on ancient star lore explores the mysterious location of Pueblos in the American Southwest, circa 1100 AD, that appear to be a mirror image of the major stars of the Orion constellation. Chapters include: Leaving Many Footprints—The Emergence and Migrations of the Anazazi; The Sky Over the Hopi Villages; Orion Rising in the Dark Crystal; The Cosmo-Magical Cities of the Anazazi; Windows Onto the Cosmos; To Calibrate the March of Time; They Came from Across the Ocean—The Patki (Water) Clan and the Snake Clan of the Hopi; Ancient and Mysterious Monuments; Beyond That Fiery Day; more.
346 pages. 6x9 Paperback. Illustrated. $19.95. Code: OZON

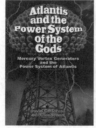

ATLANTIS & THE POWER SYSTEM
OF THE GODS
by David Hatcher Childress and Bill Clendenon

Childress' fascinating analysis of Nikola Tesla's broadcast system in light of Edgar Cayce's "Terrible Crystal" and the obelisks of ancient Egypt and Ethiopia. Includes: Atlantis and its crystal power towers that broadcast energy; how these incredible power stations may still exist today; inventor Nikola Tesla's nearly identical system of power transmission; Mercury Proton Gyros and mercury vortex propulsion; more. Richly illustrated, and packed with evidence that Atlantis not only existed—it had a world-wide energy system more sophisticated than ours today.
246 PAGES. 6x9 PAPERBACK. ILLUSTRATED. $15.95. CODE: APSG

PATH OF THE POLE
by Charles Hapgood

Hapgood researched Antarctica, ancient maps and the geological record to conclude that the Earth's crust has slipped in the inner core many times in the past, changing the position of the pole. *Path of the Pole* discusses the various "pole shifts" in Earth's past, giving evidence for each one, and moves on to possible future pole shifts. Packed with illustrations, this is the sourcebook for many other books on cataclysms and pole shifts.
356 PAGES. 6x9 PAPERBACK. ILLUSTRATED. $16.95. CODE: POP

THE MYSTERY OF THE OLMECS
by David Hatcher Childress

The Olmecs were not acknowledged to have existed as a civilization until an international archeological meeting in Mexico City in 1942. Now, the Olmecs are slowly being recognized as the Mother Culture of Mesoamerica, having invented writing, the ball game and the "Mayan" Calendar. But who were the Olmecs? Where did they come from? What happened to them? How sophisticated was their culture? Why are many Olmec statues and figurines seemingly of foreign peoples such as Africans, Europeans and Chinese? Is there a link with Atlantis? In this heavily illustrated book, join Childress in search of the lost cities of the Olmecs! Chapters include: The Mystery of Quizuo; The Mystery of Transoceanic Trade; The Mystery of Cranial Deformation; more.

296 PAGES. 6x9 PAPERBACK. COLOR SECTION. $20.00. CODE: MOLM

SUNKEN REALMS
A Survey of Underwater Ruins Around the World
By Karen Mutton

Australian researcher Mutton starts with the underwater cities in the Mediterranean, and then moves into Europe and the Atlantic. She continues with chapters on the Caribbean and then moves through the extensive sites in the Pacific and Indian Oceans. Places covered in this book include: Tartessos; Cadiz; Morocco; Alexandria; Cyprus; Malta; Thule & Hyperborea; Celtic Realms Lyonesse, Ys, and Hy Brasil; Canary and Azore Islands; Bahamas; Cuba; Bermuda; Mexico; Peru; Micronesia; California; Japan; Indian Ocean; Sri Lanka Land Bridge; India; Sumer; Lake Titicaca; more.

320 Pages. 6x9 Paperback. Illustrated. $20.00. Code: SRLM

ATLANTIS IN SPAIN

ATLANTIS IN SPAIN
A Study of the Ancient Sun Kingdoms of Spain
by E.M. Whishaw

First published in 1928, this classic book is a study of the megaliths of Spain, ancient writing, cyclopean walls, sun worshipping empires, hydraulic engineering, and sunken cities. An extremely rare book, it was out of print for 60 years. Learn about the Biblical Tartessus; an Atlantean city at Niebla; the Temple of Hercules and the Sun Temple of Seville; Libyans and the Copper Age; more. Profusely illustrated with photos, maps and drawings.

284 PAGES. 6x9 PAPERBACK. ILLUSTRATED. $15.95. CODE: AIS

RIDDLE OF THE PACIFIC
by John Macmillan Brown

Oxford scholar Brown's classic work on lost civilizations of the Pacific is now back in print! John Macmillan Brown was an historian and New Zealand's premier scientist when he wrote about the origins of the Maoris. After many years of travel thoughout the Pacific studying the people and customs of the south seas islands, he wrote *Riddle of the Pacific* in 1924. The book is packed with rare turn-of-the-century illustrations. Don't miss Brown's classic study of Easter Island, ancient scripts, megalithic roads and cities, more. Brown was an early believer in a lost continent in the Pacific.

460 PAGES. 6x9 PAPERBACK. ILLUSTRATED. $16.95. CODE: SOA

www.AdventuresUnlimitedPress.com

INVISIBLE RESIDENTS
The Reality of Underwater UFOS
by Ivan T. Sanderson

Sanderson puts forward the curious theory that "OINTS"—Other Intelligences—live under the Earth's oceans. This underwater, parallel, civilization may be twice as old as Homo sapiens, he proposes, and may have "developed what we call space flight." Sanderson postulates that the OINTS are behind many UFO sightings as well as the mysterious disappearances of aircraft and ships in the Bermuda Triangle. What better place to have an impenetrable base than deep within the oceans of the planet? Sanderson offers here an exhaustive study of USOs (Unidentified Submarine Objects) observed in nearly every part of the world.

298 PAGES. 6x9 PAPERBACK. ILLUSTRATED. $16.95. CODE: INVS

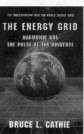

THE ENERGY GRID
Harmonic 695, The Pulse of the Universe
by Captain Bruce Cathie

This is the breakthrough book that explores the incredible potential of the Energy Grid and the Earth's Unified Field all around us. Bruce Cathie has been the premier investigator into the amazing potential of the infinite energy that surrounds our planet every microsecond. Cathie investigates the Harmonics of Light and how the Energy Grid is created. In this amazing book are chapters on UFO Propulsion, Nikola Tesla, Unified Equations, the Mysterious Aerials, Pythagoras & the Grid, Nuclear Detonation and the Grid, Maps of the Ancients, an Australian Stonehenge examined, more.

255 PAGES. 6x9 TRADEPAPER. ILLUSTRATED. $15.95. CODE: TEG

THE BRIDGE TO INFINITY
Harmonic 371244
by Captain Bruce Cathie

Cathie has popularized the concept that the earth is crisscrossed by an electromagnetic grid system that can be used for anti-gravity, free energy, levitation and more. The book includes a new analysis of the harmonic nature of reality, acoustic levitation, pyramid power, harmonic receiver towers and UFO propulsion. It concludes that today's scientists have at their command a fantastic store of knowledge with which to advance the welfare of the human race.

204 PAGES. 6x9 TRADEPAPER. ILLUSTRATED. $14.95. CODE: BTF

THE HARMONIC CONQUEST OF SPACE
by Captain Bruce Cathie

Chapters include: Mathematics of the World Grid; the Harmonics of Hiroshima and Nagasaki; Harmonic Transmission and Receiving; the Link Between Human Brain Waves; the Cavity Resonance between the Earth; the Ionosphere and Gravity; Edgar Cayce—the Harmonics of the Subconscious; Stonehenge; the Harmonics of the Moon; the Pyramids of Mars; Nikola Tesla's Electric Car; the Robert Adams Pulsed Electric Motor Generator; Harmonic Clues to the Unified Field; and more. Also included are tables showing the harmonic relations between the earth's magnetic field, the speed of light, and anti-gravity/gravity acceleration at different points on the earth's surface.

248 PAGES. 6x9. PAPERBACK. ILLUSTRATED. $16.95. CODE: HCS

ANCIENT TECHNOLOGY IN PERU & BOLIVIA
By David Hatcher Childress
Childress speculates on the existence of a sunken city in Lake Titicaca and reveals new evidence that the Sumerians may have arrived in South America 4,000 years ago. He demonstrates that the use of "keystone cuts" with metal clamps poured into them to secure megalithic construction was an advanced technology used all over the world, from the Andes to Egypt, Greece and Southeast Asia. He maintains that only power tools could have made the intricate articulation and drill holes found in extremely hard granite and basalt blocks in Bolivia and Peru, and that the megalith builders had to have had advanced methods for moving and stacking gigantic blocks of stone, some weighing over 100 tons.
340 Pages. 6x9 Paperback. Illustrated.. $19.95 Code: ATP

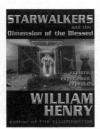

STARWALKERS AND THE DIMENSION OF THE BLESSED
By William Henry
Explore: The Egyptian belief that interdimensional beings of light created humanity; The meaning behind the 'reed,' the key term constantly repeated over thousands of years in these global myths; How the Place of Reeds, is an allegory for the opening of a gate to another realm; How the human body is capable of producing a spiritual substance that is made of space-time and through which one can see other times and places; more. Chapters include: A Cosmic Species; The Dimension of the Blessed; The Field; Up Out of Egypt; The Blessed Falcons; The Divine Spark of the Blessed; Atlantis: The Blessed Land; The Sea at the End of the World; Manna and the Blessed Realm; Blessed Sirius; Gilgamesh & Sirius; more.
270 Pages. 6x9 Paperback. Illustrated. $16.95. Code: SDOB

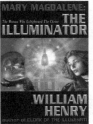

MARY MAGDALENE: THE ILLUMINATOR
The Woman Who Enlightened the Christ
By William Henry
Henry explores the core of the mysteries of Mary Magdalene to study knowledge of the 'ultimate secret' of the Tower or Ladder to God, also called the Stairway to Heaven; The alchemical secrets of Mary Magdalene's anointing oil and how it transformed Jesus; The Magdalene's connection to Ishtar, Isis and other ancient goddesses; The reality of an extraterrestrial presence in the Bible and Gnostic Christian texts; How the Knights Templar encoded the secret teaching of Jesus and Mary Magdalene in religious graffiti at Domme, France; more.
304 pages. 6x9 Paperback. Illustrated. $16.95. Code: MMTI

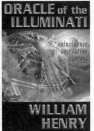

ORACLE OF THE ILLUMINATI
Coincidence, Cocreation, Contact
By William Henry
Investigative mythologist Henry on the secret codes, oracles and technology of the ancient Illuminati. His primary mission is finding and interpreting ancient gateway stories which feature advanced technology for raising spiritual vibration and increasing our body's innate healing ability. Chapters include: From Cloak to Oracle; The Return of Sophia; The Cosmic G-Spot Stimulator; The Hymn of the Pearl; The Realm of the Illuminati; Francis Bacon: Oracle; Abydos and the Head of Sophia; Enki and the Flower of Light; The God Head and the Dodecahedron; The Star Walker; The Big Secret; more.
243 Pages. 6x9 Paperback. Illustrated. $16.95. Code: ORIL

ORDER FORM

10% Discount When You Order 3 or More Items!

One Adventure Place
P.O. Box 74
Kempton, Illinois 60946
United States of America
Tel.: 815-253-6390 • Fax: 815-253-6300
Email: auphq@frontiernet.net
http://www.adventuresunlimitedpress.com

ORDERING INSTRUCTIONS

✓ Remit by USD$ Check, Money Order or Credit Card
✓ Visa, Master Card, Discover & AmEx Accepted
✓ Paypal Payments Can Be Made To:
    info@wexclub.com
✓ Prices May Change Without Notice
✓ 10% Discount for 3 or More Items

SHIPPING CHARGES

United States

✓ Postal Book Rate { $4.50 First Item / 50¢ Each Additional Item
✓ POSTAL BOOK RATE Cannot Be Tracked!
    Not responsible for non-delivery.
✓ Priority Mail { $6.00 First Item / $2.00 Each Additional Item
✓ UPS { $7.00 First Item / $1.50 Each Additional Item
NOTE: UPS Delivery Available to Mainland USA Only

Canada

✓ Postal Air Mail { $15.00 First Item / $3.00 Each Additional Item
✓ Personal Checks or Bank Drafts MUST BE
    US$ and Drawn on a US Bank
✓ Canadian Postal Money Orders OK
✓ Payment MUST BE US$

All Other Countries

✓ Sorry, No Surface Delivery!
✓ Postal Air Mail { $19.00 First Item / $7.00 Each Additional Item
✓ Checks and Money Orders MUST BE US$
    and Drawn on a US Bank or branch.
✓ Paypal Payments Can Be Made in US$ To:
    info@wexclub.com

SPECIAL NOTES

✓ RETAILERS: Standard Discounts Available
✓ BACKORDERS: We Backorder all Out-of-Stock Items Unless Otherwise Requested
✓ PRO FORMA INVOICES: Available on Request
✓ DVD Return Policy: Replace defective DVDs only
ORDER ONLINE AT: www.adventuresunlimitedpress.com

10% Discount When You Order 3 or More Items!

Please check: ☑

☐ This is my first order   ☐ I have ordered before

Name
Address
City
State/Province   Postal Code
Country
Phone: Day   Evening
Fax   Email

Item Code	Item Description	Qty	Total

Please check: ☑

	Subtotal ▶	
	Less Discount-10% for 3 or more items ▶	
☐ Postal-Surface	Balance ▶	
☐ Postal-Air Mail (Priority in USA)	Illinois Residents 6.25% Sales Tax ▶	
	Previous Credit ▶	
☐ UPS	Shipping ▶	
(Mainland USA only)	Total (check/MO in USD$ only) ▶	

☐ Visa/MasterCard/Discover/American Express

Card Number:
Expiration Date: Security Code:

✓ SEND A CATALOG TO A FRIEND:

www.AdventuresUnlimitedPress.com